When should I travel to get the best airfare?
Where do I go for answers to my travel questions?
What's the best and easiest way to plan and book my trip?

frommers.travelocity.com

Frommer's, the travel guide leader, has teamed up with **Travelocity.com,** the leader in online travel, to bring you an in-depth, easy-to-use resource designed to help you plan and book your trip online.

At **frommers.travelocity.com,** you'll find free online updates about your destination from the experts at Frommer's plus the outstanding travel planning and purchasing features of Travelocity.com. Travelocity.com provides reservations capabilities for 95 percent of all airline seats sold, more than 47,000 hotels, and over 50 car rental companies. In addition, Travelocity.com offers more than 2,000 exciting vacation and cruise packages. Travelocity.com puts you in complete control of your travel planning with these and other great features:

>**Expert travel guidance from Frommer's** – over 150 writers reporting from around the world!

>**Best Fare Finder** – an interactive calendar tells you when to travel to get the best airfare

>**Fare Watcher** – we'll track airfare changes to your favorite destinations

>**Dream Maps** – a mapping feature that suggests travel opportunities based on your budget

>**Shop Safe Guarantee** – 24 hours a day / 7 days a week live customer service, and more!

Whether traveling on a tight budget, looking for a quick weekend getaway, or planning the trip of a lifetime, Frommer's guides and Travelocity.com will make your travel dreams a reality. You've bought the book, now book the trip!

A New Star-Rating System & Other Exciting News from Frommer's!

In our continuing effort to publish the savviest, most up-to-date, and most appealing travel guides available, we've added some great new features.

Frommer's guides now include a new **star-rating system.** Every hotel, restaurant, and attraction is rated from 0 to 3 stars to help you set priorities and organize your time.

We've also added **seven brand-new features** that point you to the great deals, in-the-know advice, and unique experiences that separate travelers from tourists. Throughout the guide look for:

Finds	Special finds—those places only insiders know about
Fun Fact	Fun facts—details that make travelers more informed and their trips more fun
Kids	Best bets for kids—advice for the whole family
Moments	Special moments—those experiences that memories are made of
Overrated	Places or experiences not worth your time or money
Tips	Insider tips—some great ways to save time and money
Value	Great values—where to get the best deals

Frommer's®

PORTABLE

Vancouver Island, the Gulf Islands & the San Juan Islands

1st Edition

by Chris McBeath

WILEY
Independent Thinkers

Toronto ON

ABOUT THE AUTHOR

An award-winning writer, **Chris McBeath** is a columnist for Vancouver's most widely circulated visitor's guide and a frequent contributor of "travel getaway" pieces to a network of community newspapers. Her international features have appeared in publications worldwide. She makes her home in British Columbia.

Published by:
JOHN WILEY & SONS CANADA, LTD.
22 Worcester Road
Etobicoke, ON M9W 1L1

National Library of Canada Cataloguing in Publication Data

McBeath, Chris, 1953–
   Frommer's portable Vancouver Island, the Gulf Islands & the San Juan Islands / Chris McBeath.—1st ed.

Includes index.
ISBN 1–894413–44–X

1. Vancouver Island (B.C.)—Guidebooks. 2. Gulf Islands (B.C.)—Guidebooks. 3. San Juan Islands (Wash.)—Guidebooks. I. Title. II. Title: Portable Vancouver Island, the Gulf Islands & the San Juan Islands.

FC3844.2.M32 2002   917.11'2044   C2002–901900–1
F1089.V3M32 2002

Editorial Director: Joan Whitman
Associate Editor: Melanie Rutledge
Publishing Services Director: Karen Bryan
Cartographer: Mapping Specialists, Ltd.
Illustrations: Frommer's US and Bart Vallecoccia Illustration
Text layout: IBEX Graphic Communications
Cover design: Kyle Gell
Front cover photo: Mike Dobel/Masterfile

SPECIAL SALES

Fer reseller information, including discounts and premium sales, please call our sales department: Tel.: 416-646-4584. For press review copies, author interviews, or other publicity information, please contact our marketing department: Tel.: 416-646-4584; Fax.: 416-646-4448.

1 2 3 4 5 XX 06 05 04 03 02

Manufactured in Canada

Contents

List of Maps   vii

1   The Best of Vancouver Island, the Gulf Islands & the San Juan Islands   1

   1   The Best Family-Vacation Experiences 2
   2   The Best Adventure Activities 3
   3   The Best Soft-Adventure Activities 3
   4   The Best Drives 4
   5   The Best Hotels & Resorts 4
   6   The Best Bed-and-Breakfasts & Country Inns 5
   7   The Best Restaurants 6

2   Planning Your Trip   8

   1   The Regions in Brief 8
   2   Visitor Information 9
   3   Entry Requirements & Customs 9
   4   Money 12
   5   Insurance 13
   6   When to Go 14
     Vancouver Island, the Gulf Islands & the
     San Juan Islands Calendar of Events 16
   7   Tips for Travelers with Special Needs 20
   8   Getting There 22
   9   Getting Around 28
     Fast Facts: Vancouver Island, the Gulf Islands & the
     San Juan Islands 29

3   Victoria   32

   1   Essentials 32
     Fast Facts: Victoria 38
   2   Where to Stay 39
   3   Where to Dine 46
   4   Exploring Victoria 51
   5   Victoria After Dark 58

4 Southern Vancouver Island   61

1 The Saanich Peninsula 61
2 The Sooke Region 68
3 En Route to Nanaimo: The Cowichan Valley 77

5 Central Vancouver Island   85

1 Nanaimo 85
2 Parksville & Qualicum Beach 92
3 Heading West: Port Alberni & Bamfield 99
4 Tofino, Ucluelet & Pacific Rim National Park 103

6 Northern Vancouver Island   114

1 Courtenay & the Comox Valley 115
2 Campbell River 124
3 En Route to Port Hardy 132

7 The Gulf Islands   140

1 Salt Spring Island 145
2 The Pender Islands 153
3 Galiano Island 157
4 Mayne Island 163
5 Saturna Island 167

8 The San Juan Islands   171

1 San Juan Island 175
2 Orcas Island 182
   Shaw Island 188
3 Lopez Island 188

Index   193

General Index 193
Accommodations Index 197
Restaurant Index 199

List of Maps

Vancouver Island & the North American Mainland   15

Vancouver Island   24

Downtown Victoria   35

Southern Vancouver Island   64

Central Vancouver Island   88

Northern Vancouver Island   116

The Gulf Islands   142

The San Juan Islands   173

Here's what the critics say about Frommer's:

"Amazingly easy to use. Very portable, very complete."

—Booklist

"The only mainstream guide to list specific prices. The Walter Cronkite of guidebooks—with all that implies."

—Travel & Leisure

"Complete, concise, and filled with useful information."

—New York Daily News

"Hotel information is close to encyclopedic."

—Des Moines Sunday Register

"Detailed, accurate, and easy-to-read information for all price ranges."

—Glamour Magazine

AN INVITATION TO THE READER

In researching this book, we discovered many wonderful places—hotels, restaurants, shops, and more. We're sure you'll find others. Please tell us about them, so we can share the information with your fellow travelers in upcoming editions. If you were disappointed with a recommendation, we'd love to know that, too. Please write to:

Frommer's Portable Vancouver Island, the Gulf Islands & the
San Juan Islands, 1st Edition
John Wiley & Sons Canada, Ltd. • 22 Worcester Road • Etobicoke, ON
M9W 1L1

AN ADDITIONAL NOTE

Please be advised that travel information is subject to change at any time—and this is especially true of prices. We therefore suggest that you write or call ahead for confirmation when making your travel plans. The authors, editors, and publisher cannot be held responsible for the experiences of readers while traveling. Your safety is important to us, however, so we encourage you to stay alert and be aware of your surroundings. Keep a close eye on cameras, purses, and wallets, all favorite targets of thieves and pickpockets.

WHAT THE SYMBOLS MEAN

The following abbreviations are used for credit cards:

AE American Express	DC Diners Club	V Visa
DISC Discover	MC MasterCard	

FROMMERS.COM

Now that you have the guidebook to a great trip, visit our website at **www.frommers.com** for travel information on nearly 2,000 destinations. With features updated regularly, we give you instant access to the most current trip-planning information available. At Frommers.com, you'll also find the best prices on airfares, accommodations, and car rentals—and you can even book travel online through our travel booking partners. At Frommers.com you'll also find the following:

- Daily Newsletter highlighting the best travel deals
- Hot Spot of the Month/Vacation Sweepstakes & Travel Photo Contest
- More than 200 Travel Message Boards
- Outspoken Newsletters and Feature Articles on travel bargains, vacation ideas, tips & resources, and more!

The Best of Vancouver Island, the Gulf Islands & the San Juan Islands

There's a geological reason, having to do with movement of the earth's various surfaces that details how these islands on the Northwest coast of the North American continent came into being. But to my mind, it is the words of one island resident that best describe this creation of nature: "When God made this continent, He finished up with Vancouver Island," he explains. "But there was a little material left, so God stood up, and brushed off His hands. The results are jewels in the water that we know today as the San Juans and the Gulf Islands."

However it happened, these islands in the Pacific Northwest reflect some of the most beautiful and pristine wilderness on earth today. An archipelago that stretches along the coastline of both sides of the 49th parallel, the islands number in the hundreds. Some are large enough to sustain small communities as diverse as the islands themselves, while others are no more than seagull perches that disappear at high tide.

Vancouver Island is the largest. Separated from the British Columbia mainland by the Georgia Strait, it offers the best of all worlds. In the south, the city of Victoria has the urban sophistication of a cosmopolitan center, and lies within easy reach of soft adventure activities like hiking, whale watching, and cycling. In the north, the countryside grows untamed, opening a door to exhilarating eco-adventures such as mountaineering, spelunking, surfing, and canoeing. It is a diversity that has earned Vancouver Island high marks from leading travel publications.

The smaller Gulf and San Juan Islands are equally appealing, and their communities reflect the isolation of their water-bound environments. Each has a different history and ambience, whether it is sleepy Lopez Island or eclectic Galiano Island. It's a sense of magic, though, that is their very charm. Island residents prefer to live beyond the mainstream: they are writers, artists, and craftspeople, city retirees looking for a sense of community, or specialty producers farming everything from llama and sheep to organic orchards and cottage dairies. They've chosen to live on "island time," an easy-going tempo that bewitches visitors the moment they set foot on the soil. Although visitors are certainly welcome (in summer they swell island populations tenfold), islanders like to keep outside influences at arm's-length, lest they change that special way of life too dramatically. Islanders are self-professed stewards of the land, and as such, keepers of the island faith. When writer James Michener wanted to describe his love of islands, he made up a word for it: *nesomania,* from the Greek *neso* (island) and *mania* (extreme enthusiasm). Explore these islands, and you'll discover that nesomaniacs abound—you might even become one yourself!

1 The Best Family-Vacation Experiences

- **Visiting the Royal British Columbia Museum** (Vancouver Island; © **888/447-7977** or 250/356-7226): This place is so diverse and inspiring that kids may want to stay all afternoon. How often can you say *that* about a museum? See chapter 3.

- **Actually enjoying having stick insects navigate their way up your arm at the Victoria Bug Zoo** (Vancouver Island; © **250/384-2847**): The interaction with insects takes the creepy out of crawly. See chapter 3.

- **Exploring at Horne Lake Caves Provincial Park, near Qualicum Beach** (Vancouver Island): Armed with flashlights, helmets, and good shoes, you feel like intrepid adventurers, even though the darkened path has been well scouted before. One of the most accessible networks of caverns on the island, the caves can also accommodate extreme spelunkers. See chapter 5.

- **Wading through minnows and searching out sand dollars at Rathtrevor Beach Provincial Park, near Parksville** (Vancouver Island): This is one of the most family-friendly parks in British Columbia. The warm, ankle-deep waters go on forever. So does the sand. See chapter 5.

- **Walking the boardwalks of the Wild Pacific Trail in Ucluelet** (Vancouver Island): You can make-believe you're in training for the West Coast Trail or a trek to Cape Scott. Great for 8 and 80 year olds alike, it has all the dramatic views with none of the true-grit challenges. See chapter 5.

2 The Best Adventure Activities

- **Kayaking through the Broken Group Islands in Pacific Rim National Park** (Vancouver Island): It's an oasis of calm waters, seal colonies, and other marine life in the Pacific Ocean. Bonus points are awarded if you get there aboard the freighter *MV Lady Rose*. See chapter 5.
- **Hiking the West Coast Trail in Pacific Rim National Park** (Vancouver Island): This trek tests the mettle of the hardiest hiker; but the rewards are well worth the effort. See chapter 5.
- **Honing a new outdoor skill at Strathcona Park Lodge** (Vancouver Island; ✆ 250/286-3122): Everything from hiking to rappelling is on offer here, for both the novice and extremist. See chapter 6.

3 The Best Soft-Adventure Activities

- **Teeing off with kindred spirits at Crown Isle Resort** (Vancouver Island; ✆ 888/338-8439 or 250/703-5050): Because the entire resort is deliciously golf-nutty. See chapter 6.
- **Cruising on the *Aurora Explorer*** (Vancouver Island; ✆ 250/286-3347): A 12-passenger packet freighter that works her way up and down some of the most beautiful coastal inlets in British Columbia. Although cargo is priority, passengers are a lucrative sideline. A casual, off-beat way to travel. See chapter 6.
- **Angling for a Tyee in Campbell River** (Vancouver Island): In fact, angling for anything in these waters is sport fishing at its best. See chapter 6.
- **Scooting around San Juan Island in a Scootcar from Susie's Mopeds** (San Juan Island; ✆ 800/532-0087 or 360/378-5244): A Scootcar is a hybrid vehicle that shuttles along at a paltry speed giving you all the fun of a moped, and the cover of a car. See chapter 8.
- **Whale watching on the bluffs at Lime Kiln Point State Park** (San Juan Island; ✆ 360/378-2044): This is the only park in the world dedicated to this purpose. Your chances of spotting orca, minke, or pilot whales are particularly good in late August and early September, during the salmon runs. See chapter 8.

4 The Best Drives

- **Following the shoreline between Sooke and Port Renfrew** (Vancouver Island): The views are expansive, and the beaches along the way a delightful excuse to pull over and stretch your legs. If you can't make it all the way to Botanical Beach Provincial Park (well worth the effort), the restaurant at the **Point No Point Resort** (① **250/646-2020**) is, well, a good point to regroup, refresh, and turn around. See chapter 4.

- **Taking Highway 4 across Vancouver Island from Parksville to Tofino** (Vancouver Island): Bisecting the island east to west is a topographical treasure. You'll pass through a tableau of forests, rivers, and snow-capped mountains before hitting the windswept shores and beaches of the West Coast. See chapter 5.

- **Digressing off the main highway (Hwy. 19) and following the starfish signs along Highway 19A** (Vancouver Island): Take any exit near Parksville and meander up to Campbell River through seaside communities overlooking the Georgia Strait, past artisan studios, and across lush farmlands. A sage farmer once said that if the cows are lying down, inclement weather is brewing. Keep an eye open, and check the theory out. See chapter 6.

5 The Best Hotels & Resorts

- **The Fairmont Empress** (Vancouver Island; ① **800/441-1414** or 250/884-8111): Like a grand old dowager, this magnificent hotel commands the Victoria Inner Harbour as her fiefdom, and beckons her audience inside. If you're going for broke, stay here; the experience is what Americans think England is all about. See chapter 3.

- **The Aerie** (Vancouver Island; ① **800/518-1933** or 250/ 743-7115): This resort is appropriately named after an eagle's nest. Located on the Malahat Mountain, this is a lavish, Mediterranean-style mansion with views that will take your breath away. The Persian silk carpets are right on the mark. The crystal chandeliers, though, are a bit over the top. See chapter 4.

- **Oak Bay Beach Hotel and Marine Resort** (Vancouver Island; ① **800/668-7788** or 250/598-4556): It's so much better than it used to be, now that first-class heating upgrades have replaced the gurgling radiators. This Tudor-styled manor-resort is distinguished by intriguing corridors that lead to pubs, restaurants, lounges, and guest rooms with lead-pane windows. Best seat in the house is in front of the grand fireplace, where you can sip hot chocolate and play backgammon. See chapter 4.

- **Clayoquot Wilderness Resort** (Vancouver Island; ✆ **888/ 333-5405** or 250/725-2688): Accessible only by water, the resort is quite isolated, so you feel as if you're completely one with the wilderness. But it's the luxurious safari-style campsites that steal the show. See chapter 5.

- **Wickaninnish Inn** (Vancouver Island; ✆ **800/333-4604** or 250/725-3300): With nothing less than floor-to-ceiling triple-glazed windows standing between you and the churning Pacific Ocean, this place elevates storm watching to an art. It's a surreal experience. See chapter 5.

- **Rosario Resort** (Orcas Island; ✆ **800/562-8820** or 360/ 376-2222): Situated on a peninsula, Rosario exudes an air of 1920s grace. Listed on the National Register of Historic Places, the beautifully refurbished resort has something for everyone: elegant dining, spa services, a children's program, and a see-it-to-believe-it 1,972-pipe Aeolian organ. Concerts are nightly. See chapter 8.

6 The Best Bed-and-Breakfasts & Country Inns

- **Abigail's Hotel** (Vancouver Island; ✆ **800/561-6565** or 250/ 388-5363): This inn is the essence of old-world charm and hospitality in a phenomenal downtown Victoria location. See chapter 3.

- **Sooke Harbour House** (Vancouver Island; ✆ **800/889-9688** or 250/642-3421): Beyond its reputation as a hideaway for Hollywood's beautiful people, this place offers so much more. Many come for the food—an Epicurean feast that seems to go on for as long as you can eat. Be prepared to make reservations at the restaurant sometimes weeks in advance. See chapter 4.

- **Hastings House** (Salt Spring Island; ✆ **800/661-9255** or 250/537-2362): Everything you would want in an English country inn is here, but so much better because it is a member of the exclusive Relais & Châteaux network. Expect wonderful gardens, inspired guest rooms, and world-renowned gourmet dining. See chapter 7.

- **Island Time B&B** (Galiano Island; ✆ 877/588-3506 or 250/539-3506): Although it's brand new, this B&B has come out of the starting gate ready and raring to go. Enjoy tons of space, loads of views, and innkeepers who have stories to tell. See chapter 7.
- **Sahhali Serenity Oceanfront B&B Inn** (North Pender Island; ✆ 877/625-2583 or 250/629-3664): This B&B packs so many pampering touches into its suites, there's no need to leave. Private panoramas of sunsets, storms, and eagles are at your fingertips. See chapter 7.
- **Friday Harbor House** (San Juan Island; ✆ 360/378-8455): A modern, beautifully furnished inn sitting high above busy Friday Harbor. The views are outstanding. At night, the proverbial "twinkling lights" make the inn's restaurant a really romantic spot. See chapter 8.
- **Inn at Swifts Bay** (Lopez Island; ✆ 800/375-5285 or 360/468-3636): Pull yourself away from the squishiest, most sumptuously romantic beds in the Northwest, and you'll find breakfasts that are more than an eye-opener. They're gastronomic adventures, island-renowned for being the best on the San Juans. See chapter 8.

7 The Best Restaurants

- **Barb's Place** (Vancouver Island; ✆ 250/384-6515): Looking for fabulous fish and chips? Look no further than Barb's. The accompanying vinegar-slathered, hand-hewn chips taste so much better served in newspaper. It must be something in the ink! See chapter 3.
- **Blue Crab Bar & Grill** (Vancouver Island; ✆ 250/480-1999): This restaurant takes the cake for seafood, serving up the best selections in Victoria, made all the more mouthwatering by killer views of the harbor. See chapter 3.
- **Pagliacci's** (Vancouver Island; ✆ 250/386-1662): Go for the late-night gossip, the showmanship of owner Howie Siegal, and a great value menu named after Hollywood glitterati. See chapter 3.
- **Deep Cove Chalet** (Vancouver Island; ✆ 250/656-3541): This place makes the list for its caviar: Beluga, Ocietra, and Sevugra, from Russia, Iran, and China, which helps make the elegant French menu a standout. See chapter 4.

- **The sushi restaurant at the Inn at Tough City** (Vancouver Island; ℭ 250/725-2021): Surrounded by the bounty of the sea, you would think there would be a proliferation of sushi restaurants on the west coast of Vancouver Island. Not so, which is why this tiny cafe at the Inn at Tough City is such a treat. See chapter 5.
- **House Piccolo** (Salt Spring Island; ℭ 250/537-1844): The tiny little farmhouse in Ganges belies what you'll find inside. The restaurant was recently recognized by the prestigious Chaine des Rôtisseurs, so you know the cuisine is top-notch. See chapter 7.

2

Planning Your Trip

The islands of the Pacific Northwest are captivating, and although their charm certainly invites impromptu getaway visits, advance planning will save you time, money, and worry. This chapter covers the necessary nuts and bolts to help you plan a successful trip.

1 The Regions in Brief

As the largest of all the islands along the Pacific Northwest coast, **Vancouver Island** offers both urban sophistication and wilderness adventure; it's as cosmopolitan or as extreme as you want.

Victoria, the provincial capital of British Columbia, lies on the southern tip of Vancouver Island, not far from the international boundary. In fact, the American border scoops below the 49th parallel, keeping the island—in its entirety—in Canada. With an ambience that's more English than England ever was, Victoria's beautifully preserved turn-of-the-century buildings dominate its harbor. The city's picturesque charm draws visitors by the multitude, especially in summer. Shopping, dining, and urban attractions, such as the **Royal British Columbia Museum,** make this a first-class family destination. From Victoria, there are a number of pleasant side trips around the southern part of Vancouver Island, including to the famed **Butchart Gardens.** It is also an ideal starting point for exploring farther afield.

As you travel north, the rest of Vancouver Island ranges from rural to wild, and nowhere is this better seen than in the central part of the island. Holiday resorts line the east coast overlooking the protected Georgia Strait, while the open Pacific Ocean pounds against Canada's wildest and most westerly coast. This is where to find the unpredictable **West Coast Trail,** the awe-inspiring **Pacific Rim National Park,** and some of the untouched wilderness areas of **Clayoquot Sound.** Much of the island is home to dozens of First Nations Canadian bands; throughout your travels there'll be an opportunity to shop for native arts and to experience the many different cultures.

At **Port Hardy,** Vancouver Island's most remote and northerly community, you can board a BC Ferries vessel and take a 15-hour trip through the famed **Inside Passage** to Prince Rupert, a port town on the mainland just shy of the Alaska Panhandle. A cruise aboard BC Ferries doesn't compare with the luxurious cruise ships that ply these waters, but you'll save yourself thousands of dollars and travel through the same spectacular scenery.

The **Gulf Islands** and the **San Juan Islands** are actually a part of the same archipelago, yet, surprisingly, each group of islands has a very different feel. All are rural in character; many of the smaller islands are limited in the number of services they can provide. The one thing they do share is a milder climate than the rest of BC or Washington State.

2 Visitor Information

A great source for information on British Columbia is **Tourism British Columbia,** P.O. Box 9830, Parliament Building, Victoria, BC V8V 1X4 or P.O. Box 9830 Stn. Prov. Government, Victoria, BC V8W 9W5 (© **800/HELLOBC** (800/435-5622) or 604/ HELLOBC (604/435-5622); **www.hellobc.com**). Be prepared for lots of glossy magazines to whet your appetite.

For Vancouver Island specifics, contact the **Tourism Association of Vancouver Island,** 335 Wesley St., Suite 203, Nanaimo, BC V9R 2T5 (© **250/754-3500;** www.islands.bc.ca). Another useful website is **www.visit-vancouverisland.com**. There is a central reservations service for hotels and B&Bs in the Gulf Islands. Call © **866/539-3089.** You can also check out **www.gulfislands.com** for general information. For the San Juan Islands, contact **San Juan Islands Visitor Information Services,** P.O. Box 65, Lopez Island, WA 98261 (© **360/468-3663;** www.guidetosanjuans.com).

3 Entry Requirements & Customs

ENTERING CANADA   All visitors to Canada must carry proof of citizenship and residence. United States citizens and permanent residents do not require visas; a passport, birth certificate, or certificate of naturalization is sufficient. Traveling with some form of photo ID is highly recommended. *Note:* A current US driver's license, used on its own, is no longer accepted as proof of citizenship. Noncitizen US residents should carry their passports and resident status cards or green cards, visitor or student visas, arrival-departure records, proof of sufficient funds for a temporary stay, and evidence of return transportation.

Citizens of most European countries, former British colonies, and certain other countries do not need visas, but must carry passports. Entry visas for citizens of many other countries must be applied for and received from the Canadian embassy in your home country. For further information, check with the **Canadian Consulate** in the city nearest you or contact the Canadian government's **800-Canada information line** (© **800/OCANADA** (800/622-6232)) that will link you to numerous government services and programs, or visit **www.canada.gc.ca**.

ENTERING THE UNITED STATES   When traveling to the San Juan Islands, in Washington State, Canadian citizens must carry proof of citizenship and residence along with photo ID. All other visitors should carry passports along with arrival-departure information, proof of sufficient funds for a temporary stay, evidence of return transportation, and in many instances, student or visitor visas. Check with the **US Department of State** in the city nearest you, or visit **www.state.gov/index.cfm**.

Note: Although the border between Canada and the United States is regarded as "openly friendly," the degree of friendliness you'll encounter varies. If you're driving, random searches of your vehicle are not unusual, so be sure to bring along your car's registration papers.

TRAVELING WITH CHILDREN   United States and Canadian border officials pay particular attention to minors, especially if they are traveling solo or with a single adult. Any person 18 and under must carry a letter from a parent or guardian granting him or her permission to travel across the border, plus proof of identity. If parents are divorced, the non-traveling parent must write a similar letter granting permission for the child to accompany the ex-spouse.

TRAVELING WITH PETS   Dogs, cats, and most other pets can travel with their owners between the United States and Canada provided you have proof of rabies vaccinations within the last 36 months. In Canada, contact the **Canadian Food Inspection Agency,** 59 Camelot Dr., Ottawa, ON K1A DY9 (© **800/ OCANADA** (800/622-2342; www.inspection. gc.ca). In the US, contact the US Public Health Service, Centers for Disease Control & Prevention, Atlanta, GA 30333 (© **404/498-1670**; www.cdc.gov/ncidod/dg/animal/htm).

CUSTOMS
BRINGING GOODS HOME TO CANADA   Canadian Customs are fairly liberal except when it comes to firearms, plants, and meats. These are subject to rigorous inspection; without *precisely* the right paperwork, they won't make it across the border. Pepper sprays are also a big no. If you are over 19, you can include alcoholic beverages and tobacco products in your 48-hour exemption (you can claim C$200 (US$130) total), or your 7-day exemption (you can claim C$750 (US$487.50) total), but not in your 24-hour exemption (you can claim C$50 (US$32.50) total). All tobacco products and alcoholic beverages have to accompany you in your checked or hand luggage. Allowances are 200 cigarettes, 200 grams of manufactured tobacco, and 50 cigars or cigarillos. As of October 1, 2001, tobacco products are only partially exempt; a minimum duty must now be paid unless they are marked "CANADA-DUTY PAID · DROIT ACQUITTÉ." You will find Canadian-made products sold at duty-free shops marked this way. Alcohol includes 1.5 l (48 oz.) of wine, 1.14 l (40 oz.) of liquor, or 24 x 355 ml (24 x 12 oz.) cans/bottles of beer or ale. Gifts not exceeding C$60 (US$40) and not containing tobacco products, alcoholic beverages, or advertising material, can be brought in duty-free. For more information concerning customs regulations, contact the **Canadian Customs Office** in the city nearest you, or call © **800/461-9999** or © **204/983-3500.** The website is **www.ccra-adrc.gc.ca/customs/individuals/menu-e.html**.

BRINGING GOODS HOME TO THE UNITED STATES United States citizens who have been away for 48 hours or more are allowed to bring back, once every 30 days, C$260 (US$400) worth of merchandise duty-free. You'll be charged a flat rate of 3% duty on the next C$650 (US$1,000) worth of purchases. If travelers have been away less than 48 hours, the limit on duty-free merchandise is C$310 (US$200). Be sure to have your receipts handy. For gifts, the duty-free limit is C$150 (US$100) in a single day. If gifts are mailed or shipped, this amount increases to C$310 (US$200). When you return to the United States, mailed gifts need not be declared since they aren't accompanying you. No fresh foodstuffs are permitted. If you are over 21, these exemptions can include 1ℓ (33.8 oz.) alcohol, 200 cigarettes, and 100 cigars (except of Cuban origin). For more information, contact the **US Customs Service** in Anacortes, 519 Commercial Ave., WA 98221 (© **360/293-2331**) or in Friday Harbor, 271 Front St. North, WA 98250 (© **360/378-2080**). User-friendly details are also available at **www.customs.ustreas.gov/travel/travel.htm**.

Canadian Tax and Tax Rebates

In addition to a 7.5% **provincial sales tax** (PST) in the province of British Columbia, a 7% **Goods & Services Tax** (GST) is applied to almost all goods and services. Visitors can reclaim the GST portion of their hotel bills (if their stay is less than 30 days) and all shopping purchases bought in Canada that total a minimum of C$200 (US$130). Each receipt for eligible goods must show a minimum purchase amount of C$50 (US$32.50) before taxes. The rebate does not apply to car rentals, restaurant meals, tobacco, or alcohol. An instant GST rebate of up to C$500 (US$325) can be obtained at participating duty-free shops and rebate centers. Alternatively, visitors may file for a GST rebate once they return home. They will receive reimbursement by check within 4 to 6 weeks. Claims must be filed within a year of purchase and the original receipts must be included. Application forms are available at major hotels, information centers, and at border crossings. Note that receipts from several trips during the same year may be submitted together.

For details, contact the **GST Visitor Rebate Program,** Summerside Tax Centre, Revenue Canada, 275 Pope Road, Suite 104, Summerside, PEI C1N 6C6 (© **800-668-4748** (inside Canada) or **902/432-5608** (outside Canada); www.ccra-adrc.gc.ca/tax/nonresidents/visitors/).

4 Money

The Canadian dollar is worth about US65¢. Canadian denominations are the same as in the United States: C$5 (US$3.25), C$10 (US$6.50), C$20 (US$13.00), C$50 (US$32.50), and C$100 (US$65). Bills, however, come in different colors, which is why many Americans call them "Monopoly money"—rather a good-natured insult to Canadian ears—but at this exchange rate, shopping certainly feels like a game. Note that a single dollar is a coin, nicknamed a "loonie" for the loon on one side, and the two-toned, two-dollar coin is commonly called a "toonie" or a "doubloon."

EXCHANGE RATES In Canada, United States currency is accepted at most shops and restaurants, but because exchange rates vary, you're better off changing your funds into Canadian currency.

Banks and other financial institutions offer a standard rate of exchange based on the daily world monetary rate. **Hotels** will gladly exchange your notes, but will usually give a slightly lower exchange rate. **Stores and restaurants** can set their own exchange percentages, so these are generally the lowest of all. Your best bet is to withdraw funds from **bank ATMs**—they often provide the best rate of exchange. ATM transactions issue Canadian dollars. Your issuing company will automatically convert the transaction to your currency when you're billed.

In any transaction, always keep the rate of exchange in mind. Prices in Canada may seem on par or slightly higher, but they actually work out to be cheaper, given that the Canadian dollar is worth approximately 35% less than its American counterpart. Consequently, Canada is a real bargain for US visitors.

The prices cited in this guide are given in both Canadian and US dollars.

TRAVELER'S CHECKS, ATMs & CREDIT CARDS   Because most cities and towns have 24-hour ATMs, traveler's checks are not used as much. However, if you wish to carry larger denominations, banks, bigger stores, and hotels universally accept them. Cashing checks may sometimes incur a small fee, and you may be asked for photo ID to complete the transaction. *Note:* While ATMs are widespread on Vancouver Island, they are less prevalent on the Gulf and San Juan islands. Some of the Gulf Islands don't even have banks! If you plan to tour the Gulf and San Juan islands, be sure to travel with a **major credit card,** a **direct debit card,** or **traveler's checks,** and, of course, **cash.** Visa and MasterCard are accepted at most locations. Many businesses also accept American Express.

5 Insurance

HEALTH INSURANCE   Although Victoria and most of the major towns in the region have hospitals, some of the Gulf and San Juan islands only operate clinics. These are well equipped for most medical needs. For life-threatening emergencies, airlift services are used. Check to see if your health insurance covers potential needs away from home. Some plans offer a daily rate for the term of your trip; these include the **Canadian and American Automobile Associations** (CAA 🕾 877/325-8888 AAA 🕾 800/562-2582), **Mutual of Omaha** (🕾 800/775-6000), and your local **Thomas Cook** office. Check with your local agent for details. The standard of health care in Canada is comparable to services found in the US.

CAR INSURANCE   Car insurance is compulsory in British Columbia. Basic coverage consists of "no-fault" accident and C$200,000 (US$130,000) worth of third-party legal liability coverage. If you're driving your own vehicle, check with your insurance agent to make sure your policy meets this requirement. If you are renting, your rental agreement will outline these insurance options. *Note:* Wearing seat belts is compulsory in British Columbia. Small children must be seated in the back of the vehicle. And, whether it's a bike, scooter, or moped that you're riding, helmets are mandatory, too.

6 When to Go

CLIMATE

There's a reason for the lush, green landscape, bountiful flowers, and rich agricultural fields in the Pacific Northwest. It's called rain. So, while you're enjoying the milder temperatures, always tote an umbrella.

In **March,** Victoria boasts the first spring blooms in Canada, parading its daffodils on television newscasts across a country still bound in much chillier climes. It's also a signal for travelers to hit the road. Although weather can still be a little unsettled, the deals in accommodation and uncrowded restaurants are worth the effort of carrying an umbrella. By **May,** cherry blossoms and tulips dot the islands with a pastoral elegance, leading the way to a summer that enjoys at least 16 hours of daylight per day, temperatures that push the mercury to around 25°C/80°F, and a monthly rainfall that averages barely 1 inch. This is **high season,** when the islands seem on perpetual parade. **September or October** is a golden time to visit. The days are still long, there's warmth in the air, and the leaves turn to hues of yellow, gold, and red. With the kids back in school, attractions aren't as jam-packed; getaway packages offer great savings. The winter season, from **November to February,** sees more rain than snow, which, if it falls at all, dissolves into the atmosphere within hours. But snow does settle in the mountains and on Vancouver Island's northernmost reaches, making skiing and snowboarding popular pastimes. Along the westernmost coast of Vancouver Island, **winter storms** from the open Pacific Ocean are so dramatic that savvy marketers have successfully created a new high season specifically geared to storm watchers. Yet, for all the rain, gray days are still outnumbered by beautiful, crisp weather, especially in the San Juans.

Vancouver Island & the North American Mainland

Prince Rupert

TWEEDSMUIR

PROVINCIAL

Bella Coola

PARK

Port Hardy

VANCOUVER ISLAND

STRATHCONA PROVINCIAL PARK

PACIFIC OCEAN

VICTORIA

OLYMPIC NATIONAL PARK

LEGEND

- · — National Boundary
- 5 US Interstate Highway
- 1 Trans-Canada Highway

0   100 mi
0   100 km

Prince George

B R I T I S H

C O L U M B I A

M O U N T A I N S

To Calgary

VANCOUVER

NORTH CASCADES NATIONAL PARK

SEATTLE

WASHINGTON

Olympia

MT. RAINER NATIONAL PARK

C A S C A D E   R A N G E

Columbia River

PORTLAND

O R E G O N

SALEM

Vancouver Island's Average Temperature & Precipitation

	Jan	Feb	Mar	Apr	May	June	July	Aug	Sept	Oct	Nov	Dec
Temp. (°C)	7	8	10	13	16	20	22	22	19	14	9	7
Temp. (°F)	44	47	50	55	61	67	71	71	67	57	49	44
Precip. (mm)	147	97	83	51	40	38	23	47	45	98	132	166

Note: Temperature and precipitation may vary among different parts of Vancouver Island. For example, the west coast usually gets more precipitation than the east coast. The above chart can be used as a general gauge for conditions on the Gulf and San Juan islands, as well. For island-specific readings, contact the local chambers of commerce or visitor information centers.

HOLIDAYS

IN BRITISH COLUMBIA   Although banks, offices, and government agencies close for holiday periods, tour operators and main shops remain open in the major cities, such as Victoria, to take advantage of holiday travelers. There are nine official public holidays: New Year's Day (January 1); Good Friday; Victoria Day (the Monday on or preceding May 24); Canada Day (July 1); B.C. Day (first Monday in August); Labor Day (first Monday in September); Thanksgiving (second Monday in October); Remembrance Day (November 11); Christmas Day (December 25).

IN WASHINGTON   Banks, offices, and government agencies close for statutory holidays, as do most shops and restaurants in outlying areas such as the San Juan Islands. In the United States, there are ten public holidays: New Year's Day (January 1); Martin Luther King Jr. Day (third Monday in January); President's Day/Washington's Birthday (third Monday in February); Memorial Day (last Monday in May); Independence Day (July 4); Labor Day (first Monday in September); Columbus Day (second Monday in October); Veteran's Day (November 11); Thanksgiving (fourth Thursday in November); Christmas Day (December 25).

VANCOUVER ISLAND, THE GULF ISLANDS & THE SAN JUAN ISLANDS CALENDAR OF EVENTS

DECEMBER/JANUARY

Annual Bald Eagle Count, Goldstream Provincial Park, Vancouver Island. When the salmon swim up Goldstream Provincial Park's spawning streams, more than 300 bald eagles take up residence with an eye to a month-long feast. Call © **250/478-9414** for exact dates and events.

FEBRUARY

Chinese New Year, Victoria, Vancouver Island. This is when the Chinese traditionally pay their debts and forgive old grievances to start the new lunar year with a clean slate. The Chinese community rings it in with firecrackers, dancing dragon parades, and other festivities. Late January or early February.

Trumpeter Swan Festival, Comox Valley, Vancouver Island. A week-long festival celebrating these magnificent white birds that gather in the Comox Valley. Call the **Tourism Association of Vancouver Island** (© **250/754-3500**) for exact dates.

MARCH

Pacific Rim Whale Festival, Pacific Rim National Park Region, Vancouver Island. Every spring, mid-March through early April, more than 20,000 gray whales migrate past Vancouver Island's west coast, attracting visitors from all over the world. A colorful celebration featuring live crab races, storytelling, parades, art shows, guided whale-spotting hikes, and whale-watching excursions in zippy Zodiacs. For information, call © **250/726-4641** or 250/725-3414.

APRIL

Annual Brant Wildlife Festival, Parksville/Qualicum Beach, Vancouver Island. A birder's nirvana, this 3-day celebration focuses on the annual black brant migration through the area from Mexico to Alaska (20,000 birds). The event includes guided walks through old-growth forest and saltwater and freshwater marshes, goose-viewing stations, a birding competition, art, photography, and carving exhibitions, as well as numerous children's activities. For exact dates, call © **250/752-9171.**

MAY

Swiftsure Weekend, Victoria and Vancouver Island. More than 200 vessels navigate the unpredictable coastal waters in this, the oldest and largest offshore overnight sailing race in the Pacific Northwest. In 2003, it celebrates its 60th anniversary. It is as exciting to watch as it is to participate. Call the **Royal Victoria Yacht Club** (© **250/592-2441**) for information.

Harbour Festival, Victoria, Vancouver Island. This 10-day festival takes place in the downtown district and features heritage walks, entertainment, music, and more. Call Tourism Victoria for details (© **250/953-2033**). Last week of May.

Artists' Studios Open House, San Juan Island. An island-wide open house featuring weavers, potters, and other craftspeople. Call © **360/ 378-5594** for information. Last weekend in May.

JUNE

Jazz Fest International, Victoria, Vancouver Island. Jazz, swing, bebop, fusion, and improv artists from around the world perform at various venues in Victoria during this 10-day festival. Call ✆ 250/388-4433 for dates and information.

Boat Festival, Cowichan Bay, Vancouver Island. Classic boats, a boat-building house for children, folk singers and dancing are some of the fun activities of this festival. The Fast-and-Furious Boat Building Contest is a highlight: entrants build a boat and race it within four hours! Call the **Tourism Association of Vancouver Island** for exact dates (✆ **250/754-3500**).

Folkfest, Victoria, Vancouver Island. This free 8-day world-beat music festival takes place at the end of June or early July. Main venues are the Inner Harbour and Market Square in downtown Victoria. For dates and information, call ✆ **250/388-4728.**

JULY

Festival of the Arts, Salt Spring Island. Catch irreverent performances by the Hysterical Society. Call ✆ **250/537-4167** for information. Begins first weekend in July and runs for entire month.

Nanaimo Marine Festival, Nanaimo, Vancouver Island. Lots of activities take place around the harbor, culminating in the famous Bathtub Race between the city of Nanaimo and Kitsilano Beach, in Vancouver. Yes, it's exactly what it sounds like—racers scrunched up in racer-designed bathtub lookalikes that may or may not make it across the chop. Contact the **Nanaimo Tourism Association** (✆ **800/663-7337**) for information.

Festival of Murals, Chemainus, Vancouver Island. Chemainus is known worldwide for its ever-changing murals. During the festival, visitors have the opportunity to see local and international artists "decorate" the sides of buildings, walls, and more with new murals. From mid-July to mid-August.

All Sooke Day and Annual Festival of History, Sooke, Vancouver Island. Loggers' sports fill All Sooke Day itself, while the festival continues to the following weekend. Activities include a fishing derby, heritage events, pioneer fashion shows, tea parties, and excursions. Call ✆ **250/642-6351** for information. Third Saturday in July.

BC Open Sandcastle Competition, Parksville, Vancouver Island. Between mid- and late July, the wide sandy beaches are transformed with imagination and creativity. This event attracts more than 40,000 people. Call ✆ **250/248-3613** for exact dates and information.

AUGUST

First Peoples Festival, Victoria, Vancouver Island. This free event, held at the Royal British Columbia Museum, highlights the culture and heritage of the Pacific Northwest First Nations peoples, featuring dances, performances, carving demonstrations, and heritage displays. Call the museum for information (✆ **250/384-3211** or 250/953-3557). First weekend in August.

Canadian International Dragon Boat Festival, Victoria, Vancouver Island. Traditional dragon boat races take place in the Inner Harbour, where 120 local and international teams compete. For details, call Tourism Victoria, at ✆ **250/953-2033.** Mid-August.

Art in the Park, Orcas Island. Held at Moran Sate Park, this annual event brings together displays by local artists and traditional craftspeople that are normally scattered throughout the San Juan Islands. For information, call ✆ **360/376-2273.**

SEPTEMBER

Saanich Fall Fair, Saanichton, Vancouver Island. The oldest agricultural fair in Western Canada showcases livestock, sheep shearing, show jumping, crafts, produce, home baking, and more. Lots of candy floss and olde-style country fun, including a fiddle competition. Call ✆ **250/652-2033** for information. Early September.

Dixieland Jazz Festival & Vintage Car Rally, Nanaimo, Vancouver Island. Competitors race from Victoria, over the Malahat (the mountain north of Victoria) to Nanaimo, in vintage cars—an amazing array of classic chassis. To entertain both racers and spectators, an end-of-summer jazz festival takes place at the finish line in Nanaimo. Call ✆ **250/754-8141** or **Nanaimo Tourism Association** (✆ **800/663-7337**) for information.

OCTOBER

Royal Victorian Marathon, Victoria, Vancouver Island. This annual race attracts runners from around the world. The air is fresh, and the temperature is usually just cool enough to keep the runners moving along a course that's not too strenuous. A good trainer for the Boston Marathon course. Call ✆ **250/382-0042** for information. Canadian Thanksgiving weekend (second weekend in October).

NOVEMBER

The Great Canadian Beer Festival, Victoria, Vancouver Island. Held at the Victoria Conference Centre, some of British Columbia's best microbreweries come together in a sampling extravaganza of beers from across Western Canada. Call Tourism Victoria for information (© **250/953-2033**). Second week in November.

DECEMBER

First Night, Victoria, Vancouver Island. The city's New Year's Eve performing-arts festival and alcohol-free party, specifically designed so the whole family can enjoy a safe and fun New Year's celebration. Victoria's Inner Harbour lights up with activity with streets reserved for pedestrian revelers only. Call © **250/953-2033** for details. December 31.

7 Tips for Travelers with Special Needs

FOR TRAVELERS WITH DISABILITIES   The law requires that most hotels, restaurants, and other public places in British Columbia be **wheelchair accessible.** However, the nature of certain buildings and small-town layouts makes their compliance inconsistent, especially in the Gulf islands (and in the San Juans, for that matter). Except in towns like Ganges (on Salt Spring Island) and Friday Harbor (on San Juan Island), most streets are like country lanes. The charm or historical ambience of a building often means that access routes are difficult, which doesn't make for easy maneuverability. For information on disability travel in British Columbia, contact **Community Aboriginal Women's Services,** which covers municipal accessibility issues, P.O. Box 9490, Station Prov. Govt., Victoria BC V8W 9N7 (© **604/387-7908**). This organization handles municipal access issues. Another source is **Inquiry BC** (© **604/660-2424**). The *British Columbia Accommodations Guide* details accessibility options at lodgings throughout Western Canada. Contact **Tourism British Columbia,** P.O. Box 9820, Station Prov. Govt., 1803 Douglas St., Victoria BC VAW 9W5 (© **800/HELLOBC** (800/435-5622); www.hellobc.com).

FOR FAMILIES   Victoria is one of the most child-friendly, cosmopolitan cities on Vancouver Island, offering a great selection of family activities to enjoy. The **Victoria Bug Zoo** and **Miniature World** are wonderful diversions, come rain or shine, and children of all ages will enjoy scooting around Victoria's Inner Harbour in the 12-passenger Harbour Ferries vessel, which looks like something out of Disneyland's Cartoon Land. See chapter 3. **Tourism Victoria** (812 Wharf St. (© **250/953-2033;** www.tourismvictoria.com) publishes a good guide for parents, called *Things to Do with Kids.* Check out **www.kidfriendly.org,** too. It's a great site for child-friendly things to do in British Columbia, places to stay, and other ideas.

FOR FEMALE TRAVELERS British Columbia and the entire Pacific Northwest is safe, polite, and a great place for female travelers. As with any destination, common sense should dissuade you from hitchhiking, or walking alone late at night in a city. Otherwise, traveling should be a delight. If you're heading off the beaten track and into the wilds, hike or camp with a friend. A number of Canadian outfitters offer women-only adventure tours.

FOR GAY & LESBIAN TRAVELERS The larger cities in Western Canada are gay-tolerant, with a number of gay bars, gay-owned businesses, and after-hours clubs. In Victoria, Gay Pride stages an annual parade in early July, where transvestites and others really strut their stuff. The gay lifestyle is widely accepted throughout the islands, on either side of the border, although in some of the small, northernmost communities, discretion is advised. Public displays of affection will not be appreciated. Log into the chat channel at **www.gayvictoria.com** for updates on events, and resources around the island.

FOR SENIORS Travelers 65+ often qualify for discounts at hotels and attractions, so don't be shy about asking. Just be sure to always carry some kind of ID—such as a driver's license—that shows your date of birth. In Victoria and Nanaimo, seniors receive **discounts on public transit.** Passes for persons over 65 (with proof of age) may be purchased at shops in Victoria that display a FareDealer sign (7-Eleven stores are a good bet, as are most newsstands). To locate a FareDealer vendor, contact **BC Transit,** 520 Gorge Rd., Victoria, BC V8W 2P3 (© **250/382-6161;** www.bctransit.com).

FOR STUDENTS Council Travel Service (© **800/226-8624;** www.counciltravel.com), which operates in Canada through **Travel Cuts,** is the biggest student travel agency operation in the world. It is a great resource for travel deals, as well as basic health and life insurance. It also has a **24-hour help line.** Here's where to obtain a **Student ID card** that will be your key to discounts on plane tickets, rail passes, and more. In Canada, you can find a Travel Cuts office at most university campuses across the country. They also have offices in Victoria, at 1312 Douglas St. (© **250/995-8556**) and Vancouver, at 567 Seymour St., Vancouver BC V6B 3H6 (© **604/ 659-2830**). You can call them toll-free, at © **800/667-2887,** or go online to **www.travelcuts.com**.

8 Getting There

BY PLANE

Western Canada is linked with the United States, Europe, and Asia by frequent nonstop flights. **Vancouver International Airport** (© **604/207-7077;** www.yvr.ca) and Seattle's **Seatac International Airport** (© **206/433-5388;** www.seatac.org) are major hubs; regional airlines connect to Victoria, Bellingham, and smaller centers throughout the islands. Major carriers include: **Air Canada** (© **888/247-2262** or © 800/661-3936 (from outside Vancouver); www.aircanada.ca), **WestJet** (© **800/538-5696;** www.westjet.com), **American Airlines** (© **800/443-7300;** www.americanairlines.com), **Continental** (© **800/231-0856;** www.continentalairlines.com), **Northwest Airlines** (© **800/447-4747;** www.nwa.com), and **United Airlines** (© **800/241-6522;** www.ual.com).

Air Canada and **Horizon Air** (© **800/547-9308;** www. horizonair.com or www.alaskaair.com), Alaska Airlines' connector, offer direct connections from several American and Canadian cities such as Washington, DC, Anchorage, San Francisco, and Calgary, to Vancouver, Victoria, and Seattle. Provincial commuter airlines, including floatplanes and helicopters that fly between the Vancouver Harbour on the mainland, and Victoria's Inner Harbour, also serve the Gulf Islands. They include: **Air Canada Jazz** (a subsidiary of Air Canada) (© **888/247-2262;** www.flyjazz.ca), **Harbour Air Sea Planes** (© **604/688-1277;** www.harbour-air.com), **Helijet Airways** (© **250/382-6222** or 604/273-1414; www.helijet.com), **Kenmore Air** (© **800/543-9595;** www.kenmoreair.com), **Pacific Coastal Airlines** (© **800/663-2872** outside Vancouver or 604/ 273-8666 in Vancouver; www.pacific-coastal.com), and **West Coast Air** (Floats) (© **800/347-2222** or 604/688-9115; www.west coastair.com). Commercial Air Service between the Seattle area and the San Juan Islands includes: **Island Air** (charter only) (© **360/ 378-2376;** www.sanjuan-islandair.com), **Kenmore Air** (seaplanes) (© **800/543-9595;** www.kenmoreair.com), **Northwest Seaplanes** (© **800/690-0086** or 425/277-1590; www.nwseaplanes.com), and

West Isle Air (© 800/874-4434; www.westisleair.com). For float-plane tours and charter flights, contact **Cooper Air** (© 800/656-0766 from within Canada, or 250/656-3968; www.cooperair.com).

BY TRAIN TO VANCOUVER ISLAND

VIA Rail and **Amtrak** services end in Vancouver, so travel to Victoria and Vancouver Island requires connecting to either ferry or plane transportation. **VIA Rail** (© 800/561-8630; www.viarail.com) connects Vancouver to the rest of Canada. **Amtrak** (© 800/872-7245; www.amtrak.com) offers a daily service (a combination of train and coach) between Seattle and Vancouver. Schedules for both VIA Rail and Amtrak are posted at **Pacific Central Station,** 1150 Station St. (at the corner of Main St. and Terminal Ave.), Vancouver.

BY BUS & FERRY

TO VICTORIA   Pacific Coach Lines (© 800/661-1725 or 604/662-8074; www.pacificcoach.com) operates bus service between Vancouver and Victoria. The 4-hour trip from the **Vancouver bus terminal** (Pacific Central Station, 1150 Terminal Ave.) to the **Victoria Depot** (710 Douglas St.) includes passage on the **Tsawwassen-Swartz Bay ferry.** One-way fares are C$28 (US$18) for adults, C$20 (US$13) for BC seniors; return fares are C$54 (US$35) for adults, C$38 (US$25) for BC seniors. Discounts are not offered to out-of-province seniors. Fares for children 5 to 11 are half the adult fare. Departures are daily, every two hours, between 5:45am and 7:45pm.

The **Victoria Express** (© 800/633-1589 in season, or 360/452-8088 year-round; www.victoriaexpress.com) operates a seasonal passenger-only ferry service, June through September, between Port Angeles and Victoria. Crossing time is 1 hour. There are two crossings per day. Reservations are available. Fares are C$20 (US$13) for adults, C$11.50 (US$7.50) for children 5 to 11.

Clipper Navigation (© 800/888-2535 or 250/383-8100; www.victoriaclipper.com) runs a year-round passenger-only service between Seattle and Victoria aboard a high-speed catamaran called the **Victoria Clipper.** From mid-May to mid-September, there are up to four crossings per day. The rest of the year this is reduced to one crossing per day. One-way fares mid-May through mid-September are C$101.50 to $115 (US$66 to $75); return fares are C$168 to $192 (US$109 to $125). From mid-September to

Vancouver Island

LEGEND

✈ Airport

– – – Ferry Route

⛷ Ski Area

⑤ US Interstate Highway

🍁① Trans-Canada Highway

▓▓▓ Main Highway

▓▓▓ Secondary Highway

mid-May, in the off-season, one-way fares are C$92 (US$60); return fares are C$152 (US$99). From mid-May to mid-September, there is one daily crossing aboard the Victoria Clipper from Seattle to Friday Harbor, on San Juan Island. One-way fares for all passengers are C$59 (US$38); return fares are C$91 (US$59). Reservations are not accepted.

TO THE GULF ISLANDS Travelers should take the **Pacific Coach Lines coach** from Vancouver to Victoria, as mentioned above, but disembark in **Tsawwassen,** where **BC Ferries** (*©* **888/ BCFERRY (888/223-3779)** or 250/386-3431; www.bcferries.com) sails year-round to the island of your choice. On Vancouver Island, BC Ferries departs from **Swartz Bay,** north of Victoria. Fares and sailing times range from 1 to 3 hours depending on your final island destination. See "Getting There," in chapter 7 for information about schedules and fares to specific islands.

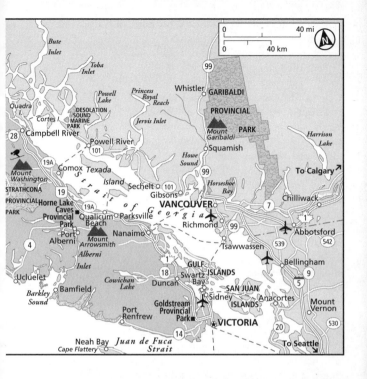

TO THE SAN JUAN ISLANDS From Seattle's **Seatac International Airport** (© 206/433-5388; www.seatac.org) and from the **Bellingham Airport** (© 360/671-5674), **Airporter Shuttle** (© 800/235-5247; www.airporter.com) and **Skagit County Bus** (© 360/757-4433; www.skat.org) transport passengers to Anacortes, north of Seattle on the Olympic Peninsula, just east of the San Juans. Connections can be made between Bellingham Airport and Vancouver on **Quick Shuttle** (© 800/665-2122; www.quick coach.com). There is no bus transportation for travelers from Anacortes to the San Juans; you either travel on foot or in your own vehicle. Once there, visitors traveling on foot have a choice of taxis, car rentals, moped rentals, or bicycle rentals. See chapter 8.

BY CAR & FERRY
TO VANCOUVER ISLAND Hopping across the United States/Canadian border by car is easy, with the main crossing located

right on the **I-5 at Peace Arch Park,** just north of **Blaine.** Once in Canada, drive to **Tsawwassen** to catch any number of ferries leaving for Vancouver, Nanaimo, and the Gulf Islands.

From the United States, daily ferry services link Port Angeles, Seattle, and Anacortes, Washington, with port facilities near Victoria. These include **Blackball Transport** (② 360/457-4491 in Washington, ② 250/386-2202 on Vancouver Island; www.ferry travel.com/coho), which runs a year-round, first-come first-served car and passenger service aboard the *MV Coho* between Port Angeles and Victoria. One-way fares are C$36 (US$30) for a standard-size vehicle and driver, C$12.50 (US$8) for adult passengers, C$6 (US$4) for children. There are four 1½-hour daily crossings, from June to mid-September. There is one crossing daily from October to January, and two crossings daily from February to May.

Washington State Ferries (② 800/843-3779 in Washington, or 888/808-7977 in Canada, or 206/464-6400; www.wsdot.wa.gov/ ferries) runs a passenger and car ferry service from Anacortes, through the San Juan Islands, to Sidney, 26km (16 miles) north of Victoria, and returns. There is only one crossing daily, so vehicle reservations are recommended in summer. Reservations must be made by 5:30pm the day prior to travel. From May to early October, one-way fares are C$19 (US$12.40) for adults, C$9.50 (US$6.20) for seniors, C$13.50 (US$8.70) for children 5 to 18, C$63 (US$41) for a standard-size vehicle and driver. From mid-October to April, return fares are C$17 (US$11) for adults, C$8.50 (US$5.50) for seniors, C$12 (US$7.70) for children; C$46 (US$29.75) for a standard-size vehicle and driver. Crossing time is 3 hours.

Alternatively, you can choose to cross the border just north of Blaine, and catch a **BC Ferries** vessel from Tsawwassen on the mainland to Swartz Bay, a 32-km (20-mile) drive from Victoria's city center, or to Duke Point Terminal, near Nanaimo. Ferries leave every hour on the hour during the summer season, June through Labor Day, and on the odd hour for the rest of the year. Extra sailings are often added for holiday periods. Reservations are available, but not always necessary. One-way fares average C$9 (US$6) for adults, C$7 (US$4.50) for students, C$4.50 (US$3) for children 4 to 11; C$30 (US$19.50) for a standard-size vehicle and driver. BC seniors travel free Monday through Thursday, except on holidays. All BC Ferries have a restaurant and/or coffee bar on board, serving a wide range of soups, sandwiches, burger platters, salads, and snack food.

TO THE GULF ISLANDS BC Ferries (© 888/BCFERRY (888/223-3779) or 250/386-3431; www.bcferries.bc.ca) operates an extensive network of ferries to the Gulf Islands, linking the islands to one another, to the BC mainland, and to Vancouver Island. There are at least two crossings daily, year-round, to each of the Gulf Islands, but departure times vary according to your destination. Ferry travel can be expensive if you're taking a vehicle, and long boarding waits are not uncommon. Ticket prices vary seasonally; mid-week travel is slightly less than on weekends and holidays. During these peak periods, book at least 3 weeks in advance to avoid disappointment. Reservations can be made by phone or online. One-way fares from Tsawwassen average C$9 (US$6) per passenger; C$35 (US$23) for a standard-size vehicle. One-way fares from Swartz Bay average C$6 (US$4) per passenger; C$21 (US$14) for a standard-size regular vehicle. Return fares are less, and vary according to which island you are returning from. Return fares from the islands to Swartz Bay are free. Inter-island trips average C$3 (US$2) per passenger; C$7 (US$4.50) for a standard-size vehicle.

TO THE SAN JUAN ISLANDS From mid-May to September, **Clipper Navigation** (© 800/888-2535 or 250/383-8100; www.victoriaclipper.com) runs one crossing daily from Seattle to Friday Harbor, on San Juan Island, aboard the **Victoria Clipper** passenger-only ferry. One-way fares are C$59 (US$38) per passenger; return fares are C$91 (US$59) per passenger. Crossing time is 2½ hours. Reservations are not accepted. **Washington State Ferries** (© 888/808-7977 or 206/464-6400; www.wsdot.wa.gov/ferries) provide multiple daily service between Anacortes and each of the larger San Juan Islands. No reservations are available. If you're taking a vehicle, you should arrive at least an hour before scheduled sailings; up to 3 hours at peak travel times on summer and holiday weekends. Some food service and a picnic area are available near the terminal. Check out **www.ferrycam.net** to see live images of the ferry lanes. From May 3 to October 1, one-way fares are C$10.50 (US$6.80) for adults, C$5.25 (US$3.40) for seniors, C$7.50 (US$4.80) for children 5 to 18, C$43.50 (US$28.25) for a standard-size vehicle and driver, C$38.25 (US$24.85) for seniors taking a vehicle. Fares are lower in the off-season, October 2 through May 2. Inter-island travel is C$17.50 (US$11.25) for a standard-size vehicle and driver. Passenger fares are as listed above.

9 Getting Around

BY CAR

All the islands are a pleasure to explore and best done by car. In Victoria and Nanaimo, you'll find a number of rental car companies, including **Avis** (© 800/879-2847; www.avis.com), **Budget** (© 800/268-8900; www.budget.com) and **Hertz** (© 800/263-0600; www.hertz.com).

ON VANCOUVER ISLAND   Although highways are well maintained on Vancouver Island, getting from point A to point B can take longer than anticipated. Traffic in and around Victoria tends to be heavy and frustratingly slow—perhaps because so many drivers appear to be slower-moving retirees. Also, many of the region's more interesting attractions are off the highway on roads that twist and turn through picturesque communities. If you have the time, this beats highway asphalt. Gas is sold by the liter, averaging around C63¢ a liter (US40¢ a liter). Speeds and distances are posted in kilometers (1 kilometer = 0.6 miles). Logging roads lead to some of the best places on the island, but if you drive on one, remember that logging trucks have absolute right of way. Members of the **American Automobile Association (AAA)** can get emergency assistance from the **British Columbia Automobile Association (BCAA)** (© 800/222-4357; www.bcaa.com).

IN VICTORIA   This is a walking city, so park your car and don a good pair of shoes. Those few attractions that are not close to the city core are only a short taxi ride away. Victoria also has a comprehensive public transit system (see chapter 3, "Essentials").

Tips Distances and Driving Times from Victoria

- Victoria to Sidney: 26km (16 miles), approximately ½ hour
- Victoria to Nanaimo: 111km (67 miles), approximately 1¾ hours
- Victoria to Port Alberni: 195km (117 miles), approximately 3 hours
- Victoria to Campbell River: 264km (158 miles), approximately 4 hours
- Victoria to Tofino: 316km (190 miles), approximately 4¾ hours
- Victoria to Port Hardy: 502km (312 miles), approximately 7 hours

---

ON THE GULF & SAN JUAN ISLANDS   The easiest way to tour these islands is by car, although some communities have rental scooters, mopeds, and bicycles. (For details, see "Essentials" in chapter 7 or 8 for the specific island.)

BY TRAIN

VIA Rail's E&N Railiner (© 800/561-8630; www.viarail.ca) travels between Victoria and Courtenay, winding through the Cowichan River Valley and Goldstream Provincial Park. Travelers on the Horseshoe Bay-Nanaimo ferry board the train in Nanaimo. It departs from Victoria's **E&N Station** (450 Pandora Ave.). The service runs Monday through Saturday, and the trip takes about 4½ hours. One-way fares from Victoria to Courtenay are C$45 (US$29) for adults, C$41 (US$27) for seniors, C$22.50 (US$14.50) for children 2 to 11. There are 7-day advance-purchase discounts and other specials available. At press time, VIA Rail had announced plans to cancel this service in summer 2002. Negotiations with local island authorities are ongoing to see that decision reversed. Contact VIA Rail for confirmation of this service prior to making your plans.

FAST FACTS: Vancouver Island, the Gulf Islands & the San Juan Islands

American Express   In Victoria, the office is at 1203 Douglas St. (© 250/385-8731) and is open Monday to Friday from 8:30am to 5pm and Saturday from 10am to 4pm. To report lost or stolen traveler's checks, call © 800/221-7282.

Business Hours   In Victoria and other major urban centers, banks are open Monday through Thursday from 10am to 3pm, Friday from 10am to 6pm. Stores are open Monday through Saturday from 10am to 6pm. Stores in Victoria are also open Sunday in summers.

Car Rentals   See "Getting Around," earlier in this chapter.

Currency Exchange   See "Money," earlier in this chapter.

Drugstores   You'll find outlets throughout the Islands. In Canada, pharmacists are extremely helpful for casual medical advice and are a good preliminary stop for minor ailments.

Electricity   Canada and the United States use the same electrical current, 110 to 115 volts, 60 cycles.

Emergencies   Dial 911 for fire, police, or ambulance, in either the US or Canada. In British Columbia, the Royal Canadian Mounted Police (RCMP) administer a **Tourist Alert** program, by posting emergency notices at visitor information centers, at provincial park sites, and on BC ferries.

Hospitals   Most major cities and towns, such as **Victoria, Nanaimo,** and **Campbell River,** have hospitals. On the Gulf and San Juan islands, however, there are only medical clinics; for life-threatening situations, they use airlift services.

Internet Access   Although you will find Internet cafes in Victoria, public Internet access becomes increasingly scarce away from the city center, particularly on the Gulf Islands and San Juan Islands.

Liquor Laws   In British Columbia, the minimum drinking age is 19. Liquor is sold only in government-run liquor stores, although in the larger communities such as Victoria and Nanaimo, you may find beer and wine sold from independent, government-licensed specialty shops. In the Gulf Islands, liquor is sold over a specific counter in one of the local stores. In Washington State, the minimum drinking age is 21. Spirits, wine, and beer are available for purchase in most grocery stores.

Post Office   Postal rates within Canada are C48¢ for standard letters and postcards, C65¢ to the US, and C$1.25 overseas. For more information, log on to **www.canadapost.ca**. Postal rates within the US are US34¢, US50¢ to Canada and Mexico, and US70¢ overseas. For more information, go to **http://pe.usps.gov**.

Smoking   British Columbia by-laws prohibit smoking in a public place, including restaurants, offices, and shopping malls. Although this is adhered to in the larger cities, individual pubs and bars in the island communities try to turn a blind eye to the legislation. Ask before you light up publicly anywhere in the province. No-smoking is also the "norm" in most public places in Washington State.

Taxes   See "Entry Requirements & Customs," earlier in this chapter.

Telephone   The Canadian and US phone systems are the same. Numbers are made up of the 3-digit area code and the 7-digit local number. On Vancouver Island and the Gulf Islands, this prefix is 250. For the San Juan Islands, the area code is 360. "1" is the long-distance prefix. For directory assistance within Canada, dial **411;** in the US, dial **1 + area code + 555-1212.** Most public phones accept prepaid phone cards, which are sold at drugstores and convenience stores.

Time Zone   British Columbia and Washington State are in the Pacific Time Zone, 3 hours behind Eastern Standard Time. Daylight saving time applies from the first Sunday in April through the last Sunday in October.

Tipping   Tipping etiquette is the same in Canada and the United States. In restaurants, tip 15 to 20% for good service. Tip 10% to hairdressers and taxi drivers. Tip on par, US or Canadian funds, for baggage handling at $1 a bag.

Weather   Call ✆ **604/664-9010** for weather updates; ✆ **604/666-3655** for marine forecasts.

3

Victoria

Whoever said Victoria was for the newly wed and nearly dead, needs to take a second look. Although it certainly has its fair share of the blue-rinse brigade, Victoria is a romantic place, and in the past decade has turned into a thriving city. Described by painter Emily Carr as "more English than England," Victoria's charm is moving beyond its rather quaint façade. Sure, there are still plenty of double-decker buses, heritage brick buildings covered with clambering vines, English-style taverns and ever-blooming gardens, but there's also a definite zip in the air. Nicknamed the "recreational capital" of British Columbia, the city's range of activities reads like an exhaustive shopping list: year-round golf, whale watching, fishing, cycling, and much more. Victoria is located around one of Canada's prettiest harbors, and the water is always busy with seaplanes, ships, and kayaks. Accommodations are first-class, many attractions are worthy of a repeat visit, shopping is varied, and restaurants are cosmopolitan, hip, and always busy.

You'll want to spend *at least* two days here, just to get a taste of what Victoria is becoming. It's also the ideal base from which to explore the rest of Vancouver Island. Extending more than 450 kilometers (280 miles) from Victoria to the northwest tip of Cape Scott, the island offers some of the most dramatic stretches of coastal wilderness you'll find in the Pacific Northwest. (See chapters 4, 5, and 6 for coverage of the rest of Vancouver Island.)

1 Essentials

GETTING THERE

BY PLANE Most visitors arrive via a connecting flight from either **Vancouver International Airport** (© 604/207-7077; www.yvr.ca), or **Seatac International Airport,** in Seattle (© 206/433-5388; www.seatac.org). Airlines flying into the rapidly expanding **Victoria International Airport** (© 250/953-7500; www.victoriaairport. com) include **Air Canada** (© 888/247-2262; www.aircanada.ca),

Horizon Air (© 800/547-9308; www.alaskaair.com), and **WestJet** (© 888/937-8538; www.westjet.com). The Victoria International Airport is near the BC Ferries terminal in Sidney, 26km (16 miles) north of Victoria off Highway 17. Highway 17 heads south to Victoria, becoming Douglas Street as you enter downtown.

Airport bus service, operated by **AKAL Airport** (© 877/386-2525 or 250/386-2526; www.victoriaairporter.com), takes about half an hour to get into town. Buses leave from the airport daily, every 30 minutes from 4:30am to midnight. The adult fare is C$13 (US$8.50) one-way, or C$23 (US$15) round-trip when purchased in advance by calling the toll-free number. The senior/student fare is C$11.70 (US$7.60); children 4 and under are free. Drop-offs and pick-ups are made at most Victoria area hotels. **Empress Cabs** (© 250/381-2222), and **Blue Bird Cabs** (© 250/382-4235) make airport runs. It costs about C$30 to 35 (US$12.50 to $23) one-way.

Several car-rental firms have desks at the Victoria International Airport, including: **Avis** (© 800/879-2847; www.avis.com), **Budget** (© 800/268-8900; www.budget.com), **Hertz** (© 800/263-0600; www.hertz.com), and **National (Tilden)** (© 800/227-7368; www.nationalcar.com). Car reservations are recommended from June to September and during peak travel times on holiday weekends.

BY TRAIN & BUS **VIA Rail** trains arrive at Victoria's **E&N Station,** 450 Pandora Ave., near the Johnson Street Bridge (© 800/561-8630 in Canada or 800/561-3941 in the US; www.viarail.com). *Note:* At press time, VIA Rail's plans to cancel this service in summer 2002 were in hot negotiation between VIA Rail officials and local communities who are fighting for its continuance. Call VIA Rail for updates.

The **Victoria Bus Depot** is at 710 Douglas St. (behind the Fairmont Empress Hotel) (© 800/663-8390 or 250/388-5248). **Pacific Coach Lines** (© 800/661-1725 within North America or 250/385-4411 in Victoria; www.pacificcoach.com), offers daily service to and from Vancouver, and includes the ferry trip across the Georgia Strait between Tsawwassen and Sidney. **Laidlaw Coach Lines/Island Coach Lines** (© 800/663-8390 or 250/385-4411; www.victoriatours.com) provides daily service from Nanaimo, Port Alberni, Campbell River, and Port Hardy.

BY FERRY   **BC Ferries** offers crossings from the mainland to various points on Vancouver Island (© **888/BCFERRY** (888/ 223-3779) in BC outside the Victoria dialing area or 250/386-3431; www.bcferries.com). For more information, see "Getting There" in chapter 2.

VISITOR INFORMATION

The **Tourism Victoria Visitor Information Centre,** 812 Wharf St., Victoria, BC V8W 1T3 (© **250/953-2033;** www.tourismvictoria. com) is an excellent resource for brochures, ideas for itineraries, and maps. If you're traveling with children, ask for *The Kids' Guide to Victoria* that details more than 50 places to go and things to do around Vancouver Island. Tourism Victoria also operates a **reservations hotline** (© **800/663-3883** or 250/953-2022) for last-minute bookings at hotels, inns, and B&Bs. The center is open September through April daily from 9am to 5pm, May and June daily from 9am to 8pm, and July and August daily from 9am to 9pm. Bus nos. 1, 27, or 28 to Douglas and Courtney streets.

GETTING AROUND

BY CAR   If you must bring your car (exploring downtown is really best done on foot), make sure your hotel has parking. Parking spaces around the city-center are at a premium. (Hotels that have parking are included in "Where to Stay.") For out-of-town activities, car-rental agencies include **Avis**, at 1001 Douglas St. (© **800/879-2847** or 250/386-8468; www.avis.com), **Budget,** at 757 Douglas St. (© **800/268-8900** or 250/253-5300; www.budget.com), **Hertz Canada,** at 2634 Douglas St. (© **800/263-0600** or 250/385-4440; www.hertz.com), and **National (Tilden),** at 767 Douglas St. (© **800/387-4747** or 250/386-1213; www.nationalcar.com). Renting a car costs approximately C$40 (US$26) per day but may be less with various discounts.

BY TAXI   **Empress Cabs** (© **250/381-2222**) and **Blue Bird Cabs** (© **250/382-4235**) are good bets. But do call ahead—very few stop for flag-downs, especially when it's raining. Rides around the downtown area average C$6 (US$4), plus 10% tip.

BY BUS   The **Victoria Regional Transit System** (operated by BC Transit) (© **250/382-6161;** www.bctransit.com) operates approximately 40 bus routes throughout **Greater Victoria** and the outer suburbs of **Sooke** and **Sidney.** Regular service on the main routes runs Monday to Friday from 6am to midnight. Call for schedules on the weekends. Consult the *Victoria Rider's Guide* for schedules and

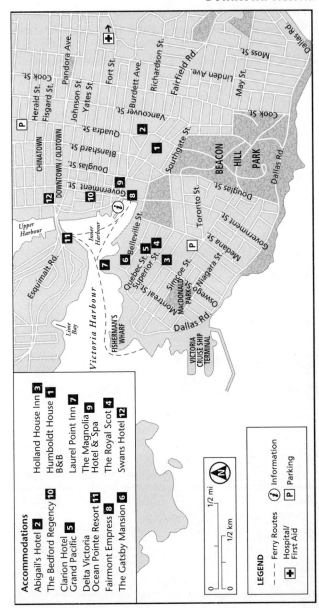

Downtown Victoria

Accommodations

Abigail's Hotel **2**

The Bedford Regency **10**

Clarion Hotel Grand Pacific **5**

Delta Victoria Ocean Pointe Resort **11**

Fairmont Empress **8**

The Gatsby Mansion **6**

Holland House Inn **3**

Humboldt House B&B **1**

Laurel Point Inn **7**

The Magnolia Hotel & Spa **9**

The Royal Scot **4**

Swans Hotel **12**

LEGEND

--- Ferry Routes

➕ Hospital/First Aid

ⓘ Information

🅿 Parking

1/2 mi

1/2 km

routes, available at the **Tourism Victoria Visitor Information Centre** (see "Visitor Information," above). The guide outlines transit routes for many of the city's neighborhoods, landmarks, and attractions. Popular routes include No. 2 (Oak Bay), No. 11 (Downtown, James Bay, Beacon Hill Park), No. 14 (Craigflower, University of Victoria), No. 23 (Art Gallery of Victoria), No. 61 (Sooke), No. 70 (Sidney, Swartz Bay), and No. 75 (Butchart Gardens). This route includes a pick-up at the Sidney ferry terminal and is handy for those arriving from the mainland without a vehicle.

Fares are based on the number of geographic zones a passenger crosses and are defined by boundaries. For example, traveling in downtown Victoria is one zone, traveling to Sooke crosses two zones, as does traveling from Sidney to Victoria. One-way, single-zone **fares** are C$1.75 (US$1.00) for adults, C$1.10 (US$0.75) for seniors and children to grade 7, but children 5 and under are free. Two-zone fares are C$2.50 (US$1.50) for adults, C$1.75 (US$1.00) for seniors and children. Transfers are good for travel in one direction with no stopovers. A **DayPass,** which costs C$5.50 (US$3.50) for adults, C$4.00 (US$2.50) for seniors and children, is available at the Tourism Victoria Visitor Information Centre, at convenience stores, and at outlets displaying the FareDealer symbol. See chapter 2, "Tips for Travelers with Special Needs."

BY FERRY   Once you're downtown, scooting across the harbor in one of the tiny, 12-passenger ferries operated by **Victoria Harbour Ferry** (© 250/708-0201) is great fun—and expedient— to get you from one part of the city to another. The squat, cartoon-style boats have big wraparound windows so everyone has a terrific view. Ferry connections to the Fairmont Empress Hotel, the Coast Harbourside Hotel, and the Delta Victoria Ocean Pointe Resort, run May through September daily every 15 minutes from 9am to 9pm. From October to April, the ferries run only on sunny weekends from 11am to 5pm. When the weather is "iffy," call the ferry office to check if the ferries are running that day. The cost per hop is C$3 (US$2) for adults, C$1.50 (US$1.00) for children. See "Organized Tours" for other ways to enjoy a ferry ride.

ORGANIZED TOURS

BUS TOURS   Gray Line of Victoria (© 250/388-5248) conducts tours of the city and, notably, of **Butchart Gardens** (see chapter 4, "The Top Attractions"). The 1½-hour **"Grand City tour"** costs C$18.50 (US$12) for adults, C$9.25 (US$6) for children 5 to 11, and is free for children 4 and under (one child per adult). From June 29 to August 25, tours are held daily, departing every 30 minutes from 9:30am to 4:30pm. From May 4 to June 28 and from August 26 to September 21, tours depart hourly from 9:30am to 3:30pm. From September 22 to November 9, tours depart at 10am, noon, and 2pm. From November 10 to March 4 tours are seasonal; call ahead to confirm exact times.

FERRY TOURS   Departing from various stops around the Inner Harbour, **Victoria Harbour Ferries** (© **250/708-0201;** vhfc@ islandnet.com) offers a terrific 45-minute tour of the harbor. See shipyards, wildlife, marinas, fishing boats, and floating homes from the water. Tours cost C$12 (US$8) for adults, C$6 (US$4) for children 11 and under. From March 1 to April 30 and for the month of October they operate daily from 11am to 5pm. From May 1 to September 30 they run daily from 9am to 9pm. Tours depart every 15 minutes. If you want to stop for food or a stroll, you can get a token good for reboarding at any time during the same day.

Victoria Harbour Ferries also runs a 50-minute tour of the gorge opposite the Johnson Street Bridge, where tidal falls reverse with each change of the tide. This tour costs C$14 (US$9) for adults, C$12 (US$8) for seniors, and C$7 (US$4.50) for children. **Gorge tours** depart from the dock in front of the Fairmont Empress Hotel from June to September, every half hour from 10am to 8pm. Tours leave less frequently from October to May, depending on the weather. Call ahead on the day to confirm schedules.

SPECIALTY TOURS   In the mood for something a little different? Climb into one of the bicycle-rickshaws operated by **Kabuki Cabs** (© **250/385-4243**). They usually park in front of the Fairmont Empress Hotel. You set your own itinerary. Tours cost C$5 (US$3.50) for 5 minutes, C$10 (US$6.50) for 10 minutes, and so on. Prices are based on two people per carriage plus a child on the lap. **Tallyho Horse Drawn Tours** (© **866/383-5067** or 250/ 383-5067; www.tallyhotours.com) has conducted horse-drawn carriage tours in Victoria since 1903. Tours start at the corner of Belleville and Menzies streets (across from the Royal London Wax Museum). Fares are C$14 (US$9) for adults, C$6 (US$4) for children 17 and under, free for children who can ride on a parent's lap. Tours operate daily in April and May from 10am to 5:30pm; from June 1 to Labor Day from 9am to 10pm; and from September to mid-October from 10am to 5:30pm. Tours depart every half hour.

FAST FACTS: Victoria

American Express   The Victoria office is located at 1203 Douglas St. (© **250/385-8731**) and is open Monday to Friday from 8:30am to 5pm and Saturday from 10am to 4pm. To report lost or stolen traveler's checks, call © **800/221-7282.**

Business Hours   **Banks** in Victoria are open Monday to Thursday from 10am to 3pm, Friday from 10am to 6pm. **Stores** are open Monday to Saturday from 10am to 6pm. Many stores are also open on Sunday in summers. Last call at the city's bars and cocktail lounges is 2am.

Currency Exchange   The best rates of exchange are at bank ATMs. Try the **Royal Bank,** 1079 Douglas St., © **250/ 356-4500,** in the heart of downtown. **Calforex Foreign Currency Services** is open 7 days a week, 724 Douglas St., © **250/384-6631.**

Dentists   Most major hotels have a dentist on call. You can also visit the **Cresta Dental Centre**, #28-3170 Tillicum Rd., at Burnside St., in Tillicum Mall. Open Monday to Friday from 8am to 9pm, Saturday from 9am to 5pm, and Sunday from 11am to 5pm. Call © **250/384-7711.**

Doctors   Hotels usually have a doctor on call. Another option is the **James Bay Treatment Centre,** at 100-230 Menzies St. Open Monday to Friday from 9am to 6pm, Saturday 10am to 4pm. Call © **250/388-9934.**

Drugstores   Pick up your allergy medication or refill your prescription at **Shoppers Drug Mart**, 1222 Douglas St. © **250/384-0544.** Open Monday to Friday from 7am to 8pm, Saturday from 9am to 7pm, and Sunday from 9am to 6pm. **McGill and Orne Rexall,** 649 Fort St., is open Monday to Saturday from 9am to 6pm, and Sunday and holidays from noon to 4pm. Call © **250/384-1195.**

Emergencies   Dial 911 for police, fire, ambulance, and poison control.

Hospitals   Local hospitals include the **Royal Jubilee Hospital,** 1900 Fort St. © **250/370-8000** or 250/370-8212 for emergencies, and **Victoria General Hospital,** 1 Hospital Way © **250/727-4212** or 250/727-4181 for emergencies.

Internet Access   Log on at **Cyberstation**, 1113 Blanshard St., (© 250/386-4687).

Newspapers   The *Victoria Times Colonist* comes out daily. The weekly entertainment paper *Monday* magazine comes out, curiously, on Thursday.

Police   The **Victoria City Police** can be reached at © 250/995-7654.

Post Office   The main **Canada Post office** is at 714 Yates St. (© 250/953-1351). The **Oak Bay post office** is at 1625 Fort St. (© 250/595-2552). There are also postal outlets in **Shoppers Drug Mart** (see "Drugstores," above).

Safety   Crime rates are quite low in Victoria, but transients panhandle throughout the downtown and Old Town areas. Lock items in the glove compartment or trunk when you park your car.

Taxes   Hotel rooms are subject to a 10% tax. The provincial sales tax (PST) is 7.5% (excluding food, restaurant meals, and children's clothing). For more information, call the **B.C. Consumer Taxation branch** © 877/388-4440 or 604/660-4500. Most goods and services are subject to the 7% federal goods and services tax (GST) (see chapter 2, "Entry Requirements & Customs," for more information).

Weather   For weather updates, call © 250/656-3978.

2 Where to Stay

Victoria has a wide choice of fine accommodations, and all are in, or within walking distance of, the **Inner Harbour** and **downtown core.** Farther afield in Sooke and on the Malahat, there are some spectacular options. In Sidney, too, you'll find one or two sweet retreats. (See chapter 4 for places to stay on the South Island.) If you're looking for a bed-and-breakfast, get in touch with **Born Free Bed & Breakfast of BC** (© 800/488-1941 (US only) or 604/298-8815; www.vancouverbandb.bc.ca), which seems to have the inside scoop on availability. **Tourism Victoria** (© 800/663-3883 or 250/953-2022; www.tourismvictoria.com) can book rooms at hotels, inns, and B&Bs. Another great source is **www.hellobc.com**, Tourism British Columbia's official site for researching and booking accommodation throughout the province.

INNER HARBOUR & NEARBY
VERY EXPENSIVE

Clarion Hotel Grand Pacific ✸✸ The "grandness" begins as you approach the hotel beneath a canopy of trees—beside ducks paddling in waterfall-fed pools. Located next to the Parliament Buildings, the Grand Pacific is the newest hotel on the harbor. Standard guest rooms are elegant and comfortable, with aromatherapy bath products, and desks that are equipped with high-speed dataports. All rooms have balconies where seagulls perch, usually waiting for a handout. One-bedroom suites include extras such as cordless phones, robes, two TVs, and deluxe sofa beds. Executive suites feature double Jacuzzis, fireplaces, multiple balconies, and wet bars. The best thing is that the wide range of accommodation means that you might be able to afford top-notch luxury for less than what's offered elsewhere. Fitness facilities are the most extensive in the city, and dining options include **The Mark,** geared to high-end, romantic encounters (see "Where to Dine").

450 Quebec St., Victoria, BC V8V 1W5. ✆ **800/663-7550** or 250/386-0450. Fax 250/380-4474. www.hotelgrandpacific.com. 304 units. July–Aug C$179–$389 (US$116–$252) deluxe room; C$259–$469 (US$168–$305) jnr. and 1-bedroom suite. Sept–mid-Oct and mid-May–June C$119–$299 (US$77–$194) deluxe room; C$199–$439 (US$129–$285) jnr. and 1-bedroom suite. Mid-Oct–mid-May C$99–$269 (US$64–$175) deluxe room; C$179–$409 (US$116–$266) jnr. and 1-bedroom suite. From C$359 (US$225.40) and way up executive suites. Children 17 and under stay free in parents' room. AE, DC, DISC, MC, V. Free parking. Bus no. 30 to Superior and Oswego sts., nos. 27 or 28. **Amenities:** 3 restaurants (all Pacific Northwest); lounge; zone-filtered lap pool; 2 squash and racquetball courts; health club & spa; concierge; secretarial services; 24-hour room service; babysitting; laundry service; dry cleaning. *In room:* A/C, TV, minibar, coffeemaker, hair dryer, iron, safe.

Delta Victoria Ocean Pointe Resort and Spa ✸✸✸ Voted one of the world's best places to stay in 2001 by *Condé Nast Traveler,* this luxurious, modern hotel sits on the north side of the Inner Harbour. Decor is clean, light, and relatively clutter-free, which highlights the gleaming woods and the soft, natural colors throughout. Many of the Inner Harbour guest rooms have floor-to-ceiling windows that view the Parliament Buildings and the Fairmont Empress. All rooms come with the usual toiletries, down duvets, and cuddly robes. The European-style spa provides the ultimate in therapeutic services. The hotel's fitness facilities will satiate the needs of most obsessives; a large indoor pool that's surrounded by glass makes you feel as if you're swimming outdoors. A popular tour company, **Springtide** (✆ **250/385-8433**), operates an activities desk in the hotel, offering whale-watching excursions, as well as bike and kayak rentals. Both hotel restaurants boast waterfront views; the **Victorian** is known for its award-winning cuisine and is considered one of the city's finest restaurants. (See "Where to Dine," later in this chapter.)

45 Songhees Rd., Victoria, BC V9A 6T3. ⓒ Delta, **800/268-1133** or 250/360-2999. Fax 250/360-1041. www.oprhotel.com. 242 units, 1 honeymoon suite, 1 penthouse suite. C$179–$269 (US$116.50–$175) double; C$299–$599 (US$194–$389) 1-bedroom suite; C$350–$550 (US$227.50–$357.50) honeymoon suite; C$550–$749 (US$357.50–$487) penthouse suite. Extra person C$30 (US$19.50). Children 11 and under stay free in parents' room. AE, DC, DISC, MC, V. Valet parking C$9 (US$6). Bus no. 24 to Colville, or no. 6. Pets accepted. **Amenities:** 2 restaurants (both Pacific Northwest); ozonated indoor swimming pool; 2 night-lit outdoor tennis courts; 1 indoor racquetball and squash court; extensive health club & spa; children's programs; car-rental desk; free shuttle to/from downtown; secretarial services; 24-hour room service; in-room massage; babysitting; laundry service; dry cleaning. *In room:* A/C, TV, dataport, minibar, coffeemaker, hair dryer, iron.

Fairmont Empress Hotel 𝞏𝞏𝞏 The grande dame of all hotels, this ivy-adorned harborside landmark is a view unto itself. Staying here is the quintessential Victoria experience, ongoing renovations maintain the old girl's elegance. Most of the deluxe guest rooms, and all of the Entrée Gold guest rooms, are superb: all have extra large beds and windows that let the light pour in. Entrée Gold rooms also have extras such as TVs in the bathrooms and CD players. Guests staying in Entrée Gold rooms are treated to their own concierge and are served breakfast in a private lounge. Many of the other guest rooms are billed as "cozy," which means that, comfort aside, the Fairmont folks couldn't make the 1908 rooms any larger. If you're slightly claustrophobic, don't even think about these. At press time, the new **Willow Stream Spa** was set to open. The Fairmont Hotel chain has proven its know-how in creating spa excellence (think of the Chateau Whistler on the mainland, or the Banff Springs in Alberta), so this one should be no exception. Dining choices include the **Bengal Lounge**—its ceiling fans and tall palms are very colonial India; the **Empress Dining Room,** and **Kipling's.** The famous afternoon tea is served year round in the Main Tea Lobby, spilling into surrounding areas as the number of tea drinkers dictate.

721 Government St., Victoria, BC V8W 1W5. ⓒ Fairmont, **800/441-1414** or 250/384-8111. Fax 250/381-5959. www.fairmont.com. 425 units, 47 suites. May–mid-Oct C$279–$479 (US$181–$311) regular room; C$429–$629 (US$279–$409) Entrée Gold room. Mid-Oct–Apr C$159–$479 (US$103.50–$311) regular room; C$239–$559 (US$155–$363) Entrée Gold room. Packages available. Children 11 and under stay free in parents' room. AE, DC, DISC, MC, V. Underground valet parking C$19

(US$12.50). Bus no. 5. Small pets accepted C$25 ($US16.25). **Amenities:** 3 restaurants (East Indian, Pacific Northwest), lounge; large heated indoor pool; health club & spa; concierge; tour desk, car-rental desk, business center; 24-hour room service; babysitting; dry cleaning. *In room:* A/C, TV w/pay movies, minibar, coffeemaker, hair dryer, safe.

EXPENSIVE

The Gatsby Mansion   Overlooking the Inner Harbour, just across from the Seattle–Port Angeles ferry, this hundred-year-old heritage mansion is trapped in a time warp, with its antique furniture, Italian stained glass, velvet tapestries, and meandering hallways. It's almost like staying in a museum. Each guest room is different and features the comforts of down duvets and fine linens. A gracious high tea is served beneath twinkling chandeliers in what was once the front parlor, drawing room, and dining rooms. Dinner is served in the same space.

309 Belleville St., Victoria, BC V8V 1X2. ℂ Belleville Park, **800/563-9656** or 250/388-9191. Fax 250/920-5651. www.bellevillepark.com. 20 units. Mid-May–Sept 30 C$245–$319 (US$159–$207) double. Oct–mid-May C$139–$185 (US$90–$120) double. Rates include full breakfast. Packages available. AE, MC, V. Free parking. Bus no. 5 to Belleville and Government sts., nos. 27, 28, or 30. **Amenities:** Restaurant (Pacific Northwest), lounge. *In room:* TV w/pay movies, coffeemaker.

Holland House Inn   The Holland is definitely the place to stay if you're looking for a classy, romantic setting. Built in 1932, this stylish inn offers all the amenities of a modern bed-and-breakfast in an atmosphere that feels like home. All guest rooms are decorated in a unique theme and sport comfortable sitting areas, as well as private bathrooms. Some rooms have balconies, canopied four-poster beds, fireplaces, and patios. The range in rates reflects this diversity. A delicious breakfast, served in the sun-filled conservatory (or on the patio if weather permits), is included.

595 Michigan St., Victoria, BC V8V 1S7. ℂ **800/335-3466** or 250/384-6644. Fax 250/384-6117. www.hollandhouse.ca. 17 units. July–Aug C$100–$175 (US$65–$114) standard and veranda room; C$230–$295 (US$149.50–$192) fireplace room and suite. Sept–June C$100–$145 (US$65–$94) standard and veranda room; C$175–$250 (US$114–$163) fireplace room and suite. Rates include full breakfast. Children 5–14 additional C$20 (US$13). Children 4 and under stay free in parents' room. AE, DISC, MC, V. Free parking. Bus no. 5 to Superior and Government sts., no. 30. **Amenities:** Concierge; tour desk. *In room:* TV.

Laurel Point Inn   One of the first modern hotels built on the Inner Harbour, the Laurel Point Inn's simple Japanese-style design still retains a certain grace. Nevertheless, and luckily for guests, it is undergoing a much-needed facelift. At press time, the hotel was installing new carpets, wallpaper, and other cosmetic necessities.

All guest rooms have spacious private terraces with panoramic views of the harbor and hills beyond. The rooms in the south wing are especially roomy, and are particularly Oriental in flavor, including shoji-style sliding doors, down duvets, and plenty of Asian art. The Japanese Garden features a large reflecting pond and a waterfall that cascades over a whopping 21,300 kilograms (47,000 lbs.) of rock. Now that's something to ponder. The two restaurants are fine, but nothing to write home about. The inn is within easy walking distance of the Parliament Buildings, the Victoria Conference Center, the Royal British Columbia Museum, and Beacon Hill Park, plus downtown shopping and entertainment venues.

680 Montreal St., Victoria, BC V8V 1Z8. © 800/663-7667 or 250/386-8721. Fax 250/386-9547. www.laurelpoint.com. 200 units: 135 harborview, 65 suites. June 1–Oct 15 C$249 (US$162) harborview C$299 (US$195) suite. Oct 16–May 31 C$144 (US$94) harborview; C$199 (US$129) suite. Packages available. Extra person C$15 (US$10). Children 11 and under stay free in parents' room. AE, DC, MC, V. Free valet parking. Small pets allowed in 1st floor harborview rooms C$25 (US$16). **Amenities:** 2 restaurants (Pacific Northwest); small heated pool; access to nearby health club; Jacuzzi; sauna; concierge; activities desk; business center; 24-hour room service; in-room massage; babysitting; laundry service; dry cleaning. *In room:* A/C, TV w/pay movies, dataport, coffeemaker, hair dryer.

MODERATE

The Royal Scot *Value* *Kids*   Situated a block from the Inner Harbour, this suite hotel provides excellent value, particularly if you're not hooked on a waterfront view. Converted from an apartment building, guest rooms are really large, with lots of cupboard space. Studio suites include a living/dining area and kitchen; one-bedroom suites have separate bedrooms with king, queen, or twin beds. Kitchens are fully equipped (including microwaves) and living areas come with sofa beds. This is an ideal home base for families; weary parents in need of a few zzzz's will love scooting their offspring into the children's games room. **Jonathan's restaurant** is fully licensed and has a summer patio. There are nine room types ranging from guest rooms to two-bedroom corner suites, so you're bound to find a good fit.

425 Quebec St., Victoria, BC V8V 1W7. © 800/663-7515 or 250/388-5463. Fax 250/388-5452. www.royalscot.com. 176 units. June 1–Sept 30 C$149 (US$97) standard; C$165–$230 (US$107–$149.50) studio suite; C$189–$299 (US$123–$194) 1-bedroom suite; C$285–$395 (US$185–$257) 2-bedroom suite. Oct 1–May 31 C$145–$175 (US$94–$114) standard; C$165–$209 (US$107–$136) studio; C$189–$219 (US$123–$142) 1-bedroom suite; C$285–$365 (US$185–$237) 2-bedroom suite. Weekly, monthly, and off-season rates available. Children 11 and under stay free in parents' room. AE, DC, MC, V. Free parking. Bus no. 30.

Amenities: Restaurant (Pacific Northwest); small heated indoor pool; hydrotherapy pool; access to nearby health club; sauna; game room; concierge; business center; 24-hour room service; babysitting; laundry service; dry cleaning. *In room*: TV, coffeemaker, hair dryer, iron.

DOWNTOWN & OLD TOWN
EXPENSIVE

Abigail's Hotel ✸✸✸   Tucked in a quiet residential cul-de-sac, only three blocks from downtown Victoria and the Inner Harbour, this European-style Tudor inn is everything you might expect to find in Olde England—and more. Guest rooms are superbly decorated with antiques, wood-burning fireplaces, two-person Jacuzzis, fresh-cut flowers, and welcoming treats such as truffles and fruit. The six "Celebration" suites, part of a recent million-dollar renovation, are especially romantic. Breakfast is fit for royalty—literally—since the chef has cooked for the Queen. Abigail's is geared to adults; children are discouraged.

906 McClure St., Victoria, BC V8V 3E7. ✆ **800/561-6565** or 250/388-5363. Fax 250/388-7787. www.abigailshotel.com. 22 units. May 16–Oct 15 C$219–$309 (US$142–$201) Country & Sunflower room; C$299–$359 (US$194–$233) Fireplace room; C$389 (US$253) Celebration suite. Oct 16–May 15 C$122–$268 (US$79–$174) Country & Sunflower room; C$166–$309 (US$108–$201) Fireplace room; C$183–$334 (US$119–$217) Celebration suite. Rates include full breakfast. Spa, Honeymoon, and Wine Tour packages available. AE, MC, V. Free Parking. Bus no. 1. **Amenities:** Concierge; business center; laundry service; dry cleaning. *In room*: Some with TV/VCR, dataport, hair dryer, iron.

Humboldt House B&B ✸ *(Finds*   Located on a quiet tree-lined street, this beautifully renovated, turn-of-the-century home overlooks the orchards of St. Ann's Academy, a heritage convent and chapel, and is only minutes away from the Inner Harbour. Each guest room has a different decor and ensures pampered privacy. A romantic champagne breakfast in bed is passed to you through a two-way pantry—no one enters your room. You don't even have to open the door. It's lovely! In-room touches include large Jacuzzis, wood-burning fireplaces, goose-down comforters, fresh flowers, and homemade chocolate truffles.

867 Humboldt St., Victoria, BC V8V 2Z6. ✆ **888-383-0327** or 250/383-0152. Fax 250/383-6402. www.humboldthouse.com. 6 units. June 16–Sept 30 C$245–$315 (US$159.50–$208) double; Oct 1–15 and May 1–June 15 C$170–$250 (US$110.50–$162.50) double; Oct 16–Apr 30 C$123–$250 (US$80–$162.50) double. Rates include full breakfast. Packages available. Children 11 and under stay free in parents' room. MC, V. Free parking. Bus nos. 1, 71. **Amenities:** Concierge; in-room massage; babysitting; laundry service; dry cleaning. *In room*: TV/ VCR, fridge, hair dryer, iron.

The Magnolia Hotel & Spa 🔆🔆   This smart boutique hotel has a terrific downtown location. Guest rooms are bright, with floor-to-ceiling windows, custom-designed furniture, two-poster beds, over-size work desks, multiline speaker phones, and cordless bedside phones. Executive Diamond suites have gas fireplaces. There's also an umbrella on hand—Victoria does get its fair share of rain, after all. Of special note is the **Aveda Lifestyle spa,** which is professional, if small. It's a shame the aroma of hair peroxide wafts towards the spa treatment rooms that otherwise provide a pampering environment. The Vichy shower facials are a treat. The hotel houses two restaurants: **Hugo's Grill** is casual, while next door, **Hugo's Brew House** is a preferred nightspot. Beer connoisseurs should try the exclusive selection of true non-pasteurized traditional beers, based on Eastern European recipes.

623 Courtney St., Victoria, BC V8W 1B8. © 877/624-6654 or 250/381-0999. Fax 250/381-0988. www.magnoliahotel.com. 64 units. June 1–Oct 15 C$259 (US$168) standard; C$299 (US$194.50) Executive Diamond suite. Oct 16–Apr15 C$169 (US$110) standard; C$219 (US$142.50) Executive Diamond suite. Apr 16–May 31 C$209 (US$136) standard; C$249 (US$162) Executive Diamond suite. Rates include continental breakfast. Children 11 and under stay free in parents' room. AE, DC, DISC, MC, V. Valet parking C$10 (US$6.50). Bus no. 5. Small pets accepted C$60 (US$39). **Amenities:** Restaurant (Pacific Northwest), pub; access to nearby health club; spa; concierge; limited secretarial services; limited room service; laundry service; dry cleaning. *In room:* A/C, TV w/pay movies, dataport, minibar, coffeemaker, hair dryer, iron.

MODERATE & INEXPENSIVE

The Bedford Regency 🔆   Located on the main commercial drag (the entrance gives the impression that you're entering a shopping mall), the Bedford is one of Victoria's oldest hotels. Although tasteful renovations have brought it up to modern standards, the quirky layout of guest rooms reflects its heritage. All are elegantly comfortable with down duvets and quality toiletries. Some are so tiny that the foot of the bed is just inches from the pedestal sink. Some have a fireplace "around the corner" beside a reading chair, while others are quite spacious, with two queen-size beds facing one another because the room is long and narrow. Bathrooms are small and very Art Deco. The 12 Superior rooms have Jacuzzis and fireplaces. Window boxes mask the busy street scene below, which in summer can be a bit noisy, at least until midnight. **Belingo 1140,** one of the newest jazz/martini lounges in town, is located on the mezzanine. If you're looking for something more casual, head for the **Garrick's Head Pub.**

1140 Government St., Victoria, BC V8W 1Y2. *C* **800/665-6500** or 250/384-6835. Fax 250/386-8930. www.bedfordregency.com. 40 units. May 16–Oct 14 C$165 (US$107) standard; C$180–$195 (US$117–$127) deluxe; C$250 (US$162) superior. Oct 15–May 15 C$79 (US$51) standard; C$89–$109 (US$58–$71) deluxe; C$139 (US$90) superior. Rates include continental breakfast. AE, MC, V. Parking C$10 (US$6.50). Bus no. 5 to Douglas and Johnson sts. **Amenities:** Restaurant (Pacific Northwest), pub, martini lounge. *In room:* TV, coffeemaker.

Swans Hotel 🐦🐦   The charming Swans offers a warm welcome in an intimately comfortable modern-day tavern. But it's more than a bed and beer experience. One of Victoria's best-loved heritage restorations, this 1913 warehouse now provides guests with 30 distinctive—and really spacious—suites. Most of the one- and two-bedroom suites are in fact two-story lofts with 11-foot ceilings and nifty layouts that have many, if not most, of the comforts of home. Accommodating up to six adults, they feature fully equipped kitchens, separate living and dining areas, and private patios. One of Canada's largest private art collections, which unfortunately sounds more impressive than it really is, adds to the atmosphere nonetheless. Check out the stylized totem pole in the restaurant lobby. The **Wild Saffron Bistro & Wine Bar** is open daily. Other facilities include Swans Pub, Buckerfields' Brewery, and **Diablo's,** a new nightclub geared to the younger crowd.

506 Pandora Ave., Victoria, BC V8W 1N6. *C* **800/668-7926** or 250/361-3310. Fax 250/361-3491. www.swanshotel.com. 30 suites. July 1–Sept 30 C$159 (US$103) studio; C$179 (US$116) 1-bedroom suite; C$249 (US$162) 2-bedroom suite. Oct 1– June 30 C$99–$125 (US$64–$81) studio; C$119–$$145 (US$77–$94) 1-bedroom suite; C$179–$205 (US$116–$133) 2-bedroom suite. Weekly and monthly rates available. Extra person C$20 (US$13). Up to 2 children 11 and under stay free in parents' room. AE, DC, MC, V. Parking C$8 (US$5.20). Bus no. 23 or 24 to Pandora Ave. **Amenities:** Restaurant (Pacific Northwest), wine bar, pub, brewery, nightclub; access to nearby health club; secretarial services; limited room service; babysitting; laundry service; dry cleaning. *In room:* TV, dataport, kitchen.

3 Where to Dine

Victoria has a cornucopia of culinary styles. With more than 700 restaurants, there's something for every taste and budget, and since they are all within walking distance of downtown hotels, you don't have to worry about who's going to be the designated driver. Although there's still a tendency for Victorians to eat early (restaurants are packed between 7 and 9pm), many trendier restaurants accept late-night reservations. For a taste of Britain in the heart of Victoria, brewpubs are great gathering-places for a before- or after-dinner pint, or an anytime pint, for that matter! Favorites include the **Swans Brewpub** (506 Pandora Ave., ✆ **250/361-3310**), in the Swans Hotel (see "Where to Stay," above), **Spinnakers** (308 Catherine St., ✆ **250/386-2739**) and the **Sticky Wicket Pub** (919 Douglas St., ✆ **250/383-7137**). And remember, no one does tea better than the Victorians. Sure, it's a bit touristy, but this isn't just dunking a tea bag in warm water. Tea in Victoria is an Epicurean affair offering a host of caloric delicacies. If you're a visitor, you must experience it at least once. In addition to the famed tea at the **Fairmont Empress** (721 Government St., ✆ **250/384-8111**) (see "Where to Stay," above), are summer teas served on the lawns at **Point Ellice House** (2616 Pleasant St., ✆ **250/380-6506**), and year-round cuppas at the **White Heather Tea Room** (1558 Oak Bay Ave., ✆ **250/595-8020**) and **Blethering Place** (2250 Oak Bay Ave., ✆ **250/598-1413**). You'll never dunk a tea bag in quite the same way again.

INNER HARBOUR & NEARBY
EXPENSIVE

Blue Crab Bar & Grill 𝕣𝕣𝕣 SEAFOOD This is the best seafood spot in the city, with killer views of the harbor to boot. Blue Crab's signature blackboards featuring seafood specials are what keep this restaurant at the top. Dishes are extraordinary inventions, such as blue crab fish pot, grilled salmon with crispy yucca root spaetzles, or smoked Alaskan black cod poached in coconut milk with a hint of red curry. There's also a good selection of landlubber dishes for those whose tastes run away from the sea. The wine list is excellent, particularly when it comes to acclaimed BC and other West Coast wines.

In the Coast Hotel, 146 Kingston St. ✆ **250/480-1999**. Reservations required. Main courses C$22–$30 (US$14.50–$19.50). AE, DC, MC, V. Daily 6:30am–3pm and 5–10pm. Nibbles available until 1am.

The Mark 𝕣𝕣 CONTINENTAL WEST COAST This just-opened restaurant in the Clarion Hotel Grand Pacific is set to rival the best. It has no view, preferring to create an intimate dining experience within the confines of a discreet, wood-paneled room. The upscale menu matches the high-end wine list with dishes such as spiced lobster, pan-seared breast of pheasant, and a milk chocolate paté that cries out calories. But the service has such finesse, indulgence is painless. The Mark is perfect for memorable and romantic encounters—it seats only 28 diners. It's *the* place to be seen.

In the Clarion Hotel Grand Pacific, 450 Quebec St. ✆ **250/386-0450**. Reservations recommended. 3–5-course prix fixe dinner C$50–$70 (US$32.50–$45.50). AE, DC, DISC, MC, V. Tues–Sat 6–10pm. Closed Sun–Mon.

The Victorian 🐸🐸🐸 PACIFIC WEST COAST   This award-winning restaurant is probably the city's finest restaurant, offering exemplary service, a casually elegant atmosphere, and right-on-the-water views. The food is also beautiful to look at and even more amazing to taste. Go for the gusto by ordering a la carte. If you're budget-conscious, the prix fixe menu offers a three-, four-, and five-course selection. The menu changes to make the most of the season's best and freshest produce, meats, and seafood. The wine list is superb.

In the Delta Victoria Ocean Pointe Resort and Spa, 45 Songhees Rd. ☎ **250/ 360-2999.** Reservations required Thurs–Sat. Main courses C$20– $35 (US$13– $23). AE, DC, MC, V. Daily 6–10:30pm. Closed Sept 30–Feb 1.

MODERATE & INEXPENSIVE

Barb's Place. 🐸🐸🐸 FISH & CHIPS   Absolutely no frills here; this floating restaurant at Fisherman's Wharf serves fish and chips at their very tastiest. Get your cod, oysters, or halibut grilled, steamed, or deep-fried "any way you like it." Barb serves it all up with hand-hewn chips in newspaper pouches. Douse your chippies in salt and vinegar, the way they do in England, and enjoy the feast at picnic tables while watching the boats, seagulls, and other harborside activities. A safe bet for hungry appetites.

Erie Street, Fisherman's Wharf (at the entrance to the Inner Harbour). ☎ **250/ 384-6515.** Reservations not accepted. Main courses C$4–$14 (US$2.50–$9). MC, V. Feb 1–Oct 31 daily 10am–sunset. Closed Nov–Jan.

The James Bay Tea Room & Restaurant 🐸🐸 *Finds* BRITISH FOOD   British cooking doesn't deserve a bad rap, at least not here. Home-style bangers and mash, Welsh rarebit, liver and bacon, and roast beef and Yorkshire pudding are hearty, wholesome, and pretty darn good. This is one of the few places that actually serves kippers for breakfast. The decor includes Tiffany lampshades, brass knick-knacks, and sepia-tinted family portraits. Tables are crowded and the atmosphere is lively with chatter. Tarot card readings are offered on the weekend.

332 Menzies St. (behind the Parliament Buildings). ☎ **250/382-8282.** Reservations recommended. Breakfast and lunch C$3.75–$7 (US$2.50–$4.50); dinner C$10–$15 (US$6.50–$10). AE, MC, V. Mon–Sat 7am–7pm; Sun 8am–7pm.

DOWNTOWN & OLD TOWN
EXPENSIVE

Cafe Brio 🐸🐸 WEST COAST   This award-winning, bistro-style restaurant serves delicious West Coast fare. An ever-changing sheet highlights whatever fresh organic produce the chef has purchased that day. A creative mix of natural flavors zings with just the right amount of added spices. Expect bold items in winter, such as venison shank, free-range chicken, and confit of duck. In summer, items are lighter: beef tartar complemented by curly-leafed frisee lettuce, goat cheese, and olive oil; Salt Spring Island mussels; and seared scallops topped with crisp potato rösti. Service is top-notch and the wine list is exceptional, with more than 200 wines by the bottle and 30 by the glass or half liter. Local artwork decorates the walls, and wide-planked wooden floors add warmth to the decor.

944 Fort St. ℂ 250/383-0009. Reservations recommended. Lunch C$8–$12 (US$5–US$8); dinner C$8–$28 (US$5–$18). MC, V. May–Sept Mon–Fri 11:45am–2pm; 5:30–9pm; Fri–Sat to10pm. Oct–Apr 5:30–9pm; Fri–Sat to10pm. Closed Dec 24–25.

Il Terrazzo Ristorante 𝕲𝕲𝕲 NORTHERN ITALIAN   Locals have voted this Victoria's best Italian restaurant for the past 7 years. Capturing the heart and soul of Tuscany and Piedmont, the restaurant's three talented chefs create specialties that include wood oven–roasted pizzas, fresh grilled seafood, and a wide variety of homemade pastas. Set in a converted heritage building, this warmly romantic restaurant features a gorgeous heated courtyard, surrounded by brick fireplaces and lit by wrought-iron candelabras. Inside, exposed brick walls, wooden beams, and intimate nooks and crannies are a delight.

555 Johnson St., Waddington Alley (off Johnson St. at Wharf St.). ℂ **250/361-0028.** Reservations recommended. Lunch C$8–$12 (US$5–$7.50); dinner C$16–$25 (US$10.50–$16.50). A, DC, MC, V. Mon–Sat 11:30am–3pm and 5pm–10pm.

Restaurant Matisse 𝕲𝕲 CLASSIC FRENCH   The world of Edith Piaf is tucked behind an entrance of wrought-iron gates, which give way to an alluring Parisian ambience. Filled with soft lights and a profusion of fresh flowers, this award-winning 40-seat restaurant has been noted for its service, elegance, and quality, and justifiably so. Savor fresh bread, rack of lamb, filet bordelaise, duck, rabbit, bouillabaisse, and possibly the best crème brûlée in the world. Menus are always *très fresh* and innovative, presenting authentic new recipes and ideas garnered during annual pilgrimages to France. Vive la France!

512 Yates St. (at Wharf St.). ℂ **250/480-0883.** Reservations recommended. Main courses C$18.95–$29.95 (US$12.50–$19.50); 3-course prix fixe dinner C$42.50 (US$27.50); 5-course prix fixe dinner C$55.50 (US$36). AE, MC, V. Wed–Sun 5:30–10pm. Closed Mon–Tues and first two weeks in May.

MODERATE & INEXPENSIVE

Bowman's Rib House *Finds* *Kids* STEAK & RIBS   The ribs
are delicious and the service fun, but that's not the only reason you
should come. First, leave your inhibitions at the door, which, by the
way, is bordered by red-and-white flashing tracer lights—definitely
not in keeping with the surrounding neighborhood. Then, wind
your way through a labyrinth of narrow corridors (Bowman's lies in
the basement of the **Cherry Bank Hotel,** one of Victoria's quirkiest
places to stay). Finally, you're in for a real treat and a fun time,
especially Thursday through Sunday when honky-tonk piano rules
the roost. Placemats are also songsheets, and everyone is expected to
sing. Kids love the atmosphere, although songs like *Ain't She Sweet*
are better geared to grannies.

In the Cherry Bank Hotel, 825 Burdett Ave. ℰ **250/385-5380.** Reservations recommended. Lunch C$5–$10 (US$3.50–$6.50); dinner C$10.95–$18.95 (US$7–$12.50).
DC, DISC, MC, V. Mon–Fri 11:30am–2pm and 5–9pm; Sat–Sun 5–10pm. Closed
statutory holidays.

Herald Street Caffe *✶✶✶* FRENCH/PACIFIC NORTHWEST
Consistently great, and sometimes inspired, the food here is
combined with an award-winning wine list. Located in a renovated
19th-century warehouse, its casual, lively atmosphere is geared to the
younger crowd. All desserts, breads, pastas, soups—even the jam—
are made in-house. Main dishes focus on fresh, local seafood and
organic produce. The clams are superb, and the crab cakes are almost
deified, having been written up by *Bon Appétit* and *Gourmet*
magazines. They've recently expanded the restaurant; it now includes
a 25-foot-long bar, ideal for a more casual dining experience, or just
a pre-dinner drink. Topped off with exceptionally good service, this
is one of the city's best restaurants.

546 Herald St. (in Chinatown). ℰ **250/381-1441.** Reservations required. Brunch
and lunch C$6–$16 (US$4–$10.50); dinner C$16–$29 (US$10.50–$19). AE, DC,
MC, V. Wed–Thurs 11:30am–3pm and 5:30–10pm; Fri–Sat 11:30am–3pm and
5:30–11pm; Sun 11am–3pm and 5:30–10pm. Closed Mon–Tues. Closed Dec 25
and Jan 1.

Hime Sushi *Value* *Finds* JAPANESE   Although low prices are
the number one attraction, this tiny 44-seat restaurant is selling itself
short. The sushi is top quality and generously served, and you'll
likely see extras to boot, such as the added pieces of sushi that appear
on your plate at no additional cost. They also do made-to-order
special requests. The decor is no frills and the tables are very small,
but it somehow creates a lively, intimate atmosphere.

680 Broughton St. ℭ **250/388-4439.** Reservations recommended. Lunch C$6.50–$10 (US$4.50–$6.50); dinner C$8.45–$25 (US$5.50–$16.50). AE, MC, V. Mon–Sat 11:30am–9pm.

Pagliacci's ℛℛℛ ITALIAN Opened in 1979 by expatriate New Yorker Howie Siegal, Pagliacci's is not your ordinary Italian restaurant. Named after the Italian word for *clown,* it's elbow-to-elbow most nights. Some might call it a "first-date" place: if your date turns out to be boring, just lean over and chat up your neighbor. Add Howie's extravagant personality to that, and terrific service that lets you mix and match selections from the menu in true *Harry Meets Sally* style, and you've got the makings of an evening to talk about. But most people come for the great food. Menu items are quirky Hollywood and tantalize the imagination: take the *Veronica Lake Salad* or the *Mae West Veal Medallions.* And if all this isn't entertainment enough, there's live jazz Sunday through Wednesday. The likes of Diana Krall and Etta James have played Pagliacci's.

1011 Broad St. ℭ **250/386-1662.** Reservations recommended. Lunch C$5–$10 (US$3.50–$6.50); dinner C$7.25–$20 (US$4.50–$13). AE, MC, V. Mon–Thurs 11:30am–11pm; Fri–Sat 11:30am–midnight; Sun 11am–11pm. Closed Dec 25 and Yom Kippur.

4 Exploring Victoria

THE TOP ATTRACTIONS

Craigdarroch Castle ℛℛ If you've got it, flaunt it. That's what coal baron Robert Dunsmuir (the wealthiest and most influential man in British Columbia back in the 1880s) decided to do. More than a home, this Highland-style castle rises 87 stairs through 5 floors of Victorian opulence and there's not an elevator to be had! Children might think it's like something out of Disneyland. The nonprofit society that runs Craigdarroch does so with impressive tender loving care, and the stained glass, Persian carpets, and intricate woodwork are treasures to behold. Visitors receive a self-guided tour booklet and volunteers delight in sharing sidebars of Dunsmuir's family history. Head to the top for a fabulous view of Victoria, the Strait of Juan de Fuca, and the Olympic Mountains. Allow about an hour to tour the castle.

1050 Joan Cres. (off Fort St.). ℭ **250/592-5323.** www.craigdarrochcastle.com. Admission C$10 (US$6.50) adults and seniors, C$5.50 (US$3.50) students, C$2.50 (US$1.50) children 6–12, free for children 5 and under. June 15–Aug 31 9am–7pm; Sept 1–June 14 10am–4:30pm. Closed Dec 25–26 and Jan 1. Take Fort St. out of downtown, just past Pandora Ave., and turn right on Joan Cres. Bus nos. 11 and 14.

Crystal Garden *(Kids*   Filled with rare and exotic tropical flora and fauna, this indoor jungle would make Tarzan proud. Originally opened in 1925 as a huge saltwater pool, the soaring glass roof of this historic conservatory now houses over 50 species of endangered exotic birds, mammals, and reptiles, including the Golden Lion Tamarin monkey, Bali Mynah, and lemurs. Your strolling safari will also take you past hundreds of tropical plants and flowers, interspersed with flamingoes, hyacinth macaws, and magnificent Koi fish. Allow about 1½ hours, especially if you're with kids.

731 Douglas St. (behind the Fairmont Empress Hotel). ✆ 250/953-8800. www.bcpcc.com/crystal. Admission C$8 (US$5) adults, C$7 (US$4.50) seniors, C$4 (US$2.50) children 5–16, free for children 4 and under, C$22 (US$14.50) family pass. Open July–Aug 8:30am–8pm; Sept–Oct and Apr–June 9am–6pm; Oct–Apr 10am–4:30pm. Bus nos. 30 and 31.

Maritime Museum of British Columbia   Located in a former Victoria courthouse, this museum celebrates British Columbia's seafaring history in film and exhibits, from whalers and grand ocean liners, to military conflict and 20th-century explorers. Highlights include a replica of the *HMS Temeraire,* constructed entirely of beef and chicken bones by French naval prisoners captured during the Napoleonic Wars. Check out the heritage courtroom renovated by Francis Rattenbury, as well as one of Victoria's most ornate elevators. Plan to stay 1½ hours, longer if you have salt in your veins; the museum maintains a registry of heritage vessels, and a wealth of resource information for maritime buffs. The gift shop also has an excellent selection of nautical paraphernalia. Kids programs include a sleepover in this purportedly haunted place!

28 Bastion Sq. ✆ 250/385-4222. www.mmbc.bc.ca. Admission C$6 (US$4) adults, C$5 (US$3.50) seniors, C$3 (US$2) students, C$2 (US$1.50) children 6–11, free for children 5 and under, C$15 (US$10) family pass. Daily 9:30am–4:30pm. Closed Dec 25. Bus no. 5 to View St.

Miniature World   If you ever wondered what Gulliver felt like in the land of the Lilliputians, this little world reveals all. Children and the young at heart will love the more than 80 miniature displays (many of them moving) of solar systems, battle scenes, fancy 18th-century dress balls, a three-ring circus, and dozens of scenes from beloved fairy tales. A big favorite is the Great Canadian Railway, one of the world's largest model railways, although close contenders are the world's smallest operational sawmill, 11 years in the making, and two of the world's largest doll houses.

649 Humboldt St., © 250/385-9731. www.miniatureworld.com. Admission C$9 (US$6) adults, C$7 (US$4.50) children 12–17, C$6 (US$4) children 3–11, free for children 2 and under. June 14–Labor Day daily 9am–9pm; Labor Day–June 13 9am–5pm. Closed Dec 25. Bus nos. 5, 27, 28, 30, and 31.

Pacific Undersea Gardens *Kids* The stark exterior looks out of place in Victoria's Inner Harbour, but descend the sloping stairway and you're in another world—below the waterline. From a glass-enclosed sunken vessel, you get up close and personal with the harbor's marine life, which swims all around you in natural aquariums. Beneath the surface, all manner of fish—from brilliant red snapper to stonefish and octopi, swim through the kelp forest. Divers descend every hour to show the audience some of the harder-to-see creatures, like starfish tucked in rocks, wolf eels, and sharks. The observatory also cares for injured and orphaned seals, many of which prefer to stay in the area after their release. Buy a bag of herring in the gift shop and feed them a feast. Plan to stay about an hour, although feeding the seals is so captivating, you may want to hang around longer.

490 Belleville St. © 250/382-5717. www.pacificunderseagardens.com. Admission C$7.50 (US$5) adults, C$6.50 (US$4.50) seniors, C$5 (US$3.50) children 12–17, C$3.50 (US$2.50) children 5–11, free for children 4 and under. July–Aug daily 10am–7pm; Sept–June daily 10am–5pm. Closed Jan–Feb Tue–Wed. Bus nos. 5, 27, 28, or 30.

Parliament Buildings By night, this architectural gem is lit by thousands of lights so that it looks more like the Hogwarts School for Wizards than the provincial Parliament Buildings. Designed by then 25-year-old Francis Rattenbury, one of the most sought-after architects of the day, the buildings were constructed between 1893 and 1898 at a cost of nearly C$1 million. The interior is equally mystical, filled with mosaics, marble, woodwork, and stained glass. If the Legislature is sitting, head up to the visitor's gallery. There's not a lot of room there, but it's fun to watch politicians in action. British Columbia is known for its eccentric politics, and question period, in the early afternoon, can be particularly entertaining. The "been there, done it" crowd could do this in 20 minutes; guided tours (summer only) last about 40 minutes.

501 Belleville St. © 250/387-3046. www.parl-bldgs.gov.bc.ca. Admission free. Daily 9am–5pm. Bus nos. 5, 27, 28, or 30.

Royal British Columbia Museum *Kids* To be succinct, this museum is one of the best regional museums in the world and is worthy of at least a half day. The dioramas are so lifelike, you'll feel as if you're stepping back in time—whether it's coming face to tusk with a wooly mammoth, or meandering down the cobblestone streets of a pioneer town. Feel the train rattle the timbers of the old train station each time it passes, or enjoy old Charlie Chaplin movies in the movie theater. Just like an IKEA store, the museum has a route that doesn't bypass a thing, so start at the top in the Modern History Gallery, and work your way down through the second-floor Natural History Gallery and the First Peoples Gallery with its totems, Native longhouses, and artifacts. The museum also has an IMAX theater, showing an ever-changing variety of large-screen movies (© **250/953-IMAX** (250/953-4629); www.imaxvictoria.com). Thunderbird Park, beside the museum, houses a cedar longhouse, where Native carvers work on new totem poles. *Note:* Admission rates are sometimes higher during special exhibitions.

675 Belleville St. © **250/356-7226.** www.royalbcmuseum.bc.ca. Admission C$9 (US$6) adults, C$6 (US$4) seniors and students, C$6 (US$4) children 6–18, free for children 5 and under, C$24 (US$15.50) family pass. Daily 9am–5pm. Closed Dec 25 and Jan 1. Bus nos. 5, 28, or 30.

Royal London Wax Museum *Kids*   If you've been to Madame Tussaud's in London, then you'll be disappointed, but at least this effort gives you an idea of what you're missing. Like God's cocktail party, you'll find celebrities, world leaders, and historical figures mixing and mingling in groupings never dreamed of. There's a plethora of waxy royal figures along **Royalty Row,** an Einstein-esque Wizard of Oz in **Storybook Land,** and a host of significant others. The **Chamber of Horrors** doesn't exactly scare up a flutter, even in the faint of heart. The average price tag for each figure is C$10,000, depending on how popular it is. US presidents go cheap; Canadian prime ministers are pricey. Plan to spend 1½ hours.

470 Belleville St. © **250/388-4461.** www.waxworld.com. Admission C$8.50 (US$5.50) adults, C$7.50 (US$5) seniors, C$6.50 (US$4.50) students, C$4 (US$2.50) children 6–12, free for children 5 and under. May–Sept daily 9:30am–8:30pm; Oct–Apr daily 9:30am-5pm. Bus nos. 5, 27, 28, or 30.

Victoria Bug Zoo *Kids Kids*   Enter an amazing world of international insects: walking sticks, praying mantis, tarantulas, and scorpions, to name a few. Although all the creepy-crawlies are behind glass, an entomologist (bug scientist) is on hand to answer questions and show you how to handle some of the multilegged creatures, which include a 400-leg millipede that stretches the length of your forearm. Even if you're spider-wary, this is a fascinating place.

1107 Wharf St. © **50/384-2847.** www.bugzoo.bc.ca. Admission C$6 (US$4) adults, C$4 (US$2.50) children 3–16, free for children 2 and under. Daily Mon–Sat 9:30am–5:30pm and Sun 11am–5:30pm. Closed Dec 25 and Jan 1. Bus no. 6.

om); and the **Victoria Marine Adventure Centre,**
© **800-575-6700** or 250/995-2211; www.marine-
. The **Pride of Victoria Cruise,** which departs from
each Hotel, 1175 Beach Dr. (© **250/592-3474;**
chhotel.com), offers 3½-hour whale-watching
om March through October on either a 45-foot
28-foot converted pleasure cruiser. Both have wash-
und bar service. Fares are C$79 (US$51.50) for
S$32) for children 12 and under. The cruise lunch
) per person. There's a complimentary shuttle from
to make arrangements for pick-up.

fter Dark

ne (**www.monday.com**) covers everything going on
nightclubs and the performing arts, to films and
You name it, *Monday*'s got it. You can also call the
ts **Council of Greater Victoria**'s events hotline, at
'S (250/381-2787). Tickets and schedules are also
Tourism Victoria Travel Visitor Information
arf St., (© **250/953-2033**).

MING ARTS

atre, 805 Broughton St. (© **250/361-0800**), dates
1900s. Renovated in the 1970s, it hosts concerts
ctoria Symphony) dance recitals, and touring plays,
nances by Pacific Opera Victoria. The **McPherson**
ntennial Sq. (© **250/361-0800**), was built in 1914
ges Vaudeville Theatre. It hosts smaller stage plays
s by the Victoria Operatic Society. The Royal and
share a box office at the **McPherson Playhouse**
21 or 250/386-6121; www.rmts.bc.ca). Box office
ay to Saturday from 9:30am to 5:30pm, and on per-
or the two hours prior to showtime. Take Bus no. 6
Government streets.

MUSIC   The **Victoria Symphony Orchestra,**
. (© **250/385-9771;** www.victoriasymphony.bc.ca),
n in August with **Symphony Splash,** a free concert
barge in the Inner Harbour. The **Victoria Inter-**
l is held in July and August. Concerts, ballet, and
presented at various locations. Contact **Tourism**
/953-2033) for details.

SHOPPING HIGHLIGHTS

Victoria has dozens of specialty shops that make browsing a real
delight. Most visitors head up the brick-paved **Government Street
promenade,** about 5 blocks north from the Inner Harbour. Many of
the stores are housed in beautiful heritage buildings and stepping
inside is like stepping back a century. **Roger's Chocolates**
(913 Government St., © **250/384-7021**) has been a Victoria establishment for more than a hundred years, and the store is filled with
original Tiffany glass, ornamental tile-work, and old-fashioned,
highly polished wooden counters. Farther along, you'll find **Munro's**
(1108 Government St., © **250/382-2464**), a bookstore that's been
described as Canada's most magnificent. Located in a heritage building built around 1909, it features a 7-m (24-ft.) coffered ceiling,
stained-glass windows, and eye-catching wall hangings. The remain-
der tables have some incredible deals. **Government Street** is a good
place to find First Nations art of the Pacific West Coast. But be
warned. Amid the jewels is a plethora of souvenir shops, each hip-
deep in bottles of maple syrup and Taiwanese knick-knacks. One of
the most respected stores for established BC First Nations artists is
Hills Native Art (1008 Government St., © **250/385-3911**). Here
you'll find exquisite traditional pieces, such as wooden masks and
carvings, Haida argillite and silver jewelry, bentwood boxes, button
blankets, drums, talking sticks, and masks. For the less serious
collector, Hills has a good selection of dream catchers and souvenir
totem poles.

Farther north, **Old Town/Market Square** features a fascinating
blend of turn-of-the-century buildings housing funky, up-to-date
shops. The area is reminiscent of San Francisco's Garibaldi Square,
but quainter, with live performances in summer. Nearby, Victoria's
Chinatown is so tiny, you might miss it in the blink of an eye.
Search out **Fan Tan Alley.** It's Canada's thinnest commercial street,
just over a meter (4 ft.) wide at either end, yet crammed with odd-
ball paraphernalia and a maze of doors leading to small courtyards—
and even more doors leading to more back alleys, stairs, and living
quarters. When the police used to raid gambling clubs, participants
could easily escape through the myriad passageways.

While you're in the area, stop by **Glass Works** (630 Yates St.,
© **250/388-7827**). Housed in a renovated bank building, this
gallery-cum-workshop is interactive shopping at its best. Watch from
the mezzanine gallery as award-winning artists transform molten glass
into unique works of art. The glasswork is incredibly imaginative

and the studio, which features some of the finest selections of glass art in Canada, is equally successful.

On the eastern edge of downtown is **Fort Street,** fondly known as **Antique Row.** Renowned for its high-quality British collectibles, you'll find everything from estate jewelry and silverware to heritage china and furniture. **Classic Silverware** (826 Fort St., © 250/ 383-6860) is a gorgeous shop that specializes in discontinued sterling silver and silver-plated flatware and tea service sets. It also maintains a registry for missing and discontinued china. **Vanity Fair Antique Mall** (1044 Fort St., © 250/380-7274), brings together more than 40 dealers of crystal, glassware, furniture, and jewelry. Some items require a mortgage to purchase; others are really very reasonable and will leave change in your pocket.

The Victoria **Eaton Centre** anchors the city core and is where to shop for top-name fashions and mainstream goods. Be sure to explore the many side streets around the Eaton Centre, such as **Trounce Alley** and **Broad Street,** as they'll lead you into many a shopping discovery. **The Bay** is also a popular department store; it got its start over 330 years ago as a series of trading posts across the country and is the oldest corporation in North America. Besides designer labels and general housewares, you can still buy their famous red-green-and-yellow-striped point blanket, an item that was originally traded for beaver pelts.

OUTDOOR ACTIVITIES

FISHING Saltwater fishing is "big" in this part of the world. Guides will show you the current hot spots. **Adam's Fishing Charters** (© 250/370-2326, www.adamsfishingcharters.com) and the diverse **Marine Adventure Centre,** 950 Wharf St. (© 800/ 575-6700 or 250/995-2211; www.marine-adventures.com), both on the Inner Harbour, are good starting points. Fishing charters run around C$75 (US$48.50) an hour, with a minimum of 3 or 4 hours. To fish, you need a **non-resident saltwater fishing license,** available at Adam's and the Marine Adventure Centre. A 1-day license costs C$7.49 (US$5), a 3-day license costs C$20.33 (US$13), and a 5-day license C$34.17 (US$22). There is a salmon surcharge of C$6.42 (US$4). If you're interested in taking the wheel yourself, the Marine Adventure Centre also rents small powerboats at C$45 (US$29.50) an hour, as well as kayaks, from C$15 (US$10) per hour. For fly-fishing, **Robinson's Outdoor Store,** 1307 Broad St. (© 250/ 385-3429; www.robinsonsoutdoors.com), is an excellent resource

for information and gear from reels, and a number of resource ing licenses. For non-residents,

GOLF Victoria has an envia are reasonable, the scenery year-round. The **Olympic V** (© 800/I-GOLFBC (800/44 olympicview.bc.ca), is one of th 2 waterfalls and 12 lakes sharin May to October, daytime gre November to April, they're C$ remain the same year-round, junior is C$25 (US$16.50). (US$81.50) per person, which balls. The **Cedar Hill Munici** (© 250/595-3103) is a more only 3.5km (2 miles) from d C$34 (US$22), twilight and **Cordova Bay Golf Course** 380-4653 or 250/658 4444; between the Victoria Internati it's about a 20-minute drive fr fairways and 66 sand traps. P daytime green fees are C$54 (US$32) from Monday to Th Tee times outside of 5 days are mid-October to late March, g ends (including Friday), C$37 time, call the **Last Minute C** 604/878-1833 for substantial courses in and around Victori

WHALE WATCHING Or lions, porpoises, and gray wh whale-watching outfitters abo (expect to pay about C$55 (U real choice is between riding t or in a larger, more leisurely **Orca Spirit Adventures** (© which departs from the Coas **Whales,** 812 Wharf St. (© 88

princeofwhale 950 Wharf St adventures.co the Oak Bay www.oakbayl charters daily **catamaran** or room facilitie adults, C$49 is C$7.50 (US downtown. C.

5 Victoria

Monday mag in town, from poetry reading **Community** © 250-381-A available at t **Centre,** 812 V

THE PERFO

The **Royal Th** from the early (including the as well as perf **Playhouse,** 3 (as the first Pa and performar the McPherso (© 888/717-6 hours are Mon formance days to Pandora an

CLASSICAL

846 Broughton kicks off its sea performed on **national Festi** other events a **Victoria** (© 2!

COMEDY & SPOKEN WORD   The **Mocambo,** 1028 Blanshard. (© **250/384-4468**), a coffeehouse near the Victoria Public Library, hosts a range of spoken-word events through the week. Friday nights feature poetry readings, and on Saturday, it breaks loose with improv comedy. No cover. Open from Monday to Thursday from 6:45am to 6pm, Friday to 11pm, Saturday to 10pm.

DANCE   Dance recitals and full-scale performances by local and international dance troupes such as **Danceworks** and the **Scottish Dance Society** are scheduled throughout the year. Call **Tourism Victoria** (© **250/953-2033**) or the **Community Arts Council of Greater Victoria** (© **250/381-ARTS** (250/381-2787)).

OPERA   The **Pacific Opera Victoria,** 1316B Government St. (© **250/385-0222;** box office © **250/386-6121;** www.pov.bc.ca), presents productions during the months of October, February, and April. Tickets are available at the McPherson Playhouse and Pacific Opera box offices. The **Victoria Operatic Society,** 798 Fairview Rd. (© **250/381-1021;** www.vos.bc.ca), stages old-time musicals and other popular fare year-round at the McPherson Playhouse.

THEATER   The nationally acclaimed **Belfry Theatre Society,** 1291 Gladstone St. (© **250/385-6815;** www.belfry.bc.ca), stages productions in an intimate playhouse that was once a church. The **Intrepid Theatre Company,** 301-1205 Broad St. (© **250/383-2663;** www.intrepidtheatre.com), runs two theater festivals annually. In late April/early May it's the **Uno Festival of Solo Performance,** a unique event of strictly one-person performances. From late August to early September, Intrepid stages the **Victoria Fringe Festival** (© **250/383-2663**), an amazingly eclectic selection of alternative theatre. More than 30 performances from all over the world are staged in four venues around the city, including the Victoria Conservatory of Music, St. Andrew's School, and the Downtown Community Activities Centre. **Theatre Inconnu** (© **250/360-0234;** www.islandnet.com/~tinconnu) produces Victoria's annual **Shakesperean Festival,** which takes place in July and August. The **Langham Court Theatre,** 805 Langham Ct. (© **250/384-2142**), performs works produced by the **Victoria Theatre Guild,** a local amateur society dedicated to presenting a wide range of dramatic and comedic works.

THE CLUB SCENE

Pubs like the **Harbour Canoe Club,** 450 Swift St. (© 250/ 361-1940), **Spinnakers,** 308 Catherine St. (© 250/386-2739), **Swans Brewpub,** 506 Pandora Ave. (© 250/361-3310), and **Hugo's,** 623 Courtney St. (© 250/920-4844), are all hot spots for whiling away an evening over a lively brewskey or two. The rowdiest is, perhaps, **Big Bad Johns,** at the popular 5-storey Strathcona Hotel complex, 919 Douglas St. (© 250/383-7137). Despite a decor that includes an ever-increasing collection of bras hanging from the ceiling, and a floor inches deep in discarded peanut shells, it's a clean-cut place where half the fun is letting it all hang out. *The* place for martinis and Sinatra-flavored schmoozing is **Suze Lounge & Restaurant,** 515 Yates St. (© 250/383-2829), particularly if you get a seat at the 7.6-m (25-ft.) mahogany bar. **Legends,** 919 Douglas St. (© 250/383-7137; www.legendsnightclub.com), the nightclub at "the Strath" is, well, legendary. Quality live music makes this a pop-music palace, running the gamut from afro-pop to blues, to R&B and zydeco. **Diablo's,** 506 Pandora Ave. (© 250/351-3310), in the basement of **Swans Pub,** is the latest club to hit the late-night scene. At press time, it was still finding its feet, but its range of music—bebop, Latino, and blues—was pulling in the twenty- to thirtysomething crowds. **Sweetwater's Niteclub,** 27-570 Store St., at Market Square (© 250/383-7844), is an elegant singles spot for those in their late 20s to early 40s, while **The Jet Lounge,** 751 View St. (© 250/920-7797), is the plush place for Victoria's upscale Gen-Xers. **The Lucky Bar,** 517 Yates St. (© 250/382-5825), next door to popular Suze and owned by the same people, is probably one of the hottest nightspots. The long, darkly lit lounge is a natural follow-through to a meal at Suze, or you can go just for the martinis and music, which is a mix of DJ-spun and live bands.

GAY & LESBIAN BARS

The dance floot at **Hush,** 1325 Government St. (© 250/385-0566), is packed on weekends. Music is a mix of live and DJ presentations plus a sprinkling of special productions, such as shows put on by Drag-o-Rama. **Rosie's,** 615 Johnson St. (© 250/381-2277), is a kitschy 1950s/60s-style diner with classic songs and videos of that era playing continuously from opening at 9am till closing at 2am. **BJ's Lounge,** 642 Johnson St. (© 250/388-0505), has a full menu and lounge decor. A perfect place to do some Streisand karaoke.

4

Southern Vancouver Island

Exploring the South Island is a relaxing change of pace from downtown Victoria. Since the entire area can be reached within a day, out-of-town itineraries are easy to plan. Or, you can stay in the city and make an afternoon of it, touring the countryside. Places like **East Sooke Regional Park,** the **Fort Rodd Hill & Fisgard Lighthouse National Historic Site,** and the world famous **Butchart Gardens,** are about 21km (13 miles) from Victoria; the **Juan de Fuca Trail, Goldstream Provincial Park,** and the **Cowichan Valley** each deserve a day—even more. If you're staying in Victoria but want to taste its urban wilderness or pastoral beauty, taking in the southern part of Vancouver Island is a great way to do so. If you're heading north towards Nanaimo, there are some notable attractions worth building into your itinerary (see "En Route to Nanaimo: The Cowichan Valley," later in the chapter).

1 The Saanich Peninsula

A bustling seaside village, Sidney is filled with picturesque parks and gardens, waterfront restaurants, galleries, and more bookstores than any other community on Vancouver Island. It's small-town Canada gift-wrapped in beautiful scenery. Sidney is located 26km (16 miles) north of Victoria, and approximately 6km (4 miles) south of the BC Ferries terminal in Swartz Bay. Washington State Ferries arriving from Anacortes dock at Sidney.

ESSENTIALS
GETTING THERE
BY CAR AND FERRY If you're driving out of Victoria, head north on **Blanshard St.,** which becomes **Highway 17,** or take BC Transit buses nos. 70, 72, or 75, from downtown Victoria. If you're driving from Swartz Bay (BC Ferries terminal), Sidney is a 6-km (4-mile) drive south on **Highway 17. BC Ferries** (© **888/223-3779** or 250/386-3431; www.bcferries.com) runs a passenger and car ferry service between Swartz Bay and **Tsawwassen,** on the mainland.

June through August, crossings are every hour on the hour, from 7am to 11pm. September through May crossings are every other hour. Additional ferries are often scheduled during holiday periods. One-way fares are C$9.50 (US$6) for adults, C$4.75 (US$3) for children 5 to 11, C$33.50 (US$22) for a standard-size vehicle. BC seniors travel free Monday through Thursday, except on holidays.

BY FERRY   The **Washington State Ferry** terminal is located in Sidney, at 2499 Ocean Ave., (© **888-808/7977** or 206/464-7977; www.wsdot.wa.gov/ferries). Ferries sail once a day, midmorning, between Sidney and Anacortes. Crossing time is 3 hours. Summer vehicle reservations are highly recommended, and must be made by 5:30pm the day prior to travel. One-way passenger fares during the high season (May 3 to October 1) are C$17 (US$11) for adults, C$11.50 (US$7.50) for students, C$8.50 (US$5.50) for seniors; C$63 (US$41) for a standard-size vehicle, C$54.50 (US$35.50) for seniors taking a vehicle. Fares are lower in the off-season (October 2 to May 2).

VISITOR INFORMATION

The **Sidney Chamber of Commerce** operates two Visitor Information Centers on the Saanich Peninsula. One is located at 10382 Pat Bay Highway, Sidney BC V8L 3S3 (© **250/656-0525;** www.spcoc.org). It is open year-round, Monday through Friday, from 8:30am to 5:30pm. The other information center is located in Sidney, **opposite the Washington State Ferry terminal,** at A-2295 Ocean Ave. (mailing address is 10382 Pat Bay Highway, Sidney BC V8L 3S3) (© **250/656-3260**). It is open April through October 15, Monday through Saturday, from 10:30am to 12:30pm, to coincide with ferry arrivals. It is closed October 16 through March.

WHERE TO STAY

Oak Bay Beach Hotel and Marine Resort ᏚᏚᏚ   Located east of Victoria, about a 15-minute drive from the downtown core, the Oak Bay Beach Hotel sits in a pretty, residential area of the city. Reportedly built in just 19 days, this Tudor-style mansion was a favorite haunt of Rudyard Kipling. Furnishings and decor are a cultivated flashback to the 1930s—complete with Edwardian and Victorian antiques—which may be why it attracts so many elderly patrons. That said, its old-world charm has appeal for romantic types. Guest rooms and suites offer a wide variety of configurations and amenities, and are priced accordingly. Popular favorites are the **fireside suites,** with double Jacuzzis beside the window. Welcoming touches include candies sprinkled on the down-comforter-clad beds, alongside cuddly, oversized stuffed animals. Another one of the draws is the hotel's proximity to the Victoria Golf Club across the street, and its on-site adventure programs, including whale watching, kayaking, and a sunset dinner cruise.

1175 Beach Dr., Victoria, BC V8S 2N2. ℂ **800/668-7758** or 250/598-4556. Fax 250/598-6180. www.oakbaybeachhotel.com. 51 units. June 15–Oct 15 C$198 (US$129) standard; C$240 (US$156) deluxe; C$240–$425 (US$156–$276) suite. Oct 16–June 14 C$129 (US$84) standard; C$240 (US$156) deluxe; C$325–$475 (US$211–$309) suite. Rates include breakfast. Adventure and custom packages available. Children 12 and under stay free in parents' room. AE, MC, V. Free parking. Bus no. 2 to Newport and Margate sts. **Amenities:** 2 restaurants, pub; access to nearby health club; game room; concierge; activities desk; free shuttle to/from downtown; 24-hour room service; babysitting; laundry service; dry cleaning. *In room:* TV, dataport, coffeemaker, hair dryer, iron.

Moments Gastronomic Safaris

These unique tours will whet your appetite:

The Ale Trail: Beer aficionados can slurp 'n burp their way to heaven, visiting four breweries to sample some of the finest all-natural, handcrafted brews in the region.

The Gourmet Trail: This guided tour takes you to wineries, herb farms, cheese-makers, and the Butchart Gardens, all of which are only preliminaries to the gourmet tables at area hotels like Sooke Harbour House, The Aerie, and the Wickaninnish Inn.

For more information, contact **First Island Tours, Ltd.** (ℂ **250/658-5367**; www.firstislandtours.com).

The Shoal Harbour Inn 🇷🇷   This new inn blends stunning West Coast scenery and the sophistication of a European boutique hotel. Owned by the same folks who have made **The Latch** a destination restaurant (see "Where to Dine," below), Shoal Harbour features warm, honey-toned woodwork and atrium-style architecture for glimpses of sky, and a view of all three floors of studio, one- and two-room suites. Guest rooms are filled with hand-picked, locally made furniture and custom-made linens. All have gas fireplaces, impressive ensuite bathrooms (complete with heated towel racks), decks, and gleaming, fully appointed kitchens.

2328 Harbour Rd., Sidney, BC V8L 2P8. ℂ **877/956-6622** or 250/656-6622. Fax 250/656-6212. www.shoalharbourinn.com. 20 units. Jun–Aug C$139–$249

Southern Vancouver Island

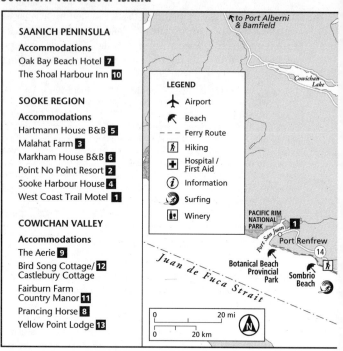

SAANICH PENINSULA

Accommodations
Oak Bay Beach Hotel **7**
The Shoal Harbour Inn **10**

SOOKE REGION

Accommodations
Hartmann House B&B **5**
Malahat Farm **3**
Markham House B&B **6**
Point No Point Resort **2**
Sooke Harbour House **4**
West Coast Trail Motel **1**

COWICHAN VALLEY

Accommodations
The Aerie **9**
Bird Song Cottage/ **12**
Castlebury Cottage
Fairburn Farm
Country Manor **11**
Prancing Horse **8**
Yellow Point Lodge **13**

LEGEND
✈ Airport
🏖 Beach
--- Ferry Route
🚶 Hiking
✚ Hospital /
First Aid
ⓘ Information
🏄 Surfing
🏛 Winery

to Port Alberni & Bamfield

Cowichan Lake

PACIFIC RIM NATIONAL PARK **1**

Port Renfrew

Botanical Beach Provincial Park

Sombrio Beach

Juan de Fuca Strait

Port San Juan

0 — 20 mi
0 — 20 km

(US$90–$162) 1-bedroom; C$189 (US$123) studio; C$359 (US$233) 2-bedroom. Apr–May, Sept–Nov C$119–$180 (US$77–$123) 1-bedroom; C$139 (US$90) studio; C$289 (US$188) 2-bedroom. Dec–Mar C$99–$169 (US$64–$110) 1-bedroom; C$139 (US$90) studio; C$299 (US$194) 2-bedroom. Rates include breakfast. Extra person C$25 (US$16.25). AE, DC, MC, V. Free parking. **Amenities:** Restaurant, lounge; concierge; business center. *In room:* A/C, TV w/pay movies, dataport, mini-bar, fridge, coffeemaker, hair dryer, iron.

WHERE TO DINE

Deep Cove Chalet 🟥🟥🟥 FRENCH   A local favorite for special occasions, this charming 1914 chalet was originally the terminus building of the BC Electric railway line. Perched on a grassy bank overlooking a beautiful inlet, the restaurant offers top-notch service, a superb menu that emphasizes local seafood, lamb, and game, and a cellar that boasts a very extensive and fairly priced collection of wines. The whole experience is very upscale. Prix fixe dinners feature

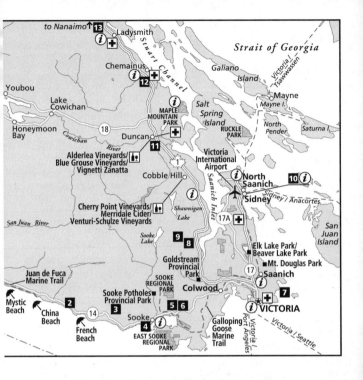

items such as roast caribou, Dungeness crab, and sometimes even a terrific selection of caviars from Russia, China, and Iran.

11190 Chalet Drive Rd. ⓒ 250/656-3541. Reservations recommended for Sunday brunch and dinner. Lunch C$25 (US$16.25); dinner C$35 (US$22.75); brunch C$26.50 (US$17.25). Prix fixe dinner C$46.60–$75 (US$30–$48.75). AE, MC. Wed–Sun Noon–2:30pm; daily 5:30–9:30pm. Closed Mon–Tues lunch.

The Latch ⭐⭐ WEST COAST   This restaurant delivers a first-class dining experience. Built in the 1920s for then Lieutenant-Governor Walter C. Nichol, The Latch was once a summer retreat for dignitaries and debutantes. Although the antiques hark back to that era, the food certainly does not. New West Coast flavors are prepared in a classic Tuscan style with an emphasis on local produce. This is an excellent choice for romantic, candlelight dining.

2328 Harbour Rd., Sidney. ⓒ 250/656-6622. Reservations recommended on weekends. Main courses C$18–$29 (US$12–$19). AE, DC, MC, V. Thurs–Sun 5–10pm.

THE TOP ATTRACTIONS

British Columbia Aviation Museum   You'll want to dig out your bomber jacket for a visit. Located in a hangar on the edge of the Victoria International Airport, this is a working museum that illustrates the province's aviation history. Volunteers restore vintage aircraft to add to the collection, which already has several reconditioned vintage airplanes, helicopters, and kit planes. Most are in working order. Look for a 1930s Bush Plane, an A26 World War II Bomber, a Gibson Twin (built in Victoria in 1911), a replica of the Chanute Glider, built in 1897, and more.

1910 Norseman Rd. © **250/655-3300**. www.bcam.net. Admission C$5 (US$3.25) adults, C$4 (US$2.60) seniors, C$3 (US$1.95) students. Children 11 and under free, but must be accompanied by an adult. Summer daily 10am–4pm; winter daily 11am–3pm. Closed Dec 25. Take the airport turnoff from Hwy. 17. The museum is on your right, as you approach the airport. Bus no. 70.

Butchart Gardens 🌟🌟🌟   Converted from an exhausted limestone quarry back in 1904, Butchart Gardens is an impressive place: 50 acres of gardens and not a blade of grass out of place! Every flower is perfectly matched to the other in height, color, and tone, including the 300,000 bulbs that bloom in spring. On summer evenings, the gardens are illuminated with softly colored lights. Musical entertainment is provided Monday through Saturday evenings June through September. Watch for fireworks every Saturday night in July and August, and in December, enjoy lavish displays of Christmas lights. An excellent lunch, dinner, and afternoon tea are offered in the **Dining Room Restaurant;** more casual fare is served in the **Blue Poppy Restaurant.** The gift shop sells seeds for some of the plants you'll see.

800 Benvenuto Ave., Brentwood Bay. © **250/652-4422**. Dining reservations © 250/652-8222. www.butchartgardens.com. Admission C$19.25 (US$12.20) adults, C$9 (US$5.85) children 13–17, C$2 (US$1.30) children 5–12, free for children 4 and under. Daily 9am–sundown (call for seasonal closing time). Take Blanshard St. (Hwy. 17) north toward the ferry terminal in Saanich, then turn left on Keating Crossroads, which leads directly to the gardens. Bus no. 75.

Sidney Historical Museum   Tucked away in the basement of the 1939 post office building, the museum's historical photographs and artifacts portray the early lives of Coast Salish, European, and Oriental local peoples. This community museum is lovingly tended and includes monthly exhibits that range in subject matter from toy collecting and quilting, to model railways and radio-controlled boats.

2423 Beacon Ave., Sidney. ℭ 250/655-6355. www.sidneybc.com/museum. Admission by donation. Suggested: C$2 (US$1.50) adults, C$5 (US$3) groups. Mar–Dec daily 10am–4pm; Jan–Feb weekends only 10am–4pm. Closed Dec 25. Take Hwy. 17 to Sidney, turning right down Beacon Ave., to 4th St. Bus no. 70 from downtown or Swartz Bay.

Sidney Marine Centre   Everything you ever wanted to know about whales and other marine creatures, you'll find in this waterfront museum. Models, fossils, skeletons, and murals trace the remarkable story of the biology and evolution of whales. There are some interactive exhibits and a few fun displays, such as a milk-filled container— 250 l (55 gallons)—which represents only half the amount of milk consumed in a day by a nursing blue whale calf.

2538 Beacon Ave., Sidney. ℭ 250/656-1322. www.sidneybc.com/museum. Admission by donation. Suggested: C$2 (US$1.50) adults, C$5 (US$3) groups. Mar–Dec daily 10am–4pm; Jan–Feb weekends only 10am–4pm. Closed Dec 25. Take Hwy. 17 to Sidney, turning right down Beacon Ave., to the water. The museum is on your left. Bus no. 70 from downtown or Swartz Bay.

Victoria Butterfly Gardens ✿✿✿ *Kids*   Hundreds of exotic species of butterflies flutter through this lush tropical greenhouse, from the tiny Central American Julia to the Southeast Asian Giant Atlas Moth (its wingspan is nearly a foot). Pick up an identification chart before you enter so you can put names to the various flying wonders around you. Then wander freely through the gardens. Along the way, you'll encounter naturalists happy to explain butterfly biology, who pepper their speech with slightly bizarre factoids, such as "Butterflies taste with their feet," and "If a human baby grew at the same rate as some caterpillars, it would weigh 8 tons in only two weeks." Hmm. Food for thought. Be sure to see the cocoon display—a metamorphic sight, literally! If you're visiting between November and February, you need to make a reservation to see the gardens.

1461 Benvenuto Ave., Brentwood Bay. ℭ 250/652-3822. www.butterflygardens. com. Admission C$8 (US$5.20) adults, C$7 (US$4.55) seniors and students, C$4.50 (US$2.90) children 5–12, free for children 4 and under. 10% discount for families. Mar 1–May 13 and Oct daily 9:30am–4:30pm; May 14–Sept 30 daily 9am–4:30pm. Closed Nov–Feb. Bus no. 75.

PARKS & BEACHES

Located off Highway 17 in Saanich, **Elk Lake/Beaver Lake Park** is a lovely place to spend an afternoon. The park's big draw is a 593-acre freshwater lake rimmed by four beaches, with plenty of play areas and picnic tables. The lake provides for all sorts of aquatic recreation, and is a particularly good place for beginner windsurfers. It is also home to the University of Victoria Rowing Club, and the site of the annual International Boat races, one of the five top rowing events in the world. Nearer to Victoria, off Cordova Bay Road, is **Mount Douglas Park,** a 25-acre park in its natural state. The **Summit Lookout** is a superb site from which to view the surrounding area, and there are several **easy hiking trails** to the mountaintop. The lower park has a beach, and a playground, while the upper park accesses the observation point. Parking is plentiful.

2 The Sooke Region

To the west of Victoria lies Southern Vancouver Island's wild side. Within a couple hours' drive out of the city, you are met with windswept beaches and trails through old-growth forest. Whether you're an urbanite looking for a spectacular afternoon side trip, a soft adventurer, or a hardy hiker, this drive along **Highway 14,** toward Port Renfrew, delivers. Set aside a day, or make the tranquility of Sooke your home base. It's about 32km (20 miles) out of Victoria, and you'll be on the edge of outdoor adventure country. Sooke is one of those wish-you-were-here coastal towns. Its name is derived from the first inhabitants of the region, the T'sou-ke band. The "e" in both T'sou-ke and Sooke is silent, just like the morning mist that lingers over the harbor.

ESSENTIALS
GETTING THERE
BY CAR   Driving from Victoria, take **Douglas Street** north and follow the signs to **Highway 1,** toward Sooke. Take the **Highway 14 (Island Highway) exit** at **Colwood,** and you're on your way. Highway 14 follows the coast all the way through Sooke, and along to Port Renfrew. Remember to get gas in Sooke; it's the last gas station before Port Renfrew. Sooke is a 32-km (20-mile) drive west from Victoria; Port Renfrew is 74km (46 miles) west from Sooke.

BY BUS   Board at the Western Exchange on Highway 14 (Island Hwy.) at Colwood, (about 20 minutes out of Victoria). Take **Bus no. 50** (get a transfer), then **Bus no. 61** to Sooke.

VISITOR INFORMATION
Head to the **Sooke Region Museum Visitors and Information Centre,** 2070 Phillips Rd., (right off Sooke Road/Highway 14) (*(C)* **866/888-4748** or 250/642-6351). It's open July through August

daily from 9am to 5:30pm. From October to May, it's open Tuesday through Sunday, from 9am to 6pm. Closed Mondays. Wheelchair accessible. The staff here is knowledgeable and very enthusiastic, with all kinds of ideas for places to stay and things to do, particularly when it comes to both soft- and rugged-adventure activities. There are options for self-guided explorations or escorted tours.

WHERE TO STAY

Hartmann House B&B 🐾🐾   Hartmann House is at its best in spring: shrouded by wisteria and surrounded by hydrangeas, peonies, rhododendrons, azaleas, and other favorite flowering plants. It has a stunning English country garden–style setting (that's very, very private), with distant views of the water. Inside is just as welcoming. The cedar finishing throughout the home has warmth and character, punctuated with overstuffed rattan couches and a roaring fireplace. Guest rooms are very romantic, with pampering touches such as soft terry robes and chilled wine waiting for you upon your arrival. Dried flowers, beamed ceilings, and handcrafted furniture are details in a lovely sun-filled dining room where breakfast is served. Choose the Honeymoon Suite, and breakfast is delivered to your door through an ingenious butler's pantry. There's also a TV/VCR, fridge, microwave, and Jacuzzi.

5262 Sooke Rd., Sooke, BC V0S 1N0. ℂ **250/642-3761.** Fax 250/642-7361. www.hartmannhouse.bc.ca. 3 units. May–Oct C$125–$225 (US$81–$146). Nov–Apr C$100–$180 (US$65–$117). Rates include full breakfast. V. **Amenities:** Lounge. *In room:* Hair dryer, no phone.

Malahat Farm 🐾   A charming, homey place, constructed in 1910 of framing lumber and grooved clapboard siding milled from timber on the property. The craftsmanship of builder William Anderson shows throughout. The curving fir staircase, for example, is made of pieces of flawless wood, without so much as a knot to be seen. Malahat Farm has been a guesthouse off and on since 1915, and today comprises two buildings: the original farmhouse, geared to adults, with two comfortable, unpretentious guest rooms, and a self-contained cottage (built in 1919), which sleeps eight and is more suitable for families. There's a library-lounge, with a coffeemaker and fridge, plus a gazebo and Jacuzzi in the garden.

2675 Anderson Rd., Sooke, BC V0S 1N0. ℂ **888-340-9911** or 250/ 642-6868. Fax 250/642-1543. www.malahatfarm.com. 2 units, cottage. C$95 (US$61.75) guest room. June–Sept C$195 (US$126.75) cottage. Oct–May C$150 (US$97.50) cottage. Rates include breakfast. Extra person C$10 (US$6.50). V. **Amenities:** Lounge; Jacuzzi. *In room:* No phone.

Markham House B&B ⭐⭐ Nestled into its 10-acre hillside, this Tudor-style home is bordered by towering firs and flowering perennials. A golf tee and bocce ball game are set up on the lawns and intriguing pathways lead to mossy bluff lookouts. Guests enjoy afternoon tea on the veranda or in the old English-style living room, filled with antiques. There's a TV, for those who need their soap opera fix. Each guest room has all the trimmings necessary for cocooning, including luxurious bathrobes and double Jacuzzis. There's a cottage separate from the main house that has its own outdoor Jacuzzi, plus full kitchen and barbecue.

1853 Connie Rd., Victoria BC V9C 4C2. © **888/256-6888** or 250-642-7542. Fax 250-642-7538. www.markhamhouse.com. 4 units, cottage. C$105–$175 (US$68.25–$114) guest room. C$215 (US$140) cottage. Special packages and off-season discounts available. AE, DC, MC, V. **Amenities:** Lounge. *In room:* VCR, coffeemaker, hair dryer, no phone.

Point No Point Resort ⭐ It's the ultimate getaway—a private cabin, the ocean as your front yard, and 40 acres or so of wilderness "out the back." Since this waterfront resort has been in business more than 50 years, the size and relative quality of the cabins vary depending on when they were built. Some are large enough for families; others are cozy retreats. All have wood-burning fireplaces, full kitchens, private bathrooms, stunning oceanviews, and a strip of private beach, which includes a beach house and fire pit. Lunch and traditional tea are served daily in a central teahouse, which overlooks the Juan de Fuca Strait. Dinner is served Wednesday through Sunday. There's usually a scramble for the binoculars when whales pass by or a bald eagle dives into the sea for his dinner.

1505 West Coast Hwy. (Hwy. 14), Sooke, BC V0S 1N0. © **250/646-2020.** Fax 250/646-2294. www.pointnopointresort.com. 24 cabins, 10 w/Jacuzzi and private deck. C$130–$220 (US$84.50–$143). 2-night minimum stay on weekends; 3-night minimum stay July–Aug, holiday weekends, Christmas. AE, MC, V. Free parking. Small pets accepted C$10 (US$6.50). **Amenities:** Restaurant. *In room:* Kitchen.

Sooke Harbour House ⭐⭐⭐ Sitting on the end of a sand spit, this little inn is a celebrity hideaway for Hollywood types such as Gillian Anderson, Robert DeNiro, Richard Gere, and others in the heavy wallet brigade. The ambience is understated elegance with a friendly, yet completely unobtrusive staff. An eclectic blend of antiques, original art, and whimsical crafts is showcased throughout the inn. Each of the 28 guest rooms is decorated in a unique way, though they all express a Northwest theme. All have wood-burning fireplaces, exquisite views, and all but one have sundecks. Many have

Jacuzzis and showers with beautiful stained-glass doors. Speaking of showers, guests will find rooms well equipped to venture outside if it rains; umbrellas, rubber boots, and rain jackets are provided for all. The experience wouldn't be complete without enjoying a meal at the **Sooke Harbour House** restaurant, which is the best in the region (see "Where to Dine," below). If you're not a guest at the hotel, dining here often means making a reservation weeks in advance, especially in summer. Be sure also to try the **Searenity Spa;** it offers an excellent range of massage and esthetic services.

1528 Whiffen Spit Rd., Sooke, BC V0S 1N0. © **800/889-9688** or 250/642-3421. Fax 250/628-6988. www.sookeharbourhouse.com. 28 units, 23 w/Jacuzzi. July–mid-Sept C$299 (US$194) standard; C$355–$445 (US$231–$289) suite; C$555 (US$361) executive suite. Mid-Sept–Oct 31 and May–June C$280 (US$182) standard; C$350–$420 (US$227.50–$273) suite; C$490 (US$318.50) executive suite. Nov–Apr C$230–$255 (US$149.50–$166) standard; C$255–$355 (US$166–$231) suite; C$355–$455 (US$231–$296) executive suite. Rates include breakfast and picnic lunch. Off-season discounts available. Children 12 and under stay free in parents' room. DC, MC, V. Free parking. Take Island Hwy. to the Sooke-Colwood turnoff (junction Hwy. 24); continue on Hwy. 14 to Sooke; turn left onto Whiffen Spit Rd. Pets accepted C$20 (US$13). **Amenities:** Restaurant; spa; 24-hour room service; babysitting. *In room:* Hair dryer, iron.

WHERE TO DINE

Mom's Cafe 𝒦𝒦 *(Finds* CASUAL FOOD   Tucked away by the community hall in downtown Sooke, Mom's Cafe is the quintessential 1950s diner, complete with jukeboxes at the booths and an atmosphere filled with bric-a-brac (you just know Mom never throws anything away). It serves up excellent home cooking, and is considered one of the top 10 diners in British Columbia. Mom's is always packed with locals and visitors alike.

2036 Shields Rd., Sooke. © **250/642-3314.** Main courses C$6.50–$12.95 (US$4.20–$8.40). MC, V. Daily 8am–8pm; to 9pm Fri–Sat. Drive into Sooke on Hwy. 14; take the first right after the traffic lights at Murray Rd.

Six Mile Pub 𝒦 PUB FARE   You'll find a good variety of brews on tap, and tasty food seasoned with fresh herbs from the pub's own garden. Part of a franchise, the Six Mile Pub is one of several "mile" pubs you'll find along Highway 1A, all of them, to some degree, incorporating an oak-beamed, fireside ambience of yesteryear. Most were once mile-measured stops for stagecoaches that traveled up island from Victoria. This pub has a particularly rich history. The building dates to 1855, and was the hub for provincial bootleggers during Prohibition. Since Victoria continued the ban on booze until the early 1950s, "mile houses," as they were known, were the only places Victorians could get a tot outside of the city. Today, the Six Mile Pub has broad appeal and a loyal local following.

494 Island Hwy. © **250/478-3121**. Main courses C$6–$12 (US$4–$8). MC, V. Sun–Thurs 11am–midnight; Fri–Sat 11am–1am. Follow Hwy. 14 to Six Mile Rd.

Sooke Harbour House ✿✿✿   GOURMET WEST COAST The cuisine has seduced thousands of palates, and the restaurant's award-winning wine cellar is regarded as one of the best on the West Coast. Its imaginative menu focuses on local seafood and organically grown produce, with dishes such as shady lane tomato soup, garden basil puree garnished with nasturtiums and fresh tuna, and halibut baked in a crust of herbs, sunflower seeds, and Parmesan. The food is so good here your best bet is the multicourse **tasting menu**—so you can sample as much as possible! Dinner is by reservation only, at least 3 days in advance (but you'd be better off calling 3 weeks in advance in the summer). Breakfast and lunch are served for hotel guests only.

In Sooke Harbour House, 1528 Whiffen Spit Rd., Sooke. © **250/642-3421**. Reservations required. Main courses C$35 (US$22.75). DC, MC, V. Daily 5:30–9:30pm. Take Island Hwy. to the Sooke-Colwood turnoff (junction Hwy. 24); continue on Hwy. 14 to Sooke; turn left onto Whiffen Spit Rd.

THE TOP ATTRACTIONS

Fort Rodd Hill & Fisgard Lighthouse National Historic Site ✿ (Kids)   The Fisgard lighthouse is the oldest lighthouse on Canada's west coast. From its vantage point atop a volcanic outcrop, it has guided ships toward Victoria's sheltered harbor since 1873. Although the beacon has long been automated, the site has been restored to its original appearance. The surrounding park is filled with old military installations: camouflaged searchlights, underground armories, and guns dating from the 1890s, which, in more than half a century, have never fired a shot in anger. Canada has designated it a National Historic Site. This is a great attraction for loners and families alike; for tossing a Frisbee, picnicking, or beach-combing.

603 Fort Rodd Hill Rd. © **250/478-5849**. www.parkscanada.pch.gc.ca. Admission C$3 (US$1.95) adults, C$2.25 (US$1.50) seniors, C$1.50 (US$1) children 6–16, free for children 5 and under, C$7.50 (US$4.90) family pass. Mar–Oct daily 10am–5:30pm, Nov–Feb daily 9am–4:30pm. Follow Hwy. 1 out of Victoria, taking the Colwood exit (#10) onto Hwy. 1A. Continue for 2km (1 mile), turn left at the third traffic light onto Ocean Boulevard. Follow the signs to the sites.

Sooke Region Museum Fittingly, the museum is housed in Moss Cottage (built in 1870), Sooke's oldest building, and somewhat of a museum piece itself. Sharing space with the Visitor Information Centre (see "Essentials," earlier in the chapter), the museum houses a charming, compact collection of entertaining exhibits and memorabilia. A stop here is well worth the extra time while you're picking up information on the area.

2070 Phillips Rd. (right off Sooke Road/Hwy. 14). ℂ 250/642-6351. Admission by donation. Suggested: C$2 (US$1–$1.50). July–Aug daily 9am–5:30pm; Sept–June Tues–Sun 9am–6pm.

HIKING TRAILS

Whether you like to cycle, hike, horseback ride, or just go for a stroll, the **Galloping Goose** and **Peninsula Trails** are the place to be. Stretching like a green ribbon from Sidney to Sooke, their 100km (60 miles) of pathways link the region's parks to form a continuous chain of green spaces. Named for the gawky and noisy gas rail car that carried passengers between Victoria and Sooke in the 1920s, the **Galloping Goose Trail** follows the abandoned rail beds and trestles of that railway legacy. **Leechtown,** once the site of a gold mining community, marks the westernmost reach, and terminus, of "The Goose," as it's affectionately called. For more information on the Galloping Goose and Peninsula Trails, contact the **Capital Region District Parks,** at ℂ 250/478-3344.

Stretching 47km (29 miles) along the near-wilderness coastline from **China Beach** to **Botanical Beach,** is the **Juan de Fuca Marine Trail** ✮✮✮. A neighbor to the famed West Coast Trail (see below), but less extreme in demands, the Juan de Fuca Marine Trail offers similar scenic beauty, yet can be completed as a comfortable, albeit strenuous, 4-day trek or as several 1-day hikes from different trailheads. Some easy to moderate day hikes head out from trailheads at **China Beach, Sombrio Beach, Parkinson Creek, and Botanical Beach, near Port Renfrew** (see "Parks & Beaches," below). If you're more interested in the 4-day trek, you can start either at **Botanical Beach** or at **China Beach.** Because this is a wilderness trail, conditions are always changing, so check the trailhead information centers for updates. Be sure to wear proper footwear and appropriate clothing. Campsites are regularly spaced along the trail. A great online resource is **www.sookenet.com/sooke/activity/trails/jdftr**. The site has maps, photos, safety pointers, and camping information, concerning the Juan de Fuca Marine Trail.

Of all the trails on Vancouver Island, the **West Coast Trail** ✦✦✦, is the most famous, and is known to be one of the most extreme, rigorous, and beautiful trails in the world. With its easternmost trailhead just outside of Port Renfrew, the West Coast Trail is virtually the town's only raison d'être. Now a part of **Pacific Rim National Park,** originally the trail was constructed for the rescue of mariners shipwrecked along the rugged west coast, appropriately referred to as the "graveyard of the Pacific." Running approximately 75km (46 miles) north between Port Renfrew and Bamfield, it takes an average of 5 to 7 days to complete, and is a challenge for even the most experienced hikers. For more information about the West Coast Trail, check out **www.sookenet.com/sooke/activity/trails/wctguide**. For general information about escorted tours along many backcountry hikes in British Columbia, including the West Coast Trail, log on to **www.boreasbackcountry.com**. See chapter 5 for more on the West Coast Trail and Pacific Rim National Park.

PARKS & BEACHES

Goldstream Provincial Park is a favorite escape for Victoria residents and visitors alike. Picnic beneath 600-year-old red cedars, or hike through beautiful rain forest. Watch out for old mine shafts where, in the late 1800s, prospectors mined for gold (hence, the park's name); or try panning for gold yourself in the river. You can take several easy loop hikes that explore a whole range of ecosystems: deep forests of Douglas fir, dry upland ridges with arbutus and Garry oak, and a salt marsh estuary at the head of Saanich Inlet. A new trail lets campers hike from the park to the famed **Butchart Gardens** (see "The Saanich Peninsula," earlier in this chapter). From mid-October through November, thousands come to Goldstream Provincial Park to watch salmon spawn, while in December and January, they come for the **Bald Eagle Count** (see the "Calendar of Events," in chapter 2). Many areas of the park are wheelchair accessible. For information on Goldstream Provincial Park and all other provincial parks on the South Island, contact **BC Parks** (© **250/391-2300;** www.gov. bc.ca/wlap). The park's **Freeman King Visitor Centre** (© **250/478-9414;** www.arenaria.com) is open daily from 9:30am to 6pm, and offers year-round guided walks, as well as programs geared to children. If you're interested in camping in the park, there are a good number of sites (159) available. Reserve a site through **Discover Camping** (© **800-689-9025** or 604-689-9025; www.discover camping.ca).

In Sooke, you'll find **Sooke Potholes Provincial Park,** featuring an unusual rock formation, over which the Sooke River flows onto a series of ledges and waist-deep swimming holes. The water quickly overflows and cascades into another series of rock pools below. In summer, the chilly waters are just about warm enough to attract a swarm of swimmers. The park has picnic facilities, while easy hiking trails are firm under foot. A network of over 50km (31 miles) of trails can be found in **East Sooke Regional Park** ⤳, lacing through the park's 3,512 acres, to beaches, secluded coves, forested areas, petroglyphs, and an abandoned copper mine. In the heart of the park, stumps of Douglas fir and red cedar—some measuring 2 to 3m (7 to 10 ft.) in diameter, hold clues to the era when loggers felled their riches with the springboard, axe, and crosscut saw. One of these trails, the **East Sooke Coast Trail,** is considered a premier day hike in Canada. Though it covers only 10km (6 miles), the trail is rough, winding, and a challenging 6- to 8-hour trip. You can access East Sooke Regional Park at **Aylard Farm,** off Becher Bay Road (popular with picnickers and those looking for easy excursions); at **Anderson Cove** (for hikers heading to Babbington Hill and Mount Maguire); or at **Pike Road,** off East Sooke Road, an old logging road that winds through forest to meadow and beach. Information posted at these trailheads will help you choose a trail suitable to your hiking ability. Many trails are wheelchair accessible.

As you wind your way west along Highway 14 (also known as the West Coast Road) towards Port Renfrew, you'll pass a series of beaches—many of which are worth pulling over to explore. Some beaches are more accessible than others, and trails often link one stretch of sand to another, but sometimes, only at low tide. *Note:* If you park your car, remove all valuables. Thefts are common; rental cars are favored targets.

The first beach you'll come to, ironically, is called **Second Beach,** a small sand and cobblestone beach, subject to strong storm and tidal action. At low tide, it's possible to walk along the beach to **Jordan River,** a popular wintertime surfing and windsurfing area, or to **China Beach,** where fine sand makes it an ideal spot for picnicking, building sandcastles, wading, and relaxing. There's a hidden waterfall at the west end of the beach. From the parking lot, follow the wide gravel trail through lush forest, to the beach itself. The trail is easy to navigate, so suitable for children as well as older travelers. It takes about 20 minutes, one-way; watch for some steep sections. China Beach is the southern terminus of the Juan de Fuca Marine

Trail. Overnight camping in your vehicle is allowed. There are also a number of campsites on the beach.

Getting to **Mystic Beach** involves a fairly strenuous, 2-km (1-mile) hike along a steep rain-forest trail, which can take up to 45 minutes to complete. But you'll be rewarded by a romantic sandy beach surrounded by sandstone cliffs, shallow waves, and a waterfall. If you can, it's a trip worth making. Beachfront campsites are available, but there are no services except for pit toilets. Bring your own water, or if you take water from the streams, remember to purify it. Farther along is **French Beach,** a sand and gravel beach that's a hot spot to watch for passing gray **whales.** Picnic tables and an adventure playground are located on an open, grassy area between the parking lot and beach, making this a good family destination. There are 69 campsites right on the beach. The winds, breakers, and rollers of the Pacific Ocean make **Sombrio Beach** a favorite spot for surfers. An old logging road winds down from Highway 14 to a large parking lot. From there, it's an easy 10-minute walk down to the beach. Sombrio Beach is another entry route to the Juan de Fuca Marine Trail. Overnight camping in your vehicle is allowed, and there are also a number of sites on the beach itself. But the real treasure is **Botanical Beach Provincial Park** ⊕⊕, about 4km (2.5 miles) south of Port Renfrew. A terrific place for kids, it's one of the richest intertidal zones on North America's west coast, and a magnet for avid poolies to gather and enjoy the ocean's bounty. Over the millennia, tidal action has carved and gouged out spectacular pits and pools filled with purple sea urchins, gooseneck barnacles, fiery red blood stars, and other marine flora and fauna. Check local tide tables: a low tide of 1m (4 feet) or less is best for viewing. In spring and fall, watch for passing gray whales. Camping is prohibited at this park.

For information about camping at any of these beaches, and to reserve campsites, contact **Discover Camping** (© **800/689-9025** or 604/689-9025; www.discovercamping.ca).

PORT RENFREW

Port Renfrew is, quite literally, a sleepy fishing village at the end of the road (Highway 14), and unless you're heading to the West Coast Trail (see "Trails," earlier in this chapter, and chapter 5), there aren't a whole lot of reasons to stay. Most accommodations are geared to hikers, and include a complete range of camping facilities for both tents and RVs. You might want to try the **Port Renfrew Recreational Retreat** (© **250/647-0058**). Full RV hookups are

C$29 (US19) per night; tents are C$5 (US$3.25) per night. There's a 6-person self-contained cabin at C$150 (US$97.50) per night. **The West Coast Trail Motel,** Parkinson Rd., (© 877/299-2288 or 250/647-5565; www.westcoasttrailmotel.com) is your best bet for anything resembling a decent hotel room. It's located next to the **Lighthouse Pub & Restaurant** (© 250/647-5543), the main gathering place in town, and a good pit stop before turning the car around for the drive back to Sooke.

3 En Route to Nanaimo: The Cowichan Valley

This blood pressure–lowering trip north along Vancouver Island's east coast to Nanaimo, can take you from 1½ hours to all day, depending on how many stops you make. The **Cowichan Valley** is an ideal side trip if you're staying in Victoria, and a wonderful meander through rich, rolling countryside. The fast track is along the Trans-Canada Highway (Highway 1), over the mountain hump of the **Malahat,** and down through the Cowichan Valley. Here, you'll find many small, family-owned farms selling superb home-made products such as jams, candles, and soaps. You'll also drive by a gamut of estate **vineyards** featuring award-winning wines, as well as potters' studios, craft stores, and galleries.

One detour of interest is the city of **Duncan,** nicknamed **"City of Totem Poles,"** for its impressive collection of, you guessed it, totem poles! This part of the world is famed for its native carving skills, yet most historic totem poles are in museums or have been reclaimed by nature beside abandoned villages. In the 1980s, the mayor of Duncan commissioned local First Nations artists to carve new totem poles, and today, the city showcases one of the world's largest collections of modern totem carving. Actually catching sight of them can be a bit hit and miss, however. Follow the **yellow shoeprints** on the pavement, or take a free **walking tour** that starts at the **Cowichan Valley Museum,** in the E&N Railway station, at Station St. and Caan Ave. Call © 250/715-1700 for information. You can also check in at the **Duncan Visitor Information Centre,** 381A Trans-Canada Hwy., Duncan, BC, V9L 3R5 (© 250/746-4636).

Another worthwhile detour is the town of **Chemainus.** When the building of the Trans-Canada Highway bypassed Chemainus, and the local lumber mill slowed to a virtual standstill, the town turned its declining fortunes around by painting the exteriors of its quaint buildings. Today, more than 300,000 visitors stop each year to see the 33 murals and 12 sculptures, particularly in July and August, when more are added. If you do decide to make a stop in Chemainus, stay in one of the heritage B&Bs (see "Where to Stay," below). Spend the evening at the **Chemainus Theatre,** 9737 Chemainus Rd. (© **800/565/7738;** www.ctheatre.bc.ca). This troupe offers professional live theatre year-round, held in the town's most eye-catching building, a late 19th-century opera house. There's a **Visitor Information Centre,** housed in an old railroad car, at 9758 Chemainus Rd. at Mill St. (© **250/246-3944**).

ESSENTIALS
GETTING THERE
BY CAR   Take Douglas St. north out of Victoria, which becomes Highway 1 (the Trans-Canada Highway). From here it's about 111km (67 miles) to Nanaimo.

BY BUS   Laidlaw Coach Lines operates between Victoria and Nanaimo, with various stops along the way. Schedules and reservations are handled by **Greyhound Canada** (© **800/663-8390** or 604/482-8747; www.greyhound.ca). There are six departures a day from Victoria, from 5:50am to 7:20pm. Fares are C$19.25 (US$12.50) for adults, C$17.35 (US$11) for seniors and students, C$9.50 (US$6) for children 5 to 11. The trip between Victoria and Nanaimo takes 2½ hours.

BY TRAIN   The E&N Railiner, run by VIA Rail (© **800/ 561-8630;** www.viarail.com) operates a daily service between Victoria and Courtenay. One-day sightseeing trips from Victoria include stops in Chemainus, Duncan, and Nanaimo. At press time, however, VIA Rail had plans to cancel this service in summer 2002, and would not commit to rate information. Check with VIA Rail before making your plans.

VISITOR INFORMATION
Obtain maps and information at the **Tourism Victoria Information Centre,** 812 Wharf St., Victoria, BC V8W 1T3, (© **250/953-2033;** www.tourismvictoria.com). The center is open daily May and June from 9am to 8pm; July and August daily from 9am to 9pm; September through April from 9am to 5pm. You can also contact **Tourism Vancouver Island,** 203-335 Wesley St., Nanaimo, BC V9R 2T5 (© **250/754-3500;** www.islands.bc.ca). The center is open year-round, Monday through Friday, from 8:30am to 5pm.

WHERE TO STAY
ON THE MALAHAT

The Aerie ★★★ An acclaimed member of the Relais & Châteaux group of hotels, the Aerie is a magnificent Mediterranean-style mansion reminiscent of grand homes in Southern Europe. Surrounded by 10 acres of meticulously kept grounds, the breathtaking view of the Olympic Mountains and the Gulf Islands is worth the trip alone, especially if you arrive by helicopter (unbelievably, there's a helipad amid the landscaped gardens). Suites are individually designed (some are multilevel); most feature Persian and Chinese silk carpets, fireplaces, Jacuzzis, decks, and four-poster queen- or king-size beds. Inspired touches include fresh flowers, terry cloth robes, CD/cassette players, and Bernard Callebaut chocolates, hand-dipped by the renowned chocolatier based in Banff, Alberta. The hotel's restaurant is not to be missed (see "Where to Dine," below).

600 Ebadora Lane (P.O. Box 108), Malahat, BC V0R 2L0. ℂ 800/518-1933 or 250/743-7115. Fax 250/743-4766. www.aerie.bc.ca. 28 units. Mid-May–mid-Oct C$285 (US$185) standard; C$325 (US$211) Jacuzzi. Mid-Oct–Nov and Apr–mid-May C$225 (US$146) standard; C$295 (US$192) Jacuzzi. Dec–Mar C$185 (US$120) standard; C$230 (US$150) Jacuzzi. From C$285 and way up (US$185) suite. Rates include full breakfast. Packages available. AE, DC, MC, V. Free parking. Take Hwy. 1 to the Spectacle Lake turnoff; take the first right and follow the winding driveway. **Amenities:** Restaurant; small heated indoor pool; outdoor tennis court; spa; Jacuzzi; sauna. *In room:* A/C, TV, dataport, minibar.

Prancing Horse ★ Perched on the Malahat summit, this red-roofed Gothic villa is eye-level to passing eagles. Like the Aerie across the road, it offers stupendous views up Finlayson Arm and of the snowcapped Olympic Mountains in the distance. A terraced rockery leads to a multitiered deck, where there's a Jacuzzi and gazebo. Trails meander through the property. Inside is all antique elegance. Guest rooms are bright, and have thoughtful touches like fresh flowers, Aveda bath products, Bernard Callebaut chocolates, and views framed by Battenberg lace drapes. The luxury suites include double-soaker bathtubs, fireplaces, and private decks. A tasty champagne breakfast is included. As home base to Victoria's Ferrari Club, chances are good that you'll see one or two of these racy vehicles.

573 Ebadora Lane (P.O. Box 11), Malahat, BC V0R 2L0. ℂ 877/887-8834 or 250/743-9378. Fax 250/743-9372. www.prancinghorse.com. 6 units. May–Sept C$175–$275 (US$114–$179) suite; C$375 (US$244) penthouse. Oct–Apr C$150–$250 (US$97.50–$162.50) suite; C$350 (US$227) penthouse. Honeymoon package available. AE, MC, V. **Amenities:** Exercise room; Jacuzzi; laundry service. *In room:* TV, VCR, fridge, coffeemaker, hair dryer.

IN DUNCAN

Fairburn Farm Country Manor ★★ *Kids*   This hotel offers guests the perfect farm experience—one that lets you share the reality of working a farm, but on a take-it-or-leave-it basis. Guests are welcome, but not obliged, to join in farm activities. You can pick apples in the orchard, collect eggs, or learn about the farm's water-buffalo dairy that produces yogurt, ice cream, and authentic mozzarella. Built in the 1880s, the rambling farmhouse has high ceilings, antique moldings, tiled fireplaces, and a broad columned porch that overlooks 130 acres of gardens and meadows, with mountain slopes visible in the distance. Inside, the lounge has a VCR, coffeemaker, and fridge. The two-bedroom cottage includes a fully equipped kitchen. Breakfasts are homemade farm-fresh feasts. The entire experience is tailor-made for family fun.

3310 Jackson Rd., Duncan, BC V9L 6N7. ℂ and fax **250/746-4637**. www.fairburn farm.bc.ca. 7 units, cottage. C$110–$155 (US$71.50–$100.75) standard; July–Aug C$850 (US$552.50) cottage based on 6-day minimum stay. Sept–Oct 15 and Apr–June C$150 (US$97.50) cottage (3-night minimum). Extra person C$20 (US$13). MC, V. Closed Oct 15–Mar 31. **Amenities:** Lounge. *In room:* Hair dryer, no phone.

IN CHEMAINUS

Bird Song Cottage/Castlebury Cottage   These separate bed-and-breakfasts adjoin one another, but could hardly be more different. Bird Song is filled with so much Victorian bric-a-brac that it's both enchanting and theatrical. The recorded sound of birds trilling teams up with loads of architectural gingerbread. Next door, medieval romantic fantasy comes alive when you step into Castlebury Cottage, with its vaulted ceilings, mullioned casement windows, and antique wrought-iron wall-lamp sconces. There's even a full-size suit of armor standing in one corner. The kitschy garb extends to the guest rooms, too: oversize beds (some four-poster) are covered in satin cushions, windows are framed with lacy chiffon, and chairs are upholstered in velvet. Bathrooms are on the small side, but anything larger would detract from the Camelot-like ambience.

9909 Maple St., Chemainus, BC V0R 1K0. ℂ **250/246-9910**. Fax 250/246-2909. www.birdsongcottage.com. 4 units, cottage. C$105 (US$68) Bird Song Cottage. C$285–C$325 (US$185–$211) Castlebury Cottage 2-night minimum stay on weekends. Rates include breakfast and afternoon tea. Extra person $25 (US$16.25). MC, V. **Amenities:** Lounge. *In room:* Hair dryer, no phone. Cottage has TV/VCR, full-service kitchen, no phone.

IN LADYSMITH (NEAR CHEMAINUS)

Yellow Point Lodge 🐟   Yellow Point Lodge began operating in the 1930s, and its blend of summer camp and luxury resort has remained a perennial favorite. The main lodge has an enormous lobby, a huge fireplace, and a dining room with communal tables. Meals—good, home-style cooking—are included. There are a number of guest rooms in the lodge, all with oceanviews. Away from the lodge, the self-contained cabins are rustic, camp-style affairs with shared bathrooms; some are on the beach that's part of the lodge's property. The lodge is surrounded by 165 acres of private, mostly first-growth coastal rain forest, with over a mile-and-a-half of waterfront facing the Gulf Islands.

700 Yellow Point Rd., Ladysmith, BC V0R 2E0. ⓒ **250/245-7422.** Fax 250/245-7411. www.yellowpointlodge.com. 53 units. May–mid-Oct and winter weekends C$150–$190 (US$97.50–$123.50). Rates 20% lower Mid-Oct–Apr weekdays. Rates include all meals. AE, MC, V. Children 13 and under not accepted. **Amenities:** Restaurant; 2 outdoor tennis courts; Jacuzzi; sauna; bike rental. *In room:* No phone.

WHERE TO DINE
ON THE MALAHAT

The Aerie 🐟🐟🐟 WEST COAST/FRENCH   If the entire setting of the Aerie is overwhelmingly beautiful (see "Where to Stay," above), then the restaurant takes this one step further—if that's possible—with a gold-leaf ceiling, chandeliers, gilt chairs, and faux-marble columns. Some would say it's over the top. But it's a modus operandi that extends to the food, which, simply stated, is superb. The 8-course **tasting menu,** paired with exquisite wines, is the only way to go if you want to become an instant connoisseur of some of the very best tastes in life. This is a destination restaurant few Victorians miss, and you won't want to either.

600 Ebadora Lane. ⓒ **250/743-7115.** Reservations required. Lunch C$19 (US$12.35); dinner C$30 (US$19.50); 8-course prix fixe dinner C$95 (US$62). AE, MC, V. Daily 5–10pm. Take Hwy. 1 to the Spectacle Lake turnoff; take the first right and follow the winding driveway.

IN COWICHAN BAY

Crow & Gate 🐟🐟 *Value* PUB FARE   This classic Tudor-style pub was built in 1972, yet looks like it was plucked out of Cornwall, with its stone and timbered walls, leaded-glass windows, and low-slung ceilings. Even the sign outside seems authentic. Surrounded by a working farm, this popular watering hole offers the best of British pub fare, including roast beef and Yorkshire pudding, pasties, and shepherd's pie. There's a flower-laden patio in summer.

2313 Yellow Point Rd. © **250/722-3731.** Reservations recommended for dinner. Main courses C$9–$13.50 (US$5.85–$8.80). MC, V. Mon–Thurs and Sun 11am–11pm; Fri–Sat 11am–midnight.

Rock Cod Cafe ★★ *Value* FISH & CHIPS   Perched above the water, this funky cafe overlooks busy fishing docks and serves the best fish and chips in the area. After all, when the fish is pulled straight off the boats and put right into the pan, what would you expect? Check out the specials board: it's crammed with value-priced items based on whatever those boats bring in. This is a great place to fuel up for a stroll around the harbor.

1759 Cowichan Bay Rd. © **250/746-1550.** Main courses C$7–$13 (US$4.55–$8.45). MC, V. Sun–Thurs 11am–8pm; Fri–Sat 11am–9pm.

IN DUNCAN
Vinoteca ★★ LIGHT DINING   A combination wine-tasting room and tapas bar, Vinoteca is set amidst the family-owned and operated Vigneti Zanatta vineyards (see "Meandering the Wineries"). The 1903 farmhouse has been lovingly restored and is an eclectic place to dine or sip your afternoon away. The menu reflects the family's Italian heritage, incorporating food that is grown either on the farm or locally. A great place for a light meal, you'll find items such as marinated vegetables, bruschetta, as well as a daily fresh pasta selection, all of which are complemented by wines from the vineyards.

5039 Marshall Rd. (near Glenora south of Duncan). © **250/709-2279.** Reservations recommended for dinner. Lunch C$11–$16 (US$7–$10.50); dinner C$14–$20 (US$9–$13). MC, V. Wed–Sun noon–3:30pm; 5–10pm. Closed Mon–Tues. Closed Jan–Mar. Take Miller Rd. exit off Hwy. 1 to stop sign. Turn left onto Miller Rd., right on Koksilah Rd., and left onto Miller Rd. again. Turn left on Glenora; the vineyards are at the junction of Glenora and Marshall rds.

THE TOP ATTRACTIONS
All Fun Recreation Park *Kids*   Voted "Victoria's Best Place for Family Fun," this 1-km (¾-mile) water slide complex includes two miniature golf courses, a driving range, a go-cart track, batting cages, bumper boats, and more. The **Western Speedway,** "Canada's largest racing oval," has stock-car and late-model races, plus demolition derbies. Vancouver Island's largest Swap 'n Shop, a kind of classy flea market, is held at the track every Sunday, March through October. All Fun Recreation Park is 11km (7 miles) from downtown Victoria.

2207 Millstream Rd., Victoria. © **250/474-3184.** www.allfun.bc.ca. Admission C$18 (US$12) adults, C$14 (US$9) children 4–10, C$6 (US$4) observers. June–Sept daily 11am–7pm. Closed Oct–May. Take Hwy. 1 out of Victoria to exit 14, Millstream Rd. Follow sign to Millstream Rd.

BC Forest Museum Park/BC Forest Discovery Centre (Kids)

An affiliate of the Royal BC Museum, this is a fabulous learning and nature experience for the entire family. Focusing on forestry practices and preservation, you'll find an exhibit on the history of logging, a miniature town, a logging camp, and a ranger station. Don't miss the 20-minute ride on a full-size steam train.

2892 Drinkwater Rd., Duncan. © 250/715-1113. www.bcforestmuseum.com. Admission C$9 (US$5.85) adults, C$8 (US$5.20) seniors and students, C$5 (US$3.25) children 5–12, free for children 4 and under. C$29 (US$18.85) family pass. Mid-Apr–mid-Oct daily 10am–6pm daily. Closed mid-Oct–mid-Apr. Take Hwy. 1 past Duncan, watching for the double-span bridge over the Cowichan River. The centre is approximately 3km (2 miles) past the bridge, off the highway to the right, after the fourth set of traffic lights at Beverley St.

Cowichan Native Village ★★

The Cowichan were the original inhabitants of the valley that now bears their name. Their culture and way of life is creatively illustrated at the Cowichan Native Village. Storytelling, dancing, and traditional feasting are some of the activities here. Go on a guided walking tour of the village, which includes several modern longhouse structures; talk to carvers as they work, or enjoy the excellent multimedia theatre presentation that retells the Cowichan myth and history. The art gallery is the best place in the valley to buy the famous bulky, durable Cowichan sweaters, knitted with bold motifs from hand-spun raw wool.

200 Cowichan Way, Cowichan. © 250/746-8119. Admission C$10 (US$6.50) adults, C$8 (US$5.20) seniors and students, C$6 (US$3.90) children 12 and under. C$25.50 (US$16.50) family pass. Summer daily 9:30am–6pm; winter daily 10am–5pm.

MEANDERING THE WINERIES

The wine scene in British Columbia just keeps getting better and better, and although the vineyards on Vancouver Island are comparatively young to those found in the province's interior, they are beginning to produce some excellent vintages. As you make your way north through the Cowichan Valley towards Nanaimo, you might want to consider a pit stop at any one of the worthy wineries described below that dot the route northwards from Victoria.

The first pocket of wineries along the route is in Cobble Hill, south of Duncan. **Cherry Point Vineyards,** 840 Cherry Point Rd., RR#3, Cobble Hill (© 250/743-1272; www.cherrypointvineyards.com) is one of the most prominent Cowichan Valley wineries, with national awards to prove it. Cherry Point's California-like vineyards produce some of the finest Auxerrois in the country. The tasting room is a Swiss-styled chalet. The artwork of local artists adorns the walls. **Merridale Cider,** 1230 Merridale Rd., RR#1, Cobble Hill (© **800/998-9908** or 250/743-4293; www.merridale cider.com) is Canada's only orchard dedicated solely to cider and wine apples. Chat with the cider-makers, and tour the apple mills, presses, and fermentation casks. Visit in April and you'll see the orchard in magnificent bloom; turn up in October through November to watch the fragrant press. **Venturi-Schulze Vineyards,** 4235 Trans-Canada Highway, RR#1, Cobble Hill (© **250/743-5630;** www.venturischulze.com), is the smallest winery in the Cowichan Valley, and it's truly a family affair, centered on the 100-year-old farmhouse. A new winery, built partially underground, paved the way to convert the old winery into a vinegary. All wines and gourmet vinegars are grown, produced, and bottled on the property.

Another group of wineries worth visiting is found near Duncan. **Alderlea Vineyards,** 1751 Stamps Rd., TT1, Duncan (© **250/746-7122**) is located on a picturesque 10-acre site. Creating wines from grapes grown only in their own vineyard, Alderlea produces an excellent Bacchus, Pinot Gris, Hearth (a port-style dessert wine), Pinot Auxerrois, and Angelique blend. **Blue Grouse Vineyards,** 4365 Blue Grouse Rd, Duncan, (© **250/743-3834;** www.blue grousevineyards.com), is one of the founding estate wineries on Vancouver Island, and is renowned for its exclusive premium wines. All are 100% estate grown and produced. Wine tastings are held in a cozy European-style tasting room overlooking the valley. In summer, picnic tables under the arbor are perfect for a savory lunch. **Vignetti Zanatta,** 5039 Marshall Rd., RR#3, Duncan (© **250/748-2338;** www.zanatta.bc.ca), is one of the oldest vineyards on Vancouver Island. Wines here are made by an old-world Italian method using grapes grown only on the property. Try the Ortega, a dry fruity white wine; or the Glenora Fantasia, a sparkling wine. The Pinot Grigio, Auxerrois, Muscat, Merlot, and special Damasco are all worthwhile. Plan to stop for lunch or dinner at **Vinoteca** (see "Where to Dine," above), featuring many foods grown on the Zanatta's 120-acre farm.

5

Central Vancouver Island

The central part of Vancouver Island showcases some of the best of British Columbia's natural attractions—it's a real haven for eco-adventurers. But the central region is so diverse that much of it is also geared to family fun. Nanaimo, the island's second largest city and the gateway to the region, is the arrival point for visitors by ferries from the mainland. Families usually head for the neighboring communities of Parksville and Qualicum Beach, where sandy beaches, warm water temperatures, tranquil lakes, and exceptional golf courses prevail. They are a year-round vacation destination, and are increasingly attractive to active retirees; few can resist the more than 2,000 hours of sunshine the townships receive each year.

Things begin to change, however, as you head inland, cutting across the island to the west coast. Here lie the deep Douglas fir forests of **Cathedral Grove,** and the mill town of **Port Alberni,** from where you can explore the region's protected inlets. And once you reach the west coast, well, the changes in scenery are dramatic. The shores are windswept and wild. Fishing villages like **Tofino** (Tough City) and **Ucluelet** (*yew-kloo-let*) are home base to kayakers, hikers, surfers, naturalists, and photographers, who flock to explore **Pacific Rim National Park,** the Broken Group Islands, and Clayoquot Sound. Here you can discover some of the most pristine and accessible coastline in the province and wilderness at its very best.

1 Nanaimo

With a population close to 80,000, Nanaimo is quickly shedding its industrial roots. Once the center of vast coal-mining operations, Nanaimo developed into rather a parochial community. This image is finally beginning to change. Around the revamped waterfront, you'll find a number of galleries, intriguing shops, and quality restaurants to enjoy. The **Nanaimo District Museum** (100 Cameron Rd., © **250/753-1821;** ndmuseum@island.net) is a note-worthy attraction, even though you have to climb two steep flights of stairs to reach the entrance. Intriguing dioramas lie alongside artifacts found at the site pictured in the paintings. The recreations of a Salish Indian village, a mine, and a history of early Nanaimo have a very frontier feel. Make your own petroglyph rubbings for an unusual souvenir. The museum is open mid-May through Labor Day, Monday to Friday, from 9am to 5pm, Saturday and Sunday from 10am to 6pm; Labor Day through mid-May, Tuesday to Saturday, from 9am to 5pm. Admission is C$2 (US$1.30) adults, C$1.75 (US$1.15) for seniors and students, and less than a dollar for children 5 to 12. If you're going to stay awhile in Nanaimo, head down to the **Bastion**—the only remaining structure of its type in North America. This fort was built by the Hudson's Bay Company in 1852 to protect Nanaimo's trading post (at that time, there was particular concern with the Haida Indians, who traveled down from the northerly Queen Charlotte Islands, and mounted a series of raids). In summer, the Bastion Guards recreate the firing of the noon cannon daily at 11:45am.

ESSENTIALS
GETTING THERE

BY CAR   Nanaimo is located right off the Trans-Canada Highway (Hwy. 1), 111km (67 miles) north of Victoria.

BY PLANE   The **Nanaimo Airport** (✆ 250/245-2157) is 15km (9 miles) from downtown Nanaimo. There are approximately 20 flights daily between Nanaimo and Vancouver, as well as other cities in Canada. Airlines servicing the Nanaimo Airport include **Air Canada/Canadian** (✆ 888/247-2262 or 800/661-3936 (US/International); www.aircanada.ca), **WestJet Airlines** (✆ 800/538-5696; www.westjet.com) **North Vancouver Air** (✆ 800/228/6608; www.northvanair.com), and **Pacific Coastal Airlines** (✆ 800/663-2872; www.pacific-coastal.com). There are also several harbor-to-harbor flights between Vancouver, Nanaimo, Victoria, and Seattle. Carriers operating these include **Baxter Air** (✆ 800/661-5599; www.baxterair.com), **Harbour Air** (✆ 800/665-0212; www.harbour-air.com), **Kenmore Air** (✆ 800/543-9595; www.kenmore air.com), and **West Coast Air** (✆ 800/347-2222; www.west coastair.com).

BY BUS   **Laidlaw Coach Lines/Island Coach Lines** (✆ 800/318-0818) operates from Victoria to Nanaimo, Tofino, and Port Hardy. **Greyhound Canada** (✆ 800/661-8747; www.greyhound.ca) handles schedules and reservations. One-way fares from Victoria to

Nanaimo are C$27.50 (US$18) for adults. Fares for seniors are 10% less; fares for children 5 to 11 are 50% less.

BY TRAIN The **E&N Railiner,** operated by VIA Rail (© **800/ 561-8630;** www.viarail.com) has daily service between Victoria and Courtenay. One-day sightseeing trips from Victoria include stops in Chemainus, Duncan, and Nanaimo. At press time, however, VIA Rail had plans to cancel this service in summer 2002. Be sure to check with VIA Rail before making reservations.

BY FERRY BC Ferries (© **888/BCFERRY** (888/233-3779); www. bcferries.com) runs between **Horseshoe Bay,** in West Vancouver, and **Departure Bay,** in Nanaimo, as well as between **Tsawwassen** and **Duke's Point,** in Nanaimo. BC Ferries also services Gabriola Island, departing from an independent dock on Front St., in Nanaimo.

VISITOR INFORMATION

Tourism Nanaimo is located at Beban House, 2290 Bowen Rd., Nanaimo, BC V9T 3K7 (© **800/663-7337** or 250/756-0106; www.tourismnanaimo.com).

GETTING AROUND

Nanaimo Regional Transit System provides public transport in the Nanaimo urban area. For information about schedules and fares, call © 250/390-4531 or contact **Tourism Nanaimo** (see above). For cab service, call **AC Taxi** (© 800/753-1231 or 250/753-1231). Be alert to street signs; Nanaimo's roads go off at angles and change names along the way. For example, Bastion Street becomes Fitzwilliam Street (once Nanaimo's red-light district), which becomes 3rd Street, which leads to the Parkway, before becoming Jingle Pot Road, named for the time when miners walked the route to work, "jingling" their lunches in metal pails along the way.

WHERE TO STAY

Coast Bastion Inn 𝒜𝒜 Overlooking the Strait of Georgia, right on the inner harbor, this hotel is within minutes of championship golf courses, windsurfing, kayaking, fishing, and sailing facilities. The decor is a bit ordinary, but all guest rooms are very comfortable and have waterfront views. Some suites have Jacuzzis. The extremely courteous staff seems to enjoy fulfilling every request. There's a complimentary shuttle that runs between the hotel and downtown Nanaimo.

Central Vancouver Island

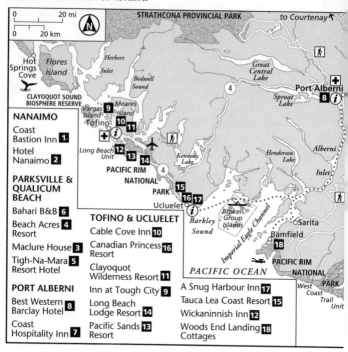

STRATHCONA PROVINCIAL PARK — to Courtenay

Hot Springs Cove
Flores Island
Herbert Inlet
Bedwell Sound
CLAYOQUOT SOUND BIOSPHERE RESERVE
Vargas Island
Meares Island
Tofino
Long Beach Unit
PACIFIC RIM NATIONAL PARK
Kennedy Lake
Ucluelet
Great Central Lake
Sproat Lake
Port Alberni
Alberni Inlet
Henderson Lake
Barkley Sound
Broken Group Islands
Imperial Eagle Channel
PACIFIC OCEAN
Sarita
Bamfield
PACIFIC RIM NATIONAL PARK
West Coast Trail Unit

NANAIMO

Coast Bastion Inn **1**

Hotel Nanaimo **2**

PARKSVILLE & QUALICUM BEACH

Bahari B&B **6**

Beach Acres Resort **4**

Maclure House **3**

Tigh-Na-Mara Resort Hotel **5**

PORT ALBERNI

Best Western Barclay Hotel **8**

Coast Hospitality Inn **7**

TOFINO & UCLUELET

Cable Cove Inn **10**

Canadian Princess Resort **16**

Clayoquot Wilderness Resort **11**

Inn at Tough City **9**

Long Beach Lodge Resort **14**

Pacific Sands Resort **13**

A Snug Harbour Inn **17**

Tauca Lea Coast Resort **15**

Wickaninnish Inn **12**

Woods End Landing Cottages **18**

---

11 Bastion St., Nanaimo, BC V9R 6E4. © **800/663-1144** or 250/753-6601. Fax 250/753-4155. www.coasthotels.com. 179 units. May–Sept C$150 (US$97.50) standard; $180 (US$117) superior. Oct–Apr C$135 (US$88) standard; C$165 (US$107) superior. Extra person C$10 (US$6.50). AE, DC, DISC, MC, V. Parking C$4.50 (US$2.95). **Amenities:** Restaurant, lounge; health club; Jacuzzi; sauna; bike rental. *In room:* A/C, TV, dataport, minibar, fridge, coffeemaker, hair dryer, iron.

Hotel Nanaimo   This is Nanaimo's newest full-service hotel. The facilities are bright and modern. Accommodations range from standard guest rooms to one-bedroom suites. All have fireplaces and kitchens or kitchenettes. Although located on the edge of the Rutherford Golf Course, the greens have been abandoned and now only offer great views and good walks. Now, golfers can tee off only at the nearby Nanaimo Golf Club. Hotel management is rather aloof and the service a bit hit-and-miss. Perhaps that's why, at time of press, the property had just lost its Four Points Sheraton franchise.

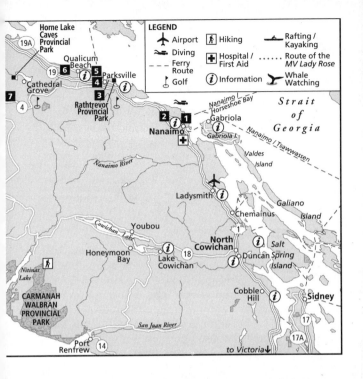

4900 Rutherford Rd., Nanaimo, BC V9T 5P1. ✆ **250/758-3000.** Fax 250/729-2808. 75 units. May–Sept C$119–$149 (US$77–$97). Oct–Apr C$89–$119 (US$58–$77). Extra person C$10 (US$6.50). AE, DC, MC, V. Underground parking. **Amenities:** Restaurant, lounge; small indoor heated pool; health club; room service. *In room:* A/C, TV, dataport, kitchen or kitchenette, coffeemaker, hair dryer, iron.

WHERE TO DINE

Mahle House 🎔🎔 PACIFIC NORTHWEST Built in 1904, Mahle (pronounced "molly") house is a lovingly restored delight overlooking an enclosed English-style garden. This family-owned restaurant has been a local favorite for more than 14 years, probably because the menu changes weekly. Items such as rabbit, free-range chicken, and venison come from local suppliers, while the herbs used to season these dishes come from the restaurant's own garden. Special evenings include wine tastings, tapas nights, and "Adventurous Wednesdays," featuring a gourmet multicourse meal for C$29.95 (US$19.50).

2104 Hemer Rd. at Cedar (10 min. south of Nanaimo). © **250/722-3621.**
Reservations recommended. Main courses C$14–$32 (US$9–$20). MC, V. Wed–Sun
5–10pm. Closed Mon–Tues.

Wesley Street Cafe 🎯🎯 PACIFIC NORTHWEST This is a
small, charming restaurant. Dining options progress from a casual
lunch that includes gourmet soups and sandwiches, to a more
sophisticated dinner menu that offers items such as roast quail with
an exotic mushroom stuffing. The chef is more than willing to adapt
menu items to accommodate allergies. There is live jazz on Friday
and Saturday nights. Dine inside or, in summer, opt for the flower-
covered patio.

1-321 Wesley St., Nanaimo. © **250/753-6057.** Lunch C$9 (US$5.85); dinner C$22
(US$14.30). AE, MC, V. Mon–Fri 11:30am–2:30pm and 5:30–10pm; Sat–Sun
noon–2:30pm and 5:30–10pm.

OUTDOOR ACTIVITIES

Scuba diving is big business in the waters around Nanaimo.
Nicknamed the "Emerald Sea," the water is clear enough to see the
likes of giant Pacific octopi, colorful sea anemones, and herds of
marine mammals that appear to just "hang around" for entertainment. **Dodds Narrows,** between Vancouver Island and Mudge
Island, is a particularly hot diving spot. Other areas include **Snake
Island Wall, Gabriola Passage,** and a number of sunken wrecks in
the region. The *HMCS Saskatchewan,* for example, is a 366-foot
Canadian Naval destroyer sunk in 1997 as part of Canada's artificial
reef project. There's also the *HMCS Cape Breton,* sunk in fall 2001.
A good diving operator, which offers guided dives, equipment
rentals, and instruction, is **Ocean Explorers Diving** (© **800/
233-4145** or 250/753-2055; www.oceanexplorersdiving.com).

Keeping your head above water delivers something quite different,
if you've got the nerve. Set high over the Nanaimo River lies the
Bungy Zone (© **800/668-7771** or 250/753-5867; www.bungy
zone.com), touted as the "Only Legal Bridge Bungy Jump Site in
North America." If free-falling 140 ft., at speeds of up to 140 km/h,
doesn't appeal, watching the bungy bravehearts is still a thrill. An
on-site gift shop sells plenty of bungy paraphernalia, so you can
always pretend you dared. Jumps range from C$50 to $180
(US$32.50 to $117) for tandems, and include an I Did It! T-shirt.

A SIDE TRIP TO GABRIOLA ISLAND

Although only a 20-minute ferry ride from the Nanaimo Harbour,
Gabriola Island feels a world away from the bustle of Vancouver

Island. Known as the "Queen of the Gulf Islands," Gabriola provides a little of everything: sandy beaches, kayaking, canoeing, fine restaurants, artisan's studios and galleries, petroglyphs, and tide pools. It is home to the **Silva Bay Shipyard School,** Canada's only traditional wooden boat-building school. Overall, Gabriola Island has a whimsical atmosphere, which you grasp as soon as you get off the ferry. When you disembark, look up at the **White Hart Pub,** next to the terminal, and you'll see an eye-catching cyclist named Mary Ann, pedaling like fury on her recycled bike. Mary Ann, a life-size polychrome folk art carving, is an example of the tongue-in-cheek wood creations scattered all over the island by **FOGO Folk Art Studio** (3065 Commodore Way, ✆ 250/247-8082). The island's biggest natural attraction are the **Malaspina Galleries,** an amazing series of sandstone formations carved by the surf into unusual caves and caverns. Most beaches are protected, providing excellent tidal pools and safe swimming, especially at **Drumbeg Park,** where the sun heats the sandstone rocks enough to dry your towels. Scuba divers also use this area, as it provides shore-based access to nearby **Gabriola Passage.** If you're tempted to stay overnight, there are a number of bed-and-breakfasts, as well as a variety of vacation homes for longer-term rentals. B&Bs include the **Hummingbird Lodge B&B,** RR#1 Site 55-C-54, Gabriola Island, BC V0R 1X0 (✆ **877/ 551-9383** or 250/247-9300), a beautiful hand-built 5,000 sq. ft. home; and the **Sunset B&B,** 969 Berry Point Rd., Gabriola Island, BC V0R 1X0 (✆ **250/247-2032;** www.islandnet.com/~sunsetcl), set on a rocky point above the Georgia Strait, with paths leading to protected coves, tidal basins, and hidden viewpoints. Meanwhile, boats can find moorage, services, and lodging at **Silva Bay,** 3383 South Rd. (✆ **250/247-8662).** The **Silva Bay Bar & Grill** is the best restaurant on the island. Head to **Pages Marina,** 3350 Coast Rd. (✆ **250/247-8931),** to buy groceries, fishing licenses, and tackle, as well as rent bicycles and diving gear. Helpful charter contacts include **Silver Blue Charters** (✆ **250/247-8807** or 250/755-6150 (boat phone); www.silverbluecharters.com) for sea fishing excursions; **Arasheena Charters** (✆ **250/247-0079;** www.arasheena.com) for island-hopping cruises and tours; and **Gabriola Reefs Dive Shop** (✆ **250/247-8443;** www.mygabriola.com/GabReefs.htm) for diving expeditions. For further information, contact Gabriola's **Visitor Information Centre,** located at the Folklore Village Centre (✆ **250/247-9332;** www.gabriolaisland.org), which isn't "folksy" at all, but quite a swish new shopping mall housed in the recycled

Folklife Pavilion from Expo 86. **BC Ferries** (© **888/223-3779** or 250/386-3431; www.bcferries.com) runs a passenger and car service between Nanaimo and Gabriola Island, with 16 daily crossings. Round-trip fares are C$5 (US$3.25) per passenger; C$13.50 (US$8.75) for a standard-size vehicle. Bicycles are carried free of charge.

2 Parksville & Qualicum Beach

Sitting side-by-side, Parksville and Qualicum Beach are probably the most popular resort towns on Vancouver Island. With miles of sand for the kids and a number of golf courses for the parents, they are the ideal base for a family vacation.

Several of the resorts in Parksville are, in fact, the town's main features. Sadly, much of Parksville's original park-like attributes have been overtaken in the past two decades by used car lots and motels that now line the highway through town, giving it a strip mall-like air. At the same time, the area's population has nearly tripled, and is expected to double again by 2016. These issues aside, though, Parksville redeems itself with its expansive **beaches.** Ebbing tides can expose up to a kilometer of shore, leaving large shallow pools in the sand, perfect for sandcastle building and collecting sand dollars. At the **International Sandcastle Competition,** held each August, sandcastle builders of all ages race to create award-winning sculptures between tides. Life thrives around the waterfront, with artsy shops, galleries, and a plethora of cafes, pubs, and restaurants. Freshwater streams west of Parksville provide trout and steelhead fishing, as well as salmon and halibut; there's cod fishing offshore. Diving abounds offshore too. When you're not near the water, take time to visit the **Old School House** ⚘, 122 Fern Rd. W. (© **250/752-6133**). The town's original school now exhibits the works of potters, weavers, painters, and other local artists. It also holds frequent workshops, classes, and concerts.

Qualicum Beach is more genteel than Parksville. Inns and restaurants are scattered along the water's edge. Formal walkways and spectacular gardens border expansive beaches. Qualicum residents are passionate gardeners, earning their community coveted awards in provincial competitions. Nowhere is this perhaps better exemplified than at **Milner Gardens & Woodland,** 2179 West Island Hwy. (© **250/752-6153;** www.milnergardens.mala.bc.ca), once the personal retreat of Queen Elizabeth II and Prince Phillip. The Cotswolds-style house and princely gardens opened to the public in

2001. The 70-acre site is a living laboratory of rare and unusual plants, combining avenues of rhododendrons (more than 500), as well as rare and exotic species, with old-growth forests full of towering Douglas firs. You can tour the gardens and the house. Admission is C$10 (US$6.50) for adults, C$6 (US$4) for students, free for children 12 and under. Open April through October, Thursday to Sunday, from 10am to 5pm. Closed November through March. This is a fabulous garden walk. But then you would expect nothing less for royals. Rule Botanica!

Other activities in the Qualicum Beach area include swimming, hiking, golf, tennis, lawn bowling, and **spelunking at Horne Lake Caves Provincial Park.**

ESSENTIALS
GETTING THERE
BY CAR   Parksville and Qualicum Beach are located 36km (22 miles) north of Nanaimo, off Highway 19. The closest airport is in Nanaimo.

BY BUS   **Laidlaw Coach Lines/Island Coach Lines** (© 800/ 318-0818 or 250/385-4411) offers service between Nanaimo and Parksville/Qualicum Beach along the Highway 1/Highway 19 corridor. One-way fares are C$8.25 (US$5) for adults. Fares for seniors are 10% less; fares for children 5 to 11 are 50% less. **Greyhound Canada** (© 800/661-8747; www.greyhound.ca) handles schedules and reservations.

BY TRAIN   VIA Rail's **E&N Railiner** (© 800/561-8630 or 250/ 383-4324; www.viarail.com) stops in Parksville and Qualicum Beach on its daily trip from Victoria to Courtenay. VIA Rail is planning to cancel this service in summer 2002; check before making your plans.

VISITOR INFORMATION
The **Parksville Visitor Information Centre** is at 1275 East Island Hwy. (P.O. Box 99), Parksville, BC V9P 2G3 (© **250/248-3613;** www.chamber.parksville.bc.ca). The **Qualicum Beach Visitor Information Centre** is at 2711 West Island Hwy., Qualicum Beach, BC V9K 2C4 (© **250/752-9532;** www.qualicum.bc.ca).

WHERE TO STAY
Bahari B&B 🎇🎇   Perched on the forested shoreline near Qualicum Beach, Bahari offers guests West Coast luxury with a Japanese ambience. A blend of raku pottery, Ikebana (a stylized Japanese floral arrangement), and modern Canadian work offsets

other objets d'art. An embroidered wedding kimono that hangs in the stairwell is a stunning centerpiece. Each of the four spacious guest rooms has custom-designed drapes, bedspreads, and accessories, with finishing touches that relegate Martha Stewart to the sidelines. Even the bathrooms contain one-of-a-kind fixtures. Guests are welcome to enjoy the uncluttered sitting room—check out the kaleidoscope display—although the TV room and library are more inviting. Relax in the garden, wander the trails down to the beach, or take in the sweeping views of the Georgia Strait from the cliffside Jacuzzi. There is also a huge two-bedroom apartment, complete with fireplace, balcony, and kitchen. The apartment is the best bet for families; children are not allowed in the main house.

5101 Island Hwy., Qualicum Beach, BC V9K 1Z1. © **877/752-9278** or 250/752-9278. Fax 250/752-9038. www.baharibandb.com. 4 units. June–Sept C$175–$210 (US$114–$136.60) standard; C$290 (US$188.50) apartment. Feb–May and Oct–Nov C$125–$175 (US$82–$114) standard; C$240 (US$156) apartment. Rates include breakfast. 2-night minimum stay in high season. Weekly rates and seasonal packages available. AE, MC, V. Closed Dec–Jan. Children 15 and under not accepted in main house. Children accepted in apartment. **Amenities:** Jacuzzi; coin-op washers and dryers. *In room:* TV, hair dryer.

Beach Acres Resort 🏕 *Kids*   Reminiscent of the great family resorts of days gone by, families return summer after summer to catch up with old friends and to make new ones. Located on Parksville's Rathtrevor Beach, the resort offers 23 acres of family fun with a carefree, summer-camp atmosphere. Children's programs include everything from scavenger hunts to sandcastle contests, and there's a supervised indoor swimming pool. While the children have fun, Mom and Dad can relax in the Jacuzzi, or challenge each other to a tennis match. Accommodations-wise, guests can choose between cottages in a forest setting with country-style furniture, one- and two-bedroom Tudor-style cottages on the beach, or oceanview townhouses. The townhouses sleep up to six people and have full kitchens and fireplaces. Beach Acres doesn't have an on-site restaurant, but it's next door to another hotel, Maclure House, which does. Most guests make the short trip over to the Maclure House Restaurant, if they aren't cooking in their rooms. (See "Where to Dine," below, for a review of the Maclure House Restaurant.)

25-1015 East Island Hwy., Parksville, BC V9P 2E4. © **800/663-7309** or 250/248-3424. Fax 250/248-6145. www.beachacresresort.com. 55 units. July–Aug C$198–$257 (US$129–$167). Sept–June C$112–$175 (US$73–$114). Weekly rates available. AE, DC, DISC, MC, V. **Amenities:** Access to restaurant at Maclure House; large heated indoor pool; 3 tennis courts; 1 outdoor basketball court; 1 outdoor volleyball court; Jacuzzi; sauna; children's programs; coin-op washers and dryers. *In room:* TV, kitchen.

Maclure House 🌟

Staying at Maclure House is rather like a "country house weekend," where a walk in bracing sea air ends with afternoon drinks on the porch, and then stretches into dinner and an early night—all amidst luxurious comfort. Built in 1921 in the style of Scottish hunting lodges, this ivy-covered mansion retains much of its traditional character, with expanses of leaded glass, 30-foot ceilings, an impressive, solid cedar staircase, and beautifully landscaped gardens. Two of the four guest rooms have oceanviews, and all are decked out in themes of the British Empire. The Ocean Suite, which boasts a large bedroom and sitting room with tiled fireplace, has a marvelous bathroom still sporting its spruced-up, original fixtures. The Maclure House Restaurant (see "Where to Dine," below) is one of the best in the area. Guests at Maclure House have access to the recreational facilities at Beach Acres Resort, next door (reviewed above).

11-1015 East Island Hwy., Parksville, BC V9P 2E4. © **250/248-3470.** Fax 250/258-5162. www.maclurehouse.com. 4 units. Mid-June–mid-Sept C$95–$140 (US$62–$91). Mid-Sept–mid-June C$80–$115 (US$52–$75). Rates include breakfast and afternoon treats. Extra person C$24 (US$16) (adult), C$12 (US$8) (child 9 and under). MC, V. **Amenities:** Restaurant; access to recreational facilities at Beach Acres Resort. *In room:* Hair dryer, no phone.

Tigh-Na-Mara Resort Hotel 🌟🌟🌟 *(Kids)*

Romantic family getaways might sound like an oxymoron, but not here at Tigh-Na-Mara, Gaelic for "the house by the sea." Established in the 1940s on a 26-acre forested waterfront beach near Rathtrevor Beach Provincial Park, this time-honored resort just keeps getting better. It offers a diverse range of quality accommodation; guests can stay in intimate one- or two-bedroom log cottages in a forest setting, splurge on the rather lavish oceanview condominiums (many with Jacuzzis), or enjoy lodge-style standard rooms. All guest accommodations are decorated with contemporary furnishings and immaculately maintained. They all have fireplaces, full bathrooms, and some kitchen facility, depending on the accommodation type. Tigh-Na-Mara's newest accommodations are three- and four-room cottages that can sleep up to eight and that are surrounded by towering arbutus and fir trees. Families flock to Tigh-Na-Mara for its supervised child-friendly programs as much as for its stunning location. Activities are numerous and even include "parents' nights out" every Tuesday and Thursday when children are entertained with movies and the like.

In addition to a full children's menu, the resort's restaurant dishes up Northwest cuisine alongside barbecues in summer. If you're child-wary, and really want to experience the full romance of Tigh-Na-Mara, seasonal specials are geared for you. A 3,059-m² (10,000-sq. ft.) full-service spa is scheduled to open in the fall of 2002.

1095 East Island Hwy., Parksville, BC V9P 2E6. ✆ 800/663-7373 or 250/248-2072. Fax 250/248-4140. www.tigh-na-mara.com. 142 units. July–Aug C$120 (US$78) lodge room; C$155–$230 US$101–$149.50) oceanview condo; C$230–$255 (US$149.50–$166) cottage; C$230–$275 (US$149.50–$179) woodlands suite. Sept–Oct, May–June C$99–110 (US$64–71.50) lodge room; C$133–215 (US$86.50–140) oceanview condo; C$155–205 (US$101–133) cottage; C$210–230 (US$136.50–149.50) woodlands suite. Nov–Apr C$83 (US$54) lodge room; C$110–165 (US$71.50–107) oceanview condo; C$140–160 (US$91–104) cottage; C$180 (US$117) woodlands suite. 3–7-night minimum stay July–Aug. Seasonal packages available. AE, DC, MC, V. Pets accepted Sept–May. **Amenities:** Restaurant, lounge; large heated indoor pool; 1 outdoor tennis court; exercise room; Jacuzzi; sauna; limited water-sports equipment rentals; business center; babysitting. *In room:* TV, kitchen, coffeemaker.

WHERE TO DINE

Beach House Cafe 𝒦𝒦 WEST COAST   Located right at the water's edge, the fully licensed Beach House Cafe is a local favorite, serving good food without a lot of frills. Its bistro-style atmosphere carries through from an easy soup-and-sandwich lunch to a casual, intimate dinner. Some lunch items are repeated at dinner, although in the evening, you'll be treated to house specialties, such as a bouilla-baisse loaded with local seafood. Homemade pies, whether steak-and-mushroom or rhubarb-and-strawberry, are a must. It's a tiny place that fills up quickly, so if you make reservations, be on time.

2775 West Island Hwy., Qualicum Beach. ✆ 250/752-9626. Reservations recommended on weekends. Lunch C$8 (US$5); dinner C$18.50 (US$12). MC, V. Daily 11am–2:30pm and 5–10pm.

Cola Diner 𝒦𝒦 *Finds* BURGERS   The experience here is pure and unadulterated retro. Built back when Coca-Cola had its own restaurant/gas station chain, the Cola Diner is housed in a roadhouse north of Qualicum Beach. It's been lovingly restored to its former glory, complete with soda fountain, jukebox, and lots of Coke memorabilia. The menu is filled with all things "greasy spoon": burgers galore, multilayered sandwiches, excellent onion rings, and chunky cut french fries.

6060 West Island Hwy., Qualicum Beach. ✆ 250/757-2029. Main courses C$5.25–$9.95 (US$3.50–$6.50). MC, V. Wed–Mon 10am–8pm. Closed Tues.

Maclure House Restaurant ✪✪ INTERNATIONAL   The setting makes this one of the loveliest restaurants in the area. Located in beautiful Maclure House (see "Where to Stay," above, for a review of this inn), the restaurant is perfect for a romantic meal or special occasion. Guests dine in the dining room, library, or music room. Each room has a view of the surrounding gardens, and an ornamental hand-carved fireplace. The snug little lounge, also with fireplace, is a wonderful place for a drink. In summer, tables spill out onto the flagstone veranda. The house specialty is rack of lamb, crusted with Dijon mustard and pecans, and served with mint au jus. It certainly lives up to its "to die for" reputation. Lunch is a more casual affair, though every bit as worthwhile.

1015 East Island Hwy., Parksville. © **250/248-3470.** Reservations recommended. Lunch C$8 (US$5); dinner C$16–$29 (US$10.50–$19). MC, V. Daily 8:30–11am, 11:30am–2pm and 5–10pm.

HORNE LAKE CAVES PROVINCIAL PARK ✪✪✪ (Kids)

This is one of Vancouver Island's best outdoor adventure destinations. Nestled in the mountains of the Beaufort Range, beside a lakeside park with camping and canoeing, Horne Lake Caves attracts spelunkers for half- or full-day adventures. Getting to the park is a bit of an adventure. Take the **Horne Lake exit** off **Highway 19** (the Island Highway) or **19A,** and follow the signs for 12km. Drive with your headlights on and watch out for logging trucks.

Two caves are open year-round for self-guided tours, although you must bring at least two sources of light, and helmets are recommended. In summer, you can rent these from the **park office.** The park also offers a number of guided tours, catering to everything from easy-going family fun to extreme experiences. The 1½-hour **Riverbend Cave Interpretive Program** is the easiest of these tours, and most popular. It starts with a short uphill hike through the forest to the cave entrance, which leads to a haven of beautiful crystal formations and ancient fossils. This tour costs C$15 (US$9.75) for adults, C$12 (US$7.80) for children 11 and under. The 3-hour **Triple Cave Adventure** is a shade more challenging, involving some tight passages and lots of cave scrambling. It costs C$39 (US$25.35) per person; ages 8 and up. In summer, tours run throughout the day, from 10am to 5pm on a first-come, first-served basis. In winter, they are by reservation only.

Where the family tour stops, a 5-hour **High Adventure** tour begins. It includes instruction in basic rock climbing and roping, which you'll need to rappel down a seven-story waterfall known as the "Rainbarrel." Sturdy footwear and warm clothing is a must, although previous climbing experience is not. The tour costs C$79 (US$51.35) for adults. The 7-hour **Underground Extreme** tour is a different story. This time, you get to *climb up* the Rainbarrel on a wild cable ladder—a real adrenaline pumper and not for the faint of heart. This tour costs C$110 (US$71.50) for adults. Two-hour **Outdoor Rappel** clinics are available, and strongly recommended for those without recent rappel experience. The clinic cost is C$32 (US$20.80). *Note:* You must be 15 years or older and sign a liability waiver form in order to participate in the High Adventure and Underground Extreme tours. For information about all tours at Horne Lake Caves, and to reserve, contact the park office (© **250/ 757-TOUR** or 250/339-0555 (reservations); www.hornelake.com).

RATHTREVOR PROVINCIAL PARK 🕱🕱🕱 (Kids

If you want to camp, this former farmstead 2km (1 mile) south of Parksville on Highway 19A is one of the best sites in the province. Located next to 2km (1 mile) of sandy shore, the park offers 175 tent and RV sites. Amenities include showers, firewood, a sani-station, and interpretive programs. This is an extremely popular campground during the summer, when school is out, so reservations are a must. There's usually a lineup of tenters and RVs in front of the park gate as early as 8am, waiting for cancellations. The early birds are often successful in securing a spot. Contact **Discover Camping** (© **800/ 689-9025** (reservations) or 250/954-4600 (information); www. discovercamping.ca).

GOLF COURSES

There are six golf courses in the Parksville-Qualicum Beach area, and over a dozen within an hour's drive. The **Eaglecrest Golf Club,** 2035 Island Hwy., Qualicum Beach (© **800/567-1320** or 250/ 752-6311), is an 18-hole, par-71 course with an emphasis on shot-making and accuracy. **Fairwinds,** 3730 Fairwinds Dr., just east of Parksville at Nanoose Bay (© **250/468-7666**), is a challenging 18-hole, par-71 course with oceanviews and lots of trees to avoid. **Glengarry Golf Links,** 1025 Qualicum Rd., Qualicum Beach (© **250/752-8786**), has nine links-style holes, plus a scenic back nine. The long established **Qualicum Beach Memorial,** 115 West Cres., Qualicum Beach (© **250/752-6312**), has nine holes, stunning oceanviews, a pro shop, and a restaurant. **Morningstar Golf Club,** 525 Lowry's Rd., Parksville (© **800/567-1320** or 250/248-

8161), is an 18-hole, 7,018-yard-long course with a par-72 rating. **Arrowsmith Golf and Country Club,** 2250 Fowler Rd., north of Qualicum Beach (*𝒞* **250/752-9727**), is a family-oriented course with 18 holes and a par-61 rating. All have a driving range, clubhouse, and pro shop. From April to October, green fees average C$60 (US$39) for adults; from November to March, they average C$35 (US$23) for adults. Children 18 and under are about C$35 (US$23) year-round, and **twilight rates,** after 3pm, average C$30 (US$19.50) for all players.

3 Heading West: Port Alberni & Bamfield

Jump into your vehicle, hit the accelerator, and begin a memorable voyage from the east to west side of central Vancouver Island. The trip is about 200km (125 miles) and takes about three hours to drive. En route, you'll pass through **Coombs,** a farming community with a good selection of country crafts boutiques. The **Old Country Market,** complete with goats on the roof, is a Kodak moment, and a chance to stretch your legs, buy a delicious ice cream, or pick up picnic supplies. There's also an intriguing gift-for-yourself emporium with teapots, marmalades, imported clothes, and baskets.

As you near the west coast, you pass waterfalls beneath a canopy of rain forest. **Port Alberni** is another stopover that's an interesting detour for a quick lunch and wander, but unless you're taking a trip on the *MV Lady Rose* to Bamfield, there's no draw to stay overnight. **Bamfield,** on the other hand, is a delightful diversion that's worth at least a day trip, if not an overnight stay. Reached only by boat, this village rests on boardwalks, with lovely coves, homes, and B&Bs tucked into the surrounding inlets.

ESSENTIALS
GETTING THERE
BY CAR   From Nanaimo, take the Island Highway (Hwy. 19) 52km (31 miles) north towards Parksville. Just before you hit Parksville, take the turnoff for Highway 4, which leads west to Port Alberni and on to the coastal towns of Tofino and Ucluelet. It's a good idea to leave Nanaimo in the morning to avoid having the afternoon sun in your eyes as you drive west (and to return in the afternoon so that the sun is behind you as you head east). A secondary highway, Highway 4, is narrow in places, as well as winding, slippery, and mountainous. Night driving isn't recommended. If you plan to drive straight through to Tofino or Ucluelet, gas up in Nanaimo. Gas stations are scarce along Highway 4.

VISITOR INFORMATION

The **Pacific Rim Tourism Association** is at 3100 Kingsway Ave.,
(The Station) Port Alberni, BC V9Y 3B1 (© **250/723-7529;**
www.pacificrimtourism.ca).

WHERE TO STAY & DINE

Best Western Barclay Hotel ℛ   Totally refurbished in 1999,
this vintage hotel now offers pleasant guest rooms, with upgraded
bathrooms and plush new mattresses. Suites have fridges, microwaves, and coffeemakers. The **Stamps Cafe** serves casual fare.
If you're looking for something more lively, there are no less than
22 TV screens in **Pastimes Sports Bar and Grill.**

4277 Stamp Ave., Port Alberni, BC V9Y 7X8. © **800/563-6590** or 250/724-7171.
Fax 250/724-9691. www.bestwesternbarclay.com. 86 units. May–Sept C$109–$139
(US$71–$90). Oct–Apr C$89–$109 (US$58–$71). Off-season discounts available.
Extra person C$10 (US$6.50). Children 17 and under stay free in parents' room.
AE, DC, DISC, MC, V. **Amenities:** Restaurant, pub, sports bar; small heated outdoor
pool; exercise room; Jacuzzi; sauna. *In room:* A/C, TV, coffeemaker, hair dryer, iron.

Coast Hospitality Inn ℛ   A cozy fireplace in the lobby welcomes
guests to this Tudor-style inn. Recently upgraded guest rooms ensure
a comfortable and relaxing stay. The **Harvest Restaurant** specializes
in home-style cooking, while **Polly's Pub** serves a lighter menu.

3835 Redford St., Port Alberni, BC V9Y 3S2. © **800/663-1144** or 250/723-8111.
Fax 250/723-0088. www.coasthotels.com. 50 units. May–Sept C$145 (US$87).
Oct–Apr C$115 (US$75). Fishing and golf packages available. Family plan, seniors
discounts, and off-season discounts available. AE, DC, MC, V. Free parking.
Amenities: Restaurant, pub; limited room service; babysitting; laundry service;
dry cleaning. *In room:* A/C, TV, dataport, coffeemaker, hair dryer, iron.

EXPLORING THE AREA

Located midway between Parksville and Port Alberni in MacMillan
Provincial Park, is the world-renowned **Cathedral Grove.** Here,
thousand-year-old forest includes Douglas fir, western hemlock,
grand fir, and western red cedar. To see where many trees like these
end up, you need look no further than Port Alberni.

  Port Alberni is a hard-working little town of nearly 20,000.
Along the waterfront, logs are milled into lumber, pulp, and paper.
Smoke from the mills spews up into the low-lying clouds that cling
to the surrounding mountains. On a dull day, the entire town is gray
with nary a hint of the fabulous views that a sunny day brings. Port
Alberni is trying to revitalize its rather industrial façade, but it's an
uphill effort despite the self-professed nickname "Positive Port
Alberni." If you need to break the drive to the coast, head down to

the redeveloped **Harbour Quay** area at the foot of **Argyle Street,** and you'll find restaurants and gift shops amid the cackle of seagulls and the full-throated honk of ship's horns. Aviation fans might want to stop at the **Home of the Mars Water Bombers,** the largest water bombing plane fleet in the world, headquartered at lovely **Sproat Lake** nearby. In summer, you can head over to the restored Port Alberni **railway station** (built around 1912) and board an antique locomotive for a ride up to the McLean Mill National Historic Site. Originally used by The Esquimalt and Nanaimo (E&N) Railway to transport logs and lumber between the mills and the harbor, the fully restored train now carries passengers. It operates Saturdays and Sundays, departing hourly from 11am to 4pm. Fares include admission to the McLean Mill: C$20 (US$13) for adults, C$15 (US$10) for seniors and children, C$45 (US$29) for a family pass. The **McLean Mill National Historic Site,** newly designated as such, preserves a family-run steam-driven sawmill built in 1926, and is a township all on its own. More than 30 buildings include an operational mill, bunkhouse accommodations for the 20-odd mill workers who once worked there, and a schoolhouse for the workers' children. It's located on Smith Road, off Beaver Creek Road, west of Port Alberni. Although only operational in summer, visitors are welcome to wander the site year-round. Admission is C$6.50 (US$4.25) for adults, C$4 (US$2.60) for seniors and youths, free for children 5 and under, C$14 (US$8.80) for a family pass. Call © **250/723-1376** for information or log on to **www.alberniheritage.com**.

Port Alberni has several small museums, but two are of particular note. **The Alberni Valley Museum,** 4255 Wallace St. (© **250/723-2181;** www.alberniheritage.com), has an excellent display of local First Nations and pioneer artifacts that is engaging and eclectic. Open year-round, Tuesday, Wednesday, Friday, and Saturday from 10am to 5pm. Open Thursday from 10am to 8pm. Admission is by donation. A new **Maritime Discovery Centre** (© **250/723-1035**), which sits in a 15-m (48-ft.) lighthouse replica at the end of a pier overlooking the town, retells Port Alberni's seafaring history. Open daily from late May to the end of September, from 9:30am to 5pm. Admission is C$2 (US$1.30) per person. For more information on Port Alberni, there's a **Visitor Information Centre** at 2533 Redford St., RR2, Site 215 C10, Port Alberni, BC V9Y 7L6 (© **250/724-6535;** www.avcoc.com).

If you're ready to leave the shore behind for a while, a truly unique way to experience the area is to take a day trip aboard either the

MV Lady Rose, or the **MV Frances Barkley** 🐟🐟🐟, both packet freighters that transport supplies to some of British Columbia's most far-flung coastal communities. Passengers observe life aboard a coastal freighter firsthand as it delivers all manner of cargo: from newspapers and groceries bound for general stores, to equipment for logging camps—even laundry. For some residents scattered along this coast, the *MV Lady Rose* and the *MV Frances Barkley* are their only links to civilization. The scenery, of course, is spectacular. Kayakers and canoeists en route to the Broken Group Islands take the *MV Lady Rose* to Sechart. Hikers bound for the West Coast Trail can catch a ride to Bamfield, a picturesque fishing village just north of the trailhead (see the upcoming section, "A Side Trip to Bamfield"). Round-trip passengers have a chance to stroll Bamfield's famous wooden boardwalks, enjoy lunch, or even stay over for some fishing, diving, or hiking. In summer, round-trippers can also take a day trip through the Broken Groups Islands to Ucluelet. Tiny galleys on board produce basic food such as weighty egg-and-bacon sandwiches, which you can't linger over since other passengers are usually lining up behind you. Wear sensible shoes and bring warm, windproof clothing. The decks are open and weather in the coastal waters can be temperamental. Reservations are required, especially for kayaks, since the freighters have limited space. Departures are from **Harbour Quay** year-round, Tuesday, Thursday, and Saturday, at 8am, returning to Port Alberni at about 5:30pm. From June through September, there are additional 8am sailings to Ucluelet, on Monday, Wednesday, and Friday, returning to Port Alberni at about 7pm. One-way adult fares to Bamfield are C$23 (US$15); return fares are C$45 (US$29.25). One-way adult fares to Ucluelet are C$25 (US$16.25); return fares are C$50 (US$32.50). Fares are half-price for children 8 to 15. Children 7 and under ride free. For ticket information and reservations, contact **Lady Rose Marine Services,** P.O. Box 188, Port Alberni BC V9Y 7M7 (© **800/663-7192** or 250/723-8313; www.ladyrosemarine.com).

A SIDE TRIP TO BAMFIELD 🐟🐟

With a population of less than 800, **Bamfield** is the Venice of Vancouver Island, and although this isolated community can be reached from Port Alberni via a 102-km (63-mile) unpaved road, most people arrive by boat or floatplane (see "Exploring the Area," above). Bamfield's high street is water-borne, lined with marine suppliers and quirky boardwalks that join weather-beaten houses, stores, and resorts. Crossing the street means hitching a ride with a local boat owner or hailing a water taxi. Day-trippers off the *MV Lady Rose* have just enough time to meander the boardwalks, buy a carving from a soapstone studio, and maybe enjoy a drink at the historic **Bamfield Inn,** before the return trip to Port Alberni. Outdoor enthusiasts tend to linger, using Bamfield as a base for fishing, diving, or kayaking. **Broken Island Adventures** (© **888/728-6200** or 250/728-3500) offers customized diving excursions in Barkley sound, kayak rentals, and kayak and wildlife viewing tours. Hikers heading for the West Coast Trail use Bamfield as a pit stop before or after a week in the rugged coastal wilderness (see "Pacific Rim National Park", later in the chapter). **The Hook and Web Pub** is a good place to eavesdrop on their harrowing stories of survival. If you just want to get away from it all, **Woods End Landing Cottages,** 168 Wild Duck Rd., Bamfield, BC V0R 1B0 (© **250/728-3383;** www.woodsend.travel.bc.ca), offers comfort and character.

4 Tofino, Ucluelet & Pacific Rim National Park

The scenic drive through the center of Vancouver Island is only a taste of what's to come once you reach the wild coast of Western Canada. Here, the Pacific Ocean rollers crash against the shore, beaches stretch for miles, and the mist clings to the rain forest like cobwebs. Most of what you'll see is part of **Pacific Rim National Park.** In winter, you'll witness some of the best storms in the world—as dramatic and angry as a Turner landscape. In summer, families play alongside surfers, kayakers, and others enjoying this Valhalla for outdoor activities. **Tofino** has long since been the commercial center of the region. As gateway to **Clayoquot Sound,** a wilderness reserve, it becomes so busy with visitors in summer that its popularity is eroding its charm. For many, the town of **Ucluelet,** 42km (27 miles) away, is a quieter haven—although judging from new developments, it's only a matter of time until it too is discovered by eco-adventurers and the like.

ESSENTIALS
GETTING THERE
BY CAR   From Port Alberni, continue west on Highway 4 for about 145km (90 miles) to a T-junction. Turn north to Tofino (34km (21 miles)), or south to Ucluelet (8km (5 miles)).

BY PLANE   North Vancouver Air (© 800/228-6608 or 604/ 278-1608) operates twin-engine, turbo-prop planes from Vancouver to Tofino from May to September daily. During the off season, October to April, it flies four times per week. One-way fares are C$185 (US$120) for adults. Fares for seniors are 15% less; fares for children 7 to 12 are 30% less. **Northwest Seaplanes** (© 800/ 690-0086 or 425/277-1590) and **Sound Flight** (© 800/825-0722 or 425/255-6500) provide floatplane service between Seattle and Tofino from mid-June to late September. One-way fares are about C$425 (US$275) for adults. Fares for seniors and children are 5 to 10% less.

BY BUS   Island Coach Lines (© 800/318-0818) operates daily service between Victoria and Tofino/Ucluelet, stopping at Nanaimo to pick up passengers arriving by ferry. One-way adult fares from Victoria to Tofino are C$52.25 (US$34); C$49.50 (US$32) from Victoria to Ucluelet; C$33 (US$21.50) from Nanaimo to Tofino; $30.25 (US$19) from Nanaimo to Ucluelet. Fares for seniors are 10% less; fares for children 5 to 11 are 50% less. The ride is 7 hours long.

VISITOR INFORMATION
The **Tofino-Long Beach Chamber of Commerce** is located at 121 Third St. (P.O. Box 249), Tofino, BC V0R 2Z0 (© 250/ 725-3414; www.island.net~tofino). The **Ucluelet Chamber of Commerce** is at the foot of Main St., P.O. Box 428, Ucluelet, BC V0R 3A0 (© 250/726-4641; www.uclueletinfo.com).

WHERE TO STAY & DINE
IN TOFINO/CLAYOQUOT SOUND
Cable Cove Inn ℛ   Where do you look first when entering this inn? At the wild oceanfront vistas outside, or at the beautiful selection of Robert Davidson and Roy Vickers prints, and First Nations masks, on the inside? It all blends together for an authentic West Coast ambience. Each of the seven romantic suites provides more than just creature comforts; featuring fireplaces, goose-down duvets draped over queen-size four-poster beds, and decks with ocean-views. Two suites have private outdoor Jacuzzis; the others have marble Jacuzzis indoors. Shared areas include a small TV lounge and a fully-stocked kitchen.

201 Main St. (P.O. Box 339), Tofino, BC V0R 2Z0. © 800/663-6449 or 259/ 725-4236. Fax 250/725-2857. www.cablecoveinn.com. 7 units. July–mid-Oct C$160–$205 (US$104–$133.25). Mid-Oct–Mar C$110–$175 (US$71.50–$114).

Apr–June C$140–$190 (US$91–$123.50). Rates include breakfast. AE, MC, V. Children not accepted. **Amenities:** Lounge; coin-op washers and dryers. *In room:* Hair dryer, no phone.

Clayoquot Wilderness Resort 🐾🐾🐾

The name says it all: splendid, luxurious isolation, floating in the middle of Quait Bay. Once you've arrived, either by floatplane or 25-minute boat ride out of Tofino, the aura of Clayoquot Sound sets in. At night, the darkness is blacker than ebony, the stars, brighter than diamonds, and the silence, deliciously deafening. The resort has created a number of trails through the surrounding virgin forest, and converted several disused logging roads into trails suitable for mountain biking and horseback riding. Other excursions offered at the resort include a trip to Hot Springs Cove as well as kayaking and wildlife-viewing excursions. Guest rooms are so comfortable that you may just want to cocoon there. On offer are squishy duvets, aromatherapy toiletries, and complimentary bathrobes. For tender-footed eco-adventurers, the resort's 10 Outposts give sleeping under canvas a new twist. Best described as 21st-century safari campsites, they have opulently furnished prospector-style tents raised on wooden platforms. In the **restaurant,** the best seats in the house are at the bar beside the open kitchen, where guests can watch the culinary antics and graze on tasty morsels that magically appear. At press time, an on-site spa was set to open in June 2002.

P.O. Box 728, Tofino, BC V0R 2Z0. © **888/333-5405** or 250/725-2688. Fax 250/ 725-2689. www.wildretreat.com. 16 units. Jul–Aug C$489 (US$318) standard. May–June and Sept–early Oct C$369 (US$240) standard. Early Oct–Nov C$269 (US$175) standard. May–Nov C$675 (US$439) outpost. Rates include 3 meals/day plus transport to and from Tofino. AE, MC, V. Parking in Tofino. Closed Nov–Feb. **Amenities:** Restaurant, lounge; extensive water-sports equipment; bike rental. *In room:* Hair dryer, no phone.

Inn at Tough City 🐾 (Finds)

Take a close look, and you'll see this inn for what it is—a recycled treasure—and one of the nicest, albeit quirkiest, small inns in Tofino. Constructed with over 45,000 recycled bricks, refurbished hardwood floors, and original stained-glass windows from as far away as Scotland, the Inn at Tough City is a find. You've got to love the vintage collection of advertising signs and old tins. All guest rooms have their own color scheme, accented with stained glass and antique furniture. They also have decks or balconies. The upstairs guest rooms have fireplaces. All have custom-made bed linens in soft, environment-friendly, unbleached cotton. The inn doesn't provide breakfast, but does have the only authentic

sushi restaurant in town. Open daily for dinner (and for lunch in summer), menu items aside from sushi include Dungeness crab, oysters, teriyaki, and other Japanese-influenced meals. A full meal averages C$24 (US$15.50).

350 Main St., (P.O. Box 8), Tofino, BC V0R 2Z0. ☎ 250/725-2021. Fax 250/725-2088. www.alberni.net/toughcity/index.htm. 8 units. Mid-May–mid-Oct C$130–$165 (US$84.50–$107.25). Mid-Oct–Feb C$75–$100 (US$49–$65). Mar–mid-May C$90–$120 (US$58.50–$78). Rates include breakfast. AE, MC, V. **Amenities:** Restaurant, library-lounge. *In room*: TV, coffeemaker, no phone.

Long Beach Lodge Resort ✺✺ Scheduled to open in July 2002, this upscale resort lies on the beach at Cox Bay, between Pacific Rim National Park and Clayoquot Sound. Set among towering trees and taking full advantage of the rugged coastline and sandy beach, the cedar-shingled lodge rivals the Wickaninnish Inn (reviewed later in this section). The welcoming Great Room, with its oversize granite fireplace and deep armchairs, is an ideal spot to relax and sample the chef's daily creations. Guest rooms include oversize beds, fireplaces, Jacuzzis or extra-deep-soaker bathtubs, and private balconies. Raingear is provided to guests who want to venture forth into the storms. Plans call for offering in-room spa services such as massage.

P.O. Box 897, Tofino, BC V0R 2Z0. ☎ 250/725-2442. Fax 250/725-2402. www.longbeachlodgeresort.com. 43 units. June–Sept C$170–$190 (US$110.50–$123.50) forest room; C$245–$400 (US$159–$260) oceanview room. Oct and Mar–May C$130–$145 (US$84.50–$94) forest room; C$185–$325 (US$120–$211) oceanview room. Nov–Feb C$110–$125 (US$71.50–$81) forest room; C$160–$300 (US$104–$195) oceanview room. **Amenities:** Restaurant, lounge. *In room*: Coffeemaker, hair dryer.

Pacific Sands Resort ✺✺ In one episode of *Seinfeld*, Kramer comes up with a wacky idea for a cologne called "The Beach," which would capture the sound, spray, and smell of the surf, the flow of the tides, and the feel of the sand under your feet. If that were possible, he would have set up a bottling plant at the Pacific Sands Resort. Nudging against the world-renowned Pacific Rim National Park, white sand beaches, islands, and old-growth rain forests are at your doorstep. In fact, the sound of the surf, although sometimes tumultuous, sets a tranquil, metronome-like quality for sleep. Accommodation ranges from one- and two-bedroom suites to oceanfront cottages, all with kitchens, fireplaces, balconies, and spectacular views. Some have Jacuzzis. Renovated in spring 2001, the Lighthouse Suites are especially comfortable. Complimentary raingear lets guests ignore the weather and ocean spray and get outside. Readers of *Beautiful British Columbia Magazine* rated the Pacific Sands their favorite hotel on the island, second only to the Fairmont Empress in Victoria.

Cox Bay, Tofino, BC V0R 2Z0. © 800/565-2322 or 250/725-2322. Fax 250/725-3155. www.pacificsands.com. 65 units. July–Sept C$195–$200 (US$127–$130) studio, standard room, cottage. Oct–Jun C$150–$160 (US$97.50–$104) studio, standard room, cottage. Year-round C$240–$395 (US$156–$257) 2-bedroom and deluxe suite. Seasonal discounts available. AE, MC, V. **Amenities:** Bike rental; children's programs; concierge. *In room:* TV.

Wickaninnish Inn 🏵🏵🏵   Perched on a rocky promontory between old-growth forest and the Pacific Ocean, this member of the renowned Relais & Châteaux network of hotels opened in 1997 to rave reviews and just keeps getting better. In summer, the sprawling sands of Chesterman Beach are littered with sandcastles, tidal pools, and sun worshippers. In winter, it's quite a different story. As thundering waves, howling winds, and sheets of rain lash up against the inn's cedar siding, storm watching becomes an art. Every guest room provides grandstand views through triple-glazed, floor-to-ceiling windows. The result is a surreal feeling of being enveloped by a storm in virtual silence, especially when snuggled up in front of the fire. Raingear is provided for those brave souls who want to take on the elements firsthand. The staff here is generally young (most are here for the surfing) and seems to relish providing good service in a rustically elegant environment. The **Ancient Cedars Spa** will mellow your mood, especially since every treatment begins with an aromatic footbath. The best treatment room is the new one out on the rocks. Cuisine is another one of the inn's draws. Reservations at the **Pointe Restaurant** are so sought-after, be sure to make them when you book your room—even if you're not staying at the Wickaninnish Inn. The menu is an imaginative showcase of fresh coastal food and seafood that's caught within a stone's throw of the inn. Chanterelles, bletus, angel wings, and pine mushrooms are brought in from neighboring forests. Gooseneck barnacles come off the rocks on the beach, and Indian Candy, made from salmon marinated and smoked for six days, comes from Tofino. If you're tired after a day's travel, head for cocktails and lighter fare in the **On the Rocks lounge** and save the Epicurean feast at the Pointe for the following day. Check the limit on your credit card.

Osprey Lane at Chesterman Beach (P.O. Box 250), Tofino, BC V0R 2Z0. © 800/ 333-4604 or 250/725-3300. Fax 250/725-3110. www.wickinn.com. 46 units. June–Sept C$380–$480 (US$247–$312). Oct–May $210–$330 (US$136.60–

$214.50). Rates may vary over holiday periods. Storm-watching and other packages available year-round. AE, MC, V. **Amenities:** Restaurant, lounge; exercise room; spa. *In room:* Coffeemaker, hair dryer.

IN UCLUELET

A Snug Harbour Inn 🌟🌟   Set on an 85-foot cliff overlooking the pounding Pacific, A Snug Harbour Inn is a romantic oasis that takes the credit for at least 50 wedding engagements! Each guest room is decorated a little differently; all have fireplaces, down duvets over queen- or king-size beds, double jet bathtubs, and private decks boasting vast oceanviews. Two new forest rooms are set to open in July 2002, one of which will allow pets. There's a gi-normous telescope in the Great Room, through which you can watch sea lions on the rocks below. Outside, there's a trail of steps down to the beach, appropriately called "Stairway from the Stars." It's worth the descent, but it's a bit of a hike back up—a good way to whet the appetite for a terrific breakfast. The new owner, Sue Brown, *loves* to cook, so mornings are filled with the aroma of freshly baked treats.

460 Marine Dr. (P.O. Box 367), Ucluelet, BC V0R 3A0. ✆ 888/936-5222 or 250/726-2686. Fax 250/726-2685. www.asnugharbourinn.com. 6 units. June–Sept C$230–$290 (US$149.50–$188.50). Oct and Mar–May C$200–$250 (US$130–$162.50). Nov–Feb C$180–$200 (US$117–$130). MC, V. Pets accepted. **Amenities:** Lounge; Jacuzzi. *In room:* Hair dryer, no phone.

Canadian Princess Resort 🌟   This former hydrographic survey ship, moored in Ucluelet's central harbor, and completely refurbished, sails to nowhere but offers no-nonsense, nautical-style accommodations. Small guest cabins offer basic bunk-style beds with washbasins; showers and bathroom facilities are shared. More comfortable onshore accommodations are also available. These guest rooms have two double beds and private bathrooms. Larger rooms sleep up to four. The vessel's dining and lounge areas are cozy and add to the seafaring atmosphere. Remember, this was once a working ship, which is a great part of its charm, and is probably why it seems to attract the fishing crowd.

Ucluelet Harbour, Ucluelet, BC V0R 3A0. ✆ 800/663-7090 or 250/726-7771. Fax 250/726-7121. www.canadianprincess.com. 76 units. Mar–mid-Sept C$75–$150 (US$48.75–$110.50) stateroom; C$145–$260 (US$94.25–$169) onshore room; C$150 (US$97.50) Captain's Cabin. Extra person C$15 (US$10). AE, MC, V. Closed mid-Sept–Feb. **Amenities:** Restaurant, 2 lounges. *In room:* TV in onshore rooms.

Tauca Lea Coast Resort 🌟🌟🌟   Overlooking the fishing boats, commercial trollers, and yachts moored in Ucluelet's inner harbor, Tauca Lea exudes a rustic, West Coast style. Its cathedral windows seem to beckon the outdoors in. The resort includes one- and two-bedroom suites, each superbly constructed and beautifully finished with a designer's eye for texture and detail. Furnishings are top-quality and include items such as leather La-Z-Boys in front of gas fireplaces, beautiful artwork, well-stocked kitchens with designer kitchenware, luxury linens, and all the amenities you would expect in a fine hotel. The **Boat Basin Lounge and Restaurant** is also first-class, serving a light West Coast menu with an Asian flair. Lighter items average C$10 (US$6.50); main courses average C$25 (US$16.25). Plans are underway to construct a 27-berth marina and full-service spa on-site.

Harbour Crescent, Ucluelet, Long Beach, BC V0R 3A0. *©* 800/979-9303 or 250/726-4224. Fax 250/726-4663. www.taucalearesort.com. 32 units. July–Sept C$230 (US$149.50) 1-bedroom; C$310 (US$201) 2-bedroom. Oct and Apr–June C$170 (US$110.50) 1-bedroom; C$230 (US$149.50) 2-bedroom. Nov–Mar C$150 (US$97.50) 1-bedroom; C$210 (US$136.50) 2-bedroom. AE, DC, MC, V. **Amenities:** Restaurant, lounge. *In room:* TV/VCR, kitchen.

EXPLORING TOFINO

Picturesque Tofino, or "Tough City," is an intriguing combination of old-growth forests, white sand beaches, and the ever-churning Pacific Ocean. It got its name from a Spanish hydrographer who had a reputation for fights and wild living. But don't let the name's origins scare you. For most of the year, Tofino is a sleepy community, but in the summer it's frenzied. As visitors flock toward the Clayoquot Sound Biosphere Reserve, boat charters, whale-watching companies, fishing boats, and seaplanes create a hubbub of activity in the harbor. If crab's your dish, you can't beat the **West Coast Crab Bar,** 604 Campbell St. (*©* **250/725-3733**), and if you're looking for First Nations art, you'll find several excellent galleries. If you've time for only one stop, it must be Roy Vicker's **Eagle Aerie Gallery** *@@,* 350 Campbell St. (*©* **250/725-3235**). As the only First Nations artist with his own gallery, Vickers and his work both inspire and dominate. The carved wooden door makes an impressive entrance and the entire gallery feels like a life-revering chapel. First Nations artists carved all woodwork within the gallery, including the rails, canoes, and eagles. A percentage of sales of certain works is given to First Peoples recovery programs.

OUTDOOR ACTIVITIES

A number of companies in the Tofino and Ucluelet area offer bear watching, whale watching, and hot springs adventures, as well as fishing charters. Reputable operators include 20-year veteran, **Jamie's Whaling Station** (© 800-667-9913 or 250-725-3919 (Tofino), © 877-470-7444 or 250-726-7444 (Ucluelet); www.jamies.com). A percentage of profits go toward gray whale research. **RainCoast Back Road Adventures** (© 250/726-7625; www.raincoastadventures.com) offers some exhilarating backroad tours, and will pick you up from any hotel in the area. **Sea Trek Tours** (© 800/811-9155 or 250/725-4412; www.seatrektours.bc.ca) also offers a good variety of eco-adventures, including a trip to Meares Island.

SIDE TRIPS FROM TOFINO

An hour's boat ride north of Tofino (even faster by seaplane), **Hot Springs Cove** is the only all-natural thermal hot springs on Vancouver Island. A beautifully maintained, 2-km (1-mile) boardwalk winds through lush rain forest to the sulfur-scented springs. Wisps of steam rise from water that is 50°C (122°F) at its source and cools as it cascades through a series of pools to the sea. It's a busy place in summer. Just 30 minutes north of Tofino, **Flores Island** is where to find the 11-km (6-mile) Ahousaht Wildside Heritage Trail, an easy hike through rain forests and along beaches. Nearby **Meares Island,** a 15-minute water taxi ride from Tofino, is worth seeing both for its beauty and its devastation because of clear-cutting. It's the site of many a tree-hugger versus logging company conflict. And finally, there's **Clayoquot Sound Biosphere Reserve,** North America's largest remaining expanse of low-elevation old-growth temperate rain forest. In 2000, UNESCO declared it a World Biosphere Reserve. It's a "living laboratory," where you'll find isolated resorts and cabins clinging to the edge of the wilderness, and bears scavenging the shoreline for tasty delicacies, flipping rocks like flapjacks.

EXPLORING UCLUELET

Smaller and less sophisticated than Tofino, Ucluelet (*yew-kloo-let*) is waking up to the extraordinary magnetism of the surrounding area. New developments are sprucing up the "downtown" core, and in its harbor, you'll now find the masts of classic fishing boats bobbing alongside moneyed, modern yachts. The village has a couple of **folk art galleries,** and there are numerous picnic areas along the beaches and rocky coast offering spectacular views. These views are best experienced on the **Wild Pacific Trail** ⚘, which is reason alone to visit

Ucluelet. If you're not hardy enough to take on the West Coast Trail, then this is a sure bet. The 14-km (8.5-mile) trail is being developed in phases, and will eventually run along the outer coast to Long Beach. So far, the first 2.5km (1.5 miles) leads along the coastline from **Amphitrite Point** and can be hiked in full or in part. Boardwalks lead you through rain forest to bluffs high above the ocean where trees, beaten back by the wind, grow at 90-degree angles. It's an easy path that gets you up close and personal to the fury of winter waves or the splendor of summer sunsets.

PACIFIC RIM NATIONAL PARK *$\star\star\star$*

Designated a national park in 1970 to protect the significant coastal environment, Pacific Rim National Park presents outstanding examples of coastal rain forest, surf-swept beaches, marine life, and the cultural history of the area's settlement. Composed of 3 "units," or sections, the **West Coast Trail Unit, the Long Beach Unit, and the Broken Group Islands,** the park spans 130km (82 miles) of shoreline. You access each unit via a different route. The variety of activities and level of services offered in each unit varies. The Long Beach Unit is the most accessible—a good choice for families and visitors who want to take it a little easier, whereas the West Coast Trail Unit is for no-nonsense hikers with nothing but trekking in mind. Contact the **Pacific Rim National Park Reserve,** P.O. Box 280, Ucluelet, BC V0R 3A0 (*$\textcircled{C}$* **250/726-7721**) for information.

WEST COAST TRAIL UNIT

The West Coast Trail is billed as one of the most grueling treks in North America. As experienced backpackers stagger out of its wilderness, muddy, bedraggled, and exhausted, you would think even that might be an understatement. This once-in-a-lifetime wilderness adventure attracts 8,000 hikers each year to do battle with the 77-km (48-mile) trail between **Port Renfrew** and **Bamfield** along the southwestern coast of Vancouver Island, known as the "graveyard of the Pacific" because of the numerous shipwrecks along the coast. The trail was originally cleared at the start of the 20th century as a lifesaving rail for shipwrecked mariners. It was upgraded in the 1970s, but trekking it still requires much experience, stamina, and strength. At any point on the trail, you may need to balance yourself on a fallen log to cross a deep gully, negotiate steep slopes, or wade thigh-deep across a river. It takes a minimum of 5 days to complete the trail end to end.

How to Book Your Hike: The West Coast Trail is open to hikers from May 1 to September 30. You should reserve up to 3 months ahead, since the number of permits issued per day is strictly limited to 52: 26 issued to hikers departing from Port Renfrew; 26 issued to hikers departing from Bamfield. To reserve, call © **800/HELLOBC** (800/435-5622). There is a nonrefundable reservation fee of C$25 (US$16.25) per hiker, which you are required to pay at time of booking. You also need to register at the park office before you set out, and be at the trailhead by noon, or lose your spot. For more information, call © **250/647-5434** (for hikers departing from Port Renfrew) or © **250/728-3234** (for hikers departing from Bamfield).

Tips Camping in Pacific Rim National Park

Pacific Rim National Park (© 250/726-7721) has 94 campsites on the bluff at **Green Point,** in the Long Beach Unit. During July and August, walk-in sites cost C$14 (US$9) per night, drive-in sites cost C$20 (US$13). From mid-March to June and September to mid-October, walk-in sites cost C$12 (US$8) per night, drive-in sites cost C$18 (US$12) per night. There are no showers or hookups. Expect to be wait-listed for up to 2 days in July and August.

BROKEN GROUP ISLANDS

Made up of more than 100 rocky islands and islets in **Barkley Sound,** the Broken Group Islands can only be reached by boat. Amidst this pristine archipelago, eagles, sea lions, and marine life abound, and tide pools and dozens of sandy pocket beaches lure nature enthusiasts, photographers, and boating sightseers. Chartered boats, guided tours, and transport for campers and kayakers can be booked in Bamfield, Tofino, and Ucluelet, or, you can arrive via the *MV Lady Rose* (see "Exploring the Area," in "Heading West: Port Alberni & Bamfield," earlier in the chapter).

Note: Only experienced boaters, canoeists, and kayakers should consider an expedition to this unit. Waters are studded with reefs, and visibility is often obscured by heavy fog. The weather in the channels that separate the islands can also be extremely variable.

LONG BEACH UNIT

Located between Tofino and Ucluelet, the Long Beach Unit is the most accessible and most developed component of the park. Named for its 20-km (12-mile) stretch of surf-swept sand, Long Beach offers outstanding beaches, surfing, and more. Open year-round, the area offers nine hiking trails, most of which are boardwalk-surfaced and wheelchair accessible. The **Wickaninnish Centre, (© 250/726-4212)** at the south end of Long Beach, is a marine interpretive center, providing information on park programs, activities, and events.

6

Northern Vancouver Island

The differences between the North and South Island are profound. The farther north you drive, the wilder Vancouver Island becomes, and as urban sophistication falls to the wayside, you'll start to discover the diversity of the region. Fewer than 3% of the island's residents live in the northern part, which is steeped in vast forests of deep green; cool, clean air heavy with the scent of trees, crystal-clear rivers and wind-ravaged beaches. It's a paradise for eco-adventurers and nature photographers—a mecca for anyone looking for a taste of Canadian wilderness. Some communities, such as Kyuquot, are accessible only by chartered floatplane or boat, and to reach them takes you through country that is quintessential West Coast Canada. Travel inland also tells a story, usually via logging roads toward off-the-beaten-track destinations. If you drive these routes, remember to use caution. Logging is a primary industry in this part of the world; logging trucks are numerous, and have the right of way.

Natural resources have long been the economic backbone of Vancouver Island, and as those resources expend, towns are looking to alternative investments. In **Courtenay-Comox,** the fastest-growing region on the island, and fish-happy **Campbell River,** resorts are springing up alongside entire retirement communities. Far-flung mining hamlets like **Zeballos,** which once made its fortune in gold, and **Holberg,** are becoming bases for eco-adventurers, and picturesque places like **Telegraph Cove,** caught in a time warp of beauty, are also starting to succumb to 21st-century development. Despite these changes, though, you'll still come across communities, such as **Port McNeill** and **Port Hardy,** that are still pretty rough-and-ready, as well as places like **Alert Bay,** whose isolation has protected its rich First Nations culture.

This great diversity is the region's primary appeal. If you're a culture buff, stay in Victoria. If you're traveling with very young children, again, stay south, unless you're heading for **Mount Washington** to ski, or to **Miracle Beach.** But if you're hankering to experience nature with no boundaries, you won't get much better than North Vancouver Island.

1 Courtenay & the Comox Valley

If you drive 62km (39 miles) north of Parksville-Qualicum Beach on Highway 19, you'll come upon Vancouver Island's other set of twin towns, Courtenay-Comox. Unlike their neighbors to the south, Courtenay and Comox are refreshingly un-touristy, and so close together that you can hop from one community to another in a matter of minutes. Courtenay, with a population of 20,000, is a center of lumber milling on Vancouver Island, and basks in a wide agricultural valley, while its sister community, Comox, with a population of 12,000, lies on the peninsula just east of Comox Harbour. Originally known as Port Augusta, it was once the only harbor from which supply ships could reach mid-island communities like Gold River.

Today, the Comox Valley is one of the fastest-growing regions on Vancouver Island. Retirees are attracted to its rural ambience and urban amenities. For travelers—particularly outdoorsy types—it is the gateway to wilderness adventure. The Beaufort Mountains, **Mount Washington Alpine Resort,** and **Strathcona Provincial Park,** are within easy reach, and the promise of alpine lakes, glacial basins, and craggy peaks brings with it abundant opportunity to view wildlife, as well as to hike, ski, kayak, and much more. If you've time, spend a day or two touring **Denman and Hornby islands,** a 10-minute ferry trip from Buckley Bay, just north of Fanny Bay. A haven for aging flower children and Vietnam draft dodgers who stayed north of the 49th parallel after amnesty, these islands have a distinct bohemian charm that's a throwback to 1960s creativity.

ESSENTIALS
GETTING THERE
BY CAR   The driving distance from Victoria to Courtenay, along Highway 19, due north, is 220km (137 miles). From Nanaimo, the distance is 113km (70 miles). From Parksville, it is 73km (45 miles). Highway 19 becomes Cliffe Avenue as it enters Courtenay.

BY PLANE   Air Canada Jazz (© 888-247-2262; www.flyjazz.ca) and **Pacific Coastal Airlines** (© 800/663-2872; www.pacific-coastal.com) operate daily flights between Victoria, Port Hardy, and Campbell River to the **Comox Valley Regional Airport** (© 250/897-3123; www.yqq-cvac.bc.ca). **WestJet Airlines** (© 888/

Northern Vancouver Island

SCOTT ISLANDS PROVINCIAL PARK
Lace I.
Cox I.
CAPE SCOTT PROVINCIAL PARK
San Josef
Holberg
Quatsino
Winter Harbour
Quatsino Sound

PACIFIC

OCEAN

0   10 mi
0   10 km

BROOKS PENINSULA PROVINCIAL MARINE PARK

Hope I.
Port Hardy I. Prince Rupert
Nigel I.
Queen Charlotte Strait
Sullivan Bay
Broughton Island
10
8 **9** Port Hardy
19
Sointula
Malcolm I.
Alert Bay
Port McNeill
Telegraph Cove
Alice Lake
Nimpkish Lake
Bonanza Lake
Port Alice
Victoria Lake
Woss
Tahsish Inlet
Woss Lake
Kyuquot
Kyuquot Sound
Zeballos
Vernon Lake
Tahsis
Esperanza Inlet
Tahsis Inlet
Nootka Island
Yuquot
Nootka Sound
Estevan Point

COURTENAY/COMOX
Coast Westerley Hotel **2**
Crown Isle Resort **3**
Kingfisher Oceanside **1**
Resort & Spa

CAMPBELL RIVER
Coast Discovery **6**
Inn & Marina
Haig-Brown House **5**
Bachmair Suite Hotel **4**
Painter's Lodge Holiday **7**
& Fishing Resort

PORT HARDY
Glen Lyon **8**
Inn & Suites
Oceanview B&B **9**
Quarterdeck **10**
Inn & Marina

937-8538 or 800-538-5696; www.westjet.com) operates nonstop flights between Comox and Calgary. Small aircraft and floatplanes can land at the **Courtenay Airpark** (© 250/334-8545).

BY BUS   Laidlaw Coach Lines (© 250/385-4411) operates between Victoria and Port Hardy, with various stops along the way. **Greyhound Canada** (© 800/663-8390 or 604/482-8747; www. greyhound.ca) handles schedules and reservations. The one-way fare from Victoria to Courtenay is C$38.50 (US$25) for adults. From Nanaimo to Courtenay, it's C$19.25 (US$12.50) for adults. Fares for seniors are 10% less; fares for children 5 to 11 are 50% less. The trip from Victoria to Courtenay takes 4½ hours; from Nanaimo, it's 2 hours.

BY TRAIN   Courtenay is the termination point of the daily service offered by the **E&N Railiner,** run by **VIA Rail** (© 800/561-8630;

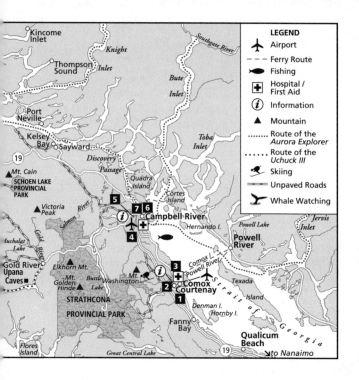

www.viarail.com) between Victoria and Courtenay. At press time, however, VIA Rail had plans to cancel this service in summer 2002, and would not commit to rate information. Check with VIA Rail before making your plans.

BY FERRY   BC Ferries (ℂ 888/223-3779; www.bcferries.com) operates two daily crossings from **Powell River,** on the BC Sunshine Coast, to **Little River,** in Comox, a 10-minute drive from Courtenay. One-way fares are C$7.50 (US$5) for adults, C$3.75 (US$2.50) for children 5 to 11, C$25 (US$16) for a standard-size vehicle. The crossing takes 1¼ hours.

VISITOR INFORMATION

The **Comox Valley Information Centre** is at 2040 Cliffe Ave., Courtenay, BC V9N 2L3 (ℂ 888/357-4471 or 250/334-3234; www.tourism-comox-valley.bc.ca). If you'd like to find out more about the Comox Valley beforehand, you can always contact the **Tourism Association of Vancouver Island,** Suite 302, 45 Bastion Sq., Victoria, BC V8W 1J1 (© 250/754-3500; www.islands.bc.ca).

GETTING AROUND

The Comox Valley Transit System (© 250/339-5453) operates local bus service in and between Courtenay, Comox, and Cumberland, a smaller community about 8km (5 miles) south of Courtenay. **United Cabs** (© 250/339-7955) provides taxi service in these same communities.

WHERE TO STAY

Coast Westerley Hotel ⚐   You can't miss it. The Coast Westerley looks like an angular three-story green house, right on Highway 19, the main route into Courtenay. Once you're past the uninviting glass façade, though, you'll find a comfortable spot to rest your road-weary bones. Guest rooms are clean, spacious, and tastefully decorated. The building is divided into two wings; the rear one is the better bet, offering rooms with balconies and views of the Courtenay River. Downstairs, there's a coffee shop, and a lively sports pub with pool tables and TVs.

1590 Cliffe Ave., Courtenay, BC V9N 2K4. © 800/668-7797 or 250/338-7741. Fax 250/338-5442. www.coasthotels.com. 108 units. C$129–$149 (US$84–$97) regular and deluxe room; C$175–$375 (US$114–$244) suite. Extra person C$10 (US$6.50). Children 18 and under stay free in parents' room. AE, DC, DISC, MC, V. **Amenities:** Restaurant, sports pub; large heated indoor pool; health club & spa; limited room service. *In room:* TV w/pay movies, dataport, minibar, coffeemaker, hair dryer, iron.

Crown Isle Resort ⚐⚐⚐   This resort breathes golf at every turn, and little wonder. Its 72-par, Platinum-rated course is suitable for golfers at all levels, and is the centerpiece of the entire development. You don't have to be a member to play, and you don't have to be a golf nut to stay. Beautifully appointed villas, housed in three buildings, make Crown Isle a luxurious stopover—whether or not you intend to tee-off. The villas are actually more like small townhouses, and come in a variety of configurations; most have fully equipped kitchens, some have wet bars and separate dining areas. Finishing touches include two-sided gas fireplaces with marble surrounds, and deep soaker Jacuzzis, over which there's a starlit ceiling that twinkles from blue to yellow. A fourth building, offering eight more villas, opens in 2002, and plans are to construct a full-service European spa in 2003. The 14,630-m² (48,000-sq. ft.) clubhouse is first class all the way, from the sweeping staircase that leads up to meeting areas,

to the cozy Timber Room pub. The atrium-style restaurant specializes in AAA-grade steak, and serves it up with some spectacular views
of the Beaufort Mountains. While you're in the main building, be
sure to see the **Classic Car Museum,** featuring a collection of pre-
dominantly fifties and sixties Chevrolets and Fords, some of which
were previously owned by the likes of Sylvester Stallone and Mary
Hart.

399 Clubhouse Dr., Courtenay, BC V9N 9G3. © **888/338-8439** or 250/703-5050.
Fax 250/703-5051. www.crownisle.com. 40 units. June–Sept C$159 (US$103) standard; C$249–$269 (US$162–$175) villa. Oct and May C$129 (US$84) standard;
C$199–$209 (US$129–$136) villa. Nov–Apr C$119 (US$77) standard; C$149–$169
(US$97–$110) villa. Golf packages available. Extra person C$15 (US$10). Children
17 and under stay free in parents' room. AE, DC, MC, V. **Amenities:** Restaurant, pub;
golf course on property; health club. *In room:* TV, hair dryer.

Kingfisher Oceanside Resort & Spa 𝕲𝕲   Located 7km (4.5 miles)
south of Courtenay, this resort is an old Best Western made exceptionally good. Consequently, the renovated older suites (with oceanviews) are extra large and sport balconies or patios. The newer
beachfront units are quite deluxe, as well. The latter come with
kitchenettes, Jacuzzis, and heated bathroom floors. There's a chaise
longue in front of the fireplace—the perfect spot to enjoy the water,
mainland, and mountain views. As delightful as the remodeled suites
are, though, most people come here for the spa, an impressive venture that has turned the Kingfisher into a destination resort.
Facilities include a heated outdoor pool with shoulder-massaging
waterfall, a cave steamroom and sauna, as well as a broad range of spa
services (at an additional cost) such as thalassotherapy wraps, hot
stone massages, Reiki, reflexology, and facials. The Kingfisher
Oceanside Restaurant is one of the better places to dine in the area,
and even though the menu descriptions hype your anticipation
beyond what is sometimes delivered, the food is still good. There's a
complimentary shuttle between the resort to downtown and to the
Comox Valley Regional Airport, as well as to **Mount Washington
Alpine Resort** (see "Mount Washington Alpine Resort," below).

4330 South Island Hwy., Courtenay, BC V9N 8H9. © **800/663-7929** or 250/338-1323.
Fax 250/338-0058. www.kingfisher-resort-spa.com. 65 units. Mid-May–Sept C$139
(US$90) oceanview suite; C$170–$250 (US$110.50–$162.50) beachfront suite;
C$290–$425 (US$19–$276) deluxe suite. Oct–mid-May C$109 (US$71) oceanview
suite; C$150–$190 (US$97.50–$123.50) beachfront suite; C$210–$350 (US$136.50–
$227.50) deluxe suite. Spa packages available. Extra person C$15 (US$10). AE, DC,
MC, V. **Amenities:** Restaurant, lounge; 1 outdoor tennis court; health club & spa;
activities desk; limited room service; laundry service; dry cleaning. *In room:* TV,
beachfront suites have VCR, dataport, kitchen, hair dryer.

WHERE TO DINE

Black Fin Pub 🏮🏮 PUB FARE   The view is to die for, stretching from a log-strewn beach, across the water and on to the distant Beaufort Mountains. The atmosphere is what you want in a stylish pub: dark wood trim complemented by deep blue upholstery with nautical bits and pieces to give it a marine atmosphere. In addition to the sunken dining area, there are plenty of chairs against the bar, and a menu of quality pub dishes like burgers, sandwiches, fish and chips, as well as yummy grazing options such as escargots, samosas, and chicken wings. Sunday brunch here is a popular favorite.

132 Port Augusta St., Comox. ℂ **250/339-5030.** Reservations not accepted. Main courses C$9.50–$12.50 (US$6–$8). AE, MC, V. Daily 11am–12:30am.

Monte Christo on the River 🏮 *Kids* WEST COAST   This period home is full of rambling rooms, each of which has been converted into individual dining areas. It's a rather bizarre yet beguiling feeling: at any one time, you're never aware of how large the place really is, or how many others are breaking bread with you. One of the rooms, about the size of a broom cupboard, is billed as the most romantic room in Courtenay; it seats two and overlooks the rest of the diners and the Courtenay River beyond through one-way glass. A patio opens in summer right on the river's edge. The broad menu selection helps to make Monte Christo a favorite for families and seniors; it includes prime beef, seafood, and pasta. A bonus for modest eaters is that most choices are available in smaller portions.

975 Comox Rd., Courtenay. ℂ **250/338-1468.** Reservations recommended. Lunch C$6–$12 (US$4–$8); dinner C$9–$40 (US$6–$26). AE, MC, V. Mon–Fri 11:30am–10pm; Sat–Sun 4–11pm.

Old House Restaurant 🏮🏮 WEST COAST   Situated on the banks of the Courtenay River, this is a lovely restaurant, complete with a siding of West Coast cedar shingles. Surrounded by exquisite, herb and flower-filled gardens, the setting comes into its own in the summer, and is best enjoyed from the patio. Inside, the ambience is that of a country getaway with rough-hewn timbers crossing the open ceiling, four fireplaces, and picturesque wooden windows. The menu is typical West Coast cuisine, offering the likes of steak and seafood. The on-site bakery produces fresh breads and mouthwatering desserts. This is *the* place to celebrate something special.

1760 Riverside Lane, Courtenay. ℂ **250/338-5406.** Reservations recommended. Lunch C$9 (US$6); dinner C$16 (US$10). AE, MC, V. Sun and Tues–Thurs 11:30am–9pm; Fri–Sat 11:30am–9:30pm.

Toscanos Trattoria *⋒⋒* ITALIAN This bright little bistro is filled with hot, cheerful colors—oranges, yellows, and reds—and wonderfully aromatic smells. It's where the trendies on a budget prefer to dine. There are good views of Augusta Bay and the distant mountains, but the bustle of the place seems to make them second to the convivial atmosphere. The menu includes huge panini, excellent pastas, and specialty entrees such as chicken breast filled with ricotta, sundried tomatoes, and spinach, and served in a basil sauce.

140 Port Augusta, Comox. © 250/890-7575. Reservations required. Main courses C$8–$15 (US$5–$10). MC, V. Mon–Sat 11am–2pm and 5–9pm.

EXPLORING THE AREA

The tallest building in **Comox** *⋒* belongs to the Logger's Union, and bears testimony to the backbone of the region's economy. The center of town bustles around a new **harborside promenade,** where fishing boats are so plentiful, you can often buy fish or prawns straight from the vessel. The **Filberg Lodge and Park,** 61 Filberg Rd. (© **250/339-2715;** www.island.net/~filberg), is a delight to explore. The handsome timbered lodge rests on piles driven into an old salt marsh and Native midden, and is surrounded by 9 acres of waterfront gardens, including a summertime petting farm, and popular teahouse. It's open May through September. Admission is C$1 (US65¢) for adults, C50¢ (US30¢) for children 6 to 12. Over the first weekend of August, the park is the site of the four-day **Filberg Festival** (© **250/334-9242;** www.filbergfestival.com), an outdoor art exhibition where up to 150 of British Columbia's top craftspeople showcase their handiwork. Tickets are C$8 (US$5) at the gate. More garden delights are to be found at **Kitty Coleman Woodland Gardens,** RR2, off Whittaker Road, just north of Seal Bay Park (© **250/338-6901;** www.woodlandgardens.ca). Named after a First Nations woman who set up residence in the area in the late 1800s, the gardens are a loving and extraordinary creation of one man, Bryan Zimmerman, who used only his hands, without the help of heavy equipment that might have destroyed the land. These spectacular, half-wild gardens must be seen to be believed—for the 3,000 rhododendrons alone! Bring along shoes with good treads, as the bark mulch trails can be slippery. Year-round admission is C$5 (US$3.25) for adults, C$2 (US$1.30) for children 5 to 12.

Courtenay's sexiest claim to fame is that it's the hometown of Kim Cattrell, from the TV show *Sex and the City.* But it just about stops there. Sure, Courtenay is a pleasant enough community, but it doesn't have a particular hub of activity, except for a few galleries and shops around 4th and 5th streets, including the **Comox Valley Art Gallery,** 367 Fourth St. (© **250/338-6211**). The **Kingfisher Oceanside Resort & Spa** and the **Crown Isle Resort** (see "Where to Stay," above) are doing their part to change all that, however. More than a place to stay, Crown Isle is an entire complex of lavish condominiums, restaurants, and lounges centered on an 18-hole links-style **championship golf course** that offers sweeping views of the Comox Glacier and Beaufort Mountains. The course is open year-round. From June to September, nonmember green fees are C$65 (US$42); from October to April, they are C$40 (US$26); in May, they are C$55 (US$36). The **Courtenay Museum & Paleontology Centre** ✦ at 360 Cliffe Ave. (© **250/334-3611;** www.courtenaymuseum.ca) is another fun place to visit. Housed in the town's old post office, the centre holds a collection of First Nations masks and basketry, pioneer artifacts, and a 12-m (40-ft.) cast skeleton of an elasmosaur, a crocodile-resembling Cretaceous-era reptile. Half- and full-day tours are offered year-round, and run the gamut from exploring the paleontology lab to digging in the riverbed. A tropical sea once covered the Comox Valley, so there's a wealth of marine fossils to be found. Take the kids. Open year-round, admission is C$15 (US$10) for adults, C$12 (US$8) for seniors and students, C$7.50 (US$5) for children 11 and under, free for children 4 and under. Multiday fossil digs are also scheduled throughout the year. Call the museum for details.

Just 16km (10 miles) south of Courtenay, in the foothills of the Beaufort Mountains, the coal-mining town of **Cumberland** still stirs the imagination with pretty heritage homes and storefronts—as evidenced by the piles of slag and sheets of rusted corrugated iron scattered around old buildings. Founded by coal baron Robert Dunsmuir, and named after the famous English coal-mining district, Cumberland was once the second largest coal producer in North America. In 1912, one mine alone produced some 2,580 kilograms (5,688 lbs.) of coal a day. Back then, the town's population was five times what it is today, made up of some 13,000 workers from around the world. Cumberland once claimed the largest Chinatown north of San Francisco. The mine was closed in 1966, but you can experience it and Cumberland's story at the **Cumberland Museum & Archives,** 2680 Dunsmuir Ave. (© **250/336-2445;** www.museum. bc.ca/cma).

MOUNT WASHINGTON ALPINE RESORT ☆☆ *(Kids)*

Drive north on Highway 19 and take Exit 130 to the Mount Washington exit, about a 30-minute drive from Courtenay-Comox. Then it's an ear-popping climb up to the base of the resort. (The road is in excellent condition.) Keep in mind, though, that Mount Washington is hardly a resort in the Whistler sense of the word. There's a handful of eateries, and no galleries or shops to speak of. But there *is* great skiing. **Skiing** is the mountain's raison d'être in winter (its success has reduced ski activities at Forbidden Plateau, the oldest ski hill in the province, to virtually nothing). **Hiking** takes over in summer. With a 488-m (1,600-ft.) vertical drop, and more than 50 groomed runs, most above 1,200m (3,937 ft.), serviced by four lifts and a beginners' tow, Mount Washington has become British Columbia's third largest ski and snowboard area. There's an 0-Zone **snow-tubing park,** a 250-m (820-ft.) **luge run,** and 30km (19 miles) of track-set **Nordic trails** connecting to Strathcona Provincial Park (see below), which are great for hiking and mountain biking in summer. To avoid crowds and lift lineups, plan to go on a weekday—the mountain is remarkably quiet. This is something that can never be said about Whistler. From December to March, day passes for skiing are C$45 (US$29) for adults, C$37 (US$24) for seniors and children 13 to 18, C$24 (US$15) for children 7 to 12, free for children 6 and under. There are about 200 condominium units for rent on the mountain. For details on lift passes, snow school programs, equipment, and condominium rentals, call the central information and reservations number: ✆ **888/231-1499** or 250/ 338-1386, or log on to **www.mtwashington.ca**.

STRATHCONA PROVINCIAL PARK ☆☆☆ *(Moments)*

Located almost in the center of Vancouver Island, Strathcona Provincial Park is a rugged wilderness of more than 617,000 acres. In the summer it can be accessed via trails from Mount Washington Alpine Resort (see above), and year-round by driving to Campbell River on Highway 19 and taking the Highway 28 Exit to Gold River. Strathcona was British Columbia's first designated wilderness and recreation area (created in 1911), and is managed by the **Ministry of Environment, Lands, and Parks (✆ 250/337-2400;** www.elp.gov.bc.ca/bcparks). The park brims with a wealth of treasures: snow-capped mountain peaks, lakes set in amphitheaters of ice, valleys filled with pristine rain forest, alpine meadows painted with heather, as well as rivers and waterfalls, including Canada's tallest waterfall, **Della Falls,** at 440m (1,445 ft.). Wildlife is plentiful, and because of Vancouver Island's separation from the mainland, there are no chipmunks, porcupines, coyotes, or grizzly bears, and species such as Roosevelt elk, black-tailed deer, marmot, and wolf, are slightly smaller than their mainland cousins. Birds are also numerous, and include the chestnut-backed chickadee, red-breasted nuthatch, winter wren, ruffed grouse, and a limited number of unique Vancouver Island **white-tailed ptarmigan.**

But Strathcona doesn't yield its wealth easily. The greatest treasures aren't exactly on display (getting to Della Falls, for example, requires a boat ride and an overnight hike), so if you really want to explore this diverse park, you'll need to hike or backpack into the alpine wilderness. The only visitor information centers exist at **Buttle Lake** and **Forbidden Plateau,** and at the privately owned **Strathcona Park Lodge & Outdoor Education Centre** 🏕🏕 25km (15 miles) west of Campbell River on Highway 28 (© **250/286-3122;** www.strathcona.bc.ca). Perched on the shores of Upper Campbell Lake, just outside the park's eastern boundary, the lodge provides not only a comfortable place to stay, from lodge rooms and cabins to chalet-type accommodation, but also a variety of opportunities for exploring the surrounding wilderness. Staying here has been described as a cross between Outward Bound and Club Med, in large part because of the array of **educational and adventure programs.** Everyone from hard-core outdoor types to parents with young children can find their niche, experiencing activities such as sailing, wilderness survival, rock climbing, backcountry hiking, fishing, swimming, canoeing, and kayaking. Special packages are available, and guides and instructors can be hired by the hour. Unless you know the park well, or are comfortably at ease trekking through backcountry, then the lodge is definitely worth checking out.

2 Campbell River

Although you could take the new inland highway, Highway 19, north from Courtenay for a fast 48-km (30-mile) drive to Campbell River, I suggest you opt for the scenic route along Highway 19A, also called the **Oceanside Route.** Exit Highway 19 at **Miracle Beach,** and head north on Highway 19A. Follow the Starfish signs past scenic coves and through small, picturesque communities. Bring your camera and enjoy weaving along the water's edge. Check out **www.oceansideroute.com** for details. Once in Campbell River, you'll be in a true North Island community with roots deep in fishing and lumber. The town center is marked by the high rigger *"Big Mike,"* a carved wooden lumberjack swinging from a harness at the top of a spar pole, while the world renowned **Tyee Club** reflects the community's obsession with fishing—commercial and recreational. Every year between July and September, the Campbell River, which in 2000 was designated a British Columbia Heritage River, swells with both visitors and fish, as salmon pass through the mile-wide passage, known as the **Discovery Channel,** en route to spawning grounds in northerly rivers. The area has historically produced vast hauls of incredibly large fish; so vast and so large that Campbell River became known as the "Salmon Fishing Capital of the World." But today, as salmon numbers diminish, catch and release programs are in force, and many fishing expeditions are billed more as wildlife adventures in an attempt to diversify their lure beyond fishing fanatics. Some local operators have already been successful in this regard. Day trips aboard the *MV Uchuck III,* from Gold River to the Tahsis, Nootka, and Kyoquot Sounds, are great family fun, and mini cruises to Bute Inlet or Kingcome Inlet aboard the *MV Aurora Explorer* reveal parts of British Columbia many visitors never get to see.

Another worthwhile diversion is a day trip out of Campbell River to **Quadra and Cortes islands,** affectionately called the Discovery Islands. The 10-minute ferry crossing lands you amidst one of the richest places to relish the area's First Nations heritage, including traditional longhouses, and the excellent **Kwagiulth Museum and Cultural Centre** (WeiWai Rd., Cape Mudge Village, Quadra Island *©* **250/285-3733**), which showcases one of the world's best collections of potlatch artifacts, ceremonial masks, and tribal costumes. There's also an opportunity to make petroglyph rubbings from fiberglass castings of ancient stone carvings. **Cortes Island,** which lies at the entrance to Desolation Sound, is a beautiful wilderness hideaway. It's also home to **Hollyhock** (P.O. Box 127, Manson's Landing, *©* **800/933-6339;** www.hollyhock.ca), the world-renowned holistic and spiritual retreat center.

ESSENTIALS
GETTING THERE
BY CAR   Driving distances up the center of Vancouver Island are fast and easy with the new inland highway (Hwy. 19) between Nanaimo and Campbell River. Campbell River is 264km (164 miles) north of Victoria (about 2½ hours' worth of driving); 153km (95 miles)

north of Nanaimo (about 1½ hours); and 48km (29 miles) north of Courtenay (about half an hour).

BY PLANE   Commercial airlines fly into the **Campbell River and District Regional Airport** (© 250/923-5012; www.district.campbell river.bc.ca). **Air Canada Jazz** (© 888 247-2262; www.flyjazz.ca), **Pacific Coastal Airlines** (© 800/663-2872; www.pacific-coastal. com), and **WestJet** (© 888-937-8538; www.westjet.com) operate daily scheduled flights from Vancouver, Calgary, Victoria, and Seattle. Car-rental companies at the airport include **Budget** (© 800/668-3233 or 250/923-4283; www.budget.com) and **National Tilden** (© 888/669-9922 or 250/923-7278; www.national carvictoria.com). Smaller carriers, such as **Air Rainbow** (© 888/ 287-8366 or 250/287-8371; www.air-rainbow.com), provide harbor-to-harbor service between Port Hardy, Campbell River, and several small island communities. **Kenmore Air** (© 800/543-9595; www.kenmoreair.com) flies from Seattle Harbor on a seasonal basis.

BY BUS   **Island Coach Lines,** operated by **Laidlaw Coach Lines,** (© 800 318-0818 or 250/385-4411; www.victoriatours.com) runs daily service from Victoria to Port Hardy, stopping in Nanaimo, Campbell River, and other towns along the way. The one-way fare from Victoria to Campbell River is C$44 (US$28) for adults. From Nanaimo to Campbell River, it's C$22.50 (US$14) for adults. Fares for seniors are 10% less; fares for children 5 to 11 are 50% less. The trip from Victoria takes 5½ hours, while the trip from Nanaimo takes 3½ hours. Contact **Greyhound Canada** (© 800/661-8747; www.greyhound.ca) for reservations.

VISITOR INFORMATION

The **Campbell River Visitor Information Centre** is located at 1235 Shoppers Row (P.O. Box 44), Campbell River, BC V9W 5B6 (© 800/ 463-4386 or 250/287-4636; www.campbellrivertourism.bc.ca).

GETTING AROUND

In Campbell River itself, **Campbell River Airporter & Taxi Service** (© 250/286-3000) offers door-to-door service anywhere. As well, **Campbell River Transit** (© 250/287-7433) operates regular bus service.

WHERE TO STAY

Coast Discovery Inn & Marina 🏵   Adjacent to a busy shopping plaza right on the main drag, this is the only deluxe hotel you'll find downtown. As you might expect, it's a bit noisy by day, but since nothing much happens in Campbell River post-10pm, the location doesn't impact a quiet night's sleep. Guest rooms and suites are rather nondescript, though roomy enough and comfortable. All guest rooms have views of the harbor, and suites have welcome extras like Jacuzzis. The marina can accommodate 70 yachts up to 46m (150 ft.), as well as smaller pleasure crafts. Moorage can be arranged through the marina. Guided fishing tours are also available. There's a restaurant, and a pub that features live evening entertainment Thursday through Saturday.

975 Shoppers Row, Campbell River, BC V9W 2C4. ℂ **800/663-1144** or 250/287-7155. Fax 250/287-2213. www.coasthotels.com. 90 units. May–Sept C$160 (US$104) standard; C$170 (US$110.50) superior; C$180–$190 (US$117–$123.50) suite. Oct–Apr C$145 (US$94) standard; C$155 (US$101) superior; C$176 (US$114) suite. Extra person C$10 (US$6.50). MC, V. Free parking. Pets accepted C$10 (US$6.50). **Amenities:** Restaurant, pub; exercise room; Jacuzzi; 24-hour room service. *In room:* AC, TV w/pay movies, dataport, minibar, coffeemaker, hair dryer.

Haig-Brown House ★★   Prolific writer, avid outdoorsman, and respected judge, Roderick Haig-Brown was also one of British Columbia's most spirited conservationists. It was largely because of him, for example, that the Fraser River, which runs down through the BC Interior to Vancouver, was never dammed. From his 1923 farmhouse, set amidst 20 acres of gardens beside the Campbell River, he wrote ardently about fly-fishing, resource management, and preserving BC's natural environment. Fully restored as a BC Heritage Property, Haig-Brown's home is a delightful B&B where you can enjoy big country breakfasts while looking out over the orchard and garden beside the river. Guest rooms are decorated with comfy furnishings, although nothing too palatial. Guests share bathroom facilities.

2250 Campbell River Rd., Campbell River, BC V9W 4N7. ℂ **250/286-6646.** 3 units. May–mid-Sept C$75–$95 (US$49–$62); mid-Sept–Apr C$65–$75 (US$42–$49). Extra person C$20 (US$13). MC, V. Children not accepted. **Amenities:** Lounge. *In room:* No phone.

Hotel Bachmair Suite Hotel ★★★ *Finds*   This lovely Bavarian-style hotel is the choice of most movie companies filming in the area, in large part because the stylish accommodation ranges from two luxurious penthouse suites (for the stars) to well-furnished standard rooms and small suites (for the crew). Most suites come with one or two bedrooms, kitchens, sitting rooms, separate dining areas, fireplaces, and views overlooking Discovery Passage. One suite sleeps eight, has its own washer-dryer, and, amazingly, a flower-filled rooftop garden. Guests have access to the restaurant, pub, and other facilities across the street at the Best Western Austrian Chalet Village (© **800/667-7207** or 250/923-4231), a first-class second choice if the Bachmair is full.

492 South Island Hwy., Campbell River, BC V9W 1A5. © **888/923-2849** or 250/923-2848. Fax 250/923-2849. www.hotelbachmair.com. 23 units. C$79–$99 (US$51–$64) standard; C$99–$120 (US$64–$78) 1-bedroom; C$110–$180 (US$71–$117) 2-bedroom; C$170 (US$110.50) loft; C$250–$450 (US$162.50–$292.50) penthouse. AE, MC, V. Indoor parking. Small pets accepted C$5 (US$3.25). **Amenities:** Restaurant; coin-op washers and dryers. *In room:* TV, kitchen, hair dryer.

Painter's Lodge Holiday & Fishing Resort 𝕣𝕣𝕣
An international favorite of avid fishermen and celebrities, Painter's Lodge has welcomed the likes of Bob Hope, Julie Andrews, Goldie Hawn, and the Prince of Luxembourg. Its location overlooking Discovery Passage is awesome, and its rustic grandeur has a terrific West Coast ambience, with comfortable lounges, large decks, and spacious guest rooms and suites decorated in natural wood and pastels. Wrapped in windows, the lodge's restaurant, **Legends,** boasts a view of the Passage from every table. The menu is varied, and, not surprisingly, includes many fish and seafood specialties. One of the neatest dining experiences is to take the speedboat trip (10 minutes in each direction) over to **April Point Lodge on Quadra Island** for a pre-dinner martini at their sushi bar before returning to Legends for the catch of the day. The trip is included in hotel rates.

1625 MacDonald Rd. (P.O. Box 460, Dept 2), Campbell River, BC V9W 4S5. © **800/663-7090** or 250/286-1102. Fax 250/286-1102. www.obmg.com. 94 units. Apr–Oct C$189 (US$123) gardenside room; C$229 (US$149) oceanside room; C$385 (US$250) suite. AE, DC, MC, V. Closed Nov–Mar. **Amenities:** Restaurant, pub, lounge; large heated outdoor pool; 2 night-lit outdoor tennis courts; health club; 2 Jacuzzis; bike rental; children's center; activities desk. *In room:* TV, coffeemaker.

WHERE TO DINE

Baan Thai 𝕣𝕣 THAI CUISINE
It's so refreshing to find a great ethnic eatery away from the big city lights. This 40-seat restaurant, located over a storefront on Shoppers Row (Campbell River's main drag) is as good as it gets. Saffron-colored walls and bistro-style tables create a cozy atmosphere, while spicy smells waft through from the kitchen. It's been said that you can judge the quality of a Thai restaurant by its pad Thai alone, which just so happens to be Bann Thai's most popular dish. They also do exceptional curries.

1090 B Shoppers Row. © **250/286-4853.** Reservations recommended. Main courses C$5.50–$15 (US$3.50–$10). MC, V. Mon–Sat 11:30am–2pm and 5:30–9pm.

Harbour Grill ✮✮✮ STEAK & SEAFOOD   You wouldn't expect to find the best restaurant in town in a shopping mall, but that's exactly where Harbour Grill recently set up shop, changing its name from Le Chateaubriand in the process. (It was a local legend under that name, and it remains one now.) Still, you would be forgiven for having your doubts about this place, given the new location. Then you find that behind the mall lies the Discovery Harbour Marina and a waterside promenade, and that the Harbour Grill has front row seats to this refurbished part of town. It's maintained its reputation for excellent steaks: peppered, béarnaised, *à la Wellington* —you name it—as well as dishes like veal Oscar and fresh-from-the-dock seafood. Service is as crisp as the white linens; the staff is friendly and professional. Lunch is more casual, adding burgers, crepes, and a terrific West Coast bouillabaisse to the mix.

In the Discovery Harbour Centre, 112-1334 Island Hwy. ✆ **250/287-4143.** Lunch C$10 (US$6.50); dinner C$18.50–$27 (US$12–$17.50). Mon–Fri 11:30 am–2pm and 5:30–10pm; Sat–Sun 5:30–10pm.

FABULOUS FISHING

Campbell River is an excellent home base for numerous sport-fishing excursions, and there are several quality outfitters and charter boat companies. These include **Calypso Charters,** 384 Simms Rd. (✆ **888/CALYPSO** (888/225-9776) or 250/923-2001; www.bctravel. com/calypsocharters/). Rates are C$70 (US$45.50) an hour (not per person), inclusive of gear and tackle. **Profish Adventures,** 533 Cormorant Rd. (✆ **250/287-3869;** www.profish.bc.ca), offers all-inclusive saltwater fishing trips at C$70 (US45.50) an hour for up to two people, minimum 4 hours, and freshwater fishing excursions at C$400 (US$260) a day, for one person; C$500 (US$325) a day, for two people. **Campbell River Sportfishing Rentals,** 1-1371 Island Highway (✆ **250/287-7279;** www.oberon.ark.com/ ~crfish/), offers boat rentals from C$17.50 (US$11) per hour, as well as 2- to 4-night packages ranging from C$370 to $1395 (US$240 to $907) per person, including pick-up and drop off at the Campbell River and District Regional Airport. Charter companies will handle licensing requirements, but if you decide to fish independently, **nonresident fishing licenses** are available at outdoor recreation stores throughout Campbell River, including **Painter's Lodge Holiday & Fishing Resort,** where you can also watch all the action from beautiful decks (see "Where to Stay," above). Licenses cost C$7.49 (US$5) per day; C$34.17 (US$22) for 5 days.

CRUISING THE QUEEN CHARLOTTE STRAIT

Aside from renting a private charter (and spending a comparative small fortune), a rather unique option exists if you want to explore the island's coastal communities. Book a trip aboard a working coastal freighter, such as the *MV Uchuck III,* which departs out of Gold River on 1- and 2-day "cruises" along the Eastern bord (see "Sidetrips from Campbell River," below), or the *MV Aurora Explorer,* a 41-m (135-ft.) landing craft that plys the western waterways on 3-, 4-, and 5-day excursions to the remote inlets of the Queen Charlotte Strait. The *MV Aurora Explorer* is the only overnight passenger-freight vessel of its kind, sailing on an itinerary that is set by the tidal currents and the cargo she carries on her open deck. This might include supplies for solitary island retreats, refrigerators for First Nations villages, heavy equipment for a logging outpost, or mail and newspapers for a floating post office. Passenger quarters, housed just below the bridge tower (to which everyone has full access), sleep 12 in cramped but hospitable cabins; some have bunk beds. Food is hearty and constant, with a daily supply of fresh baked cookies and bread. Entertainment relies on conversation, a good book, the awesome scenery, unexpected wildlife, and being part of a working vessel in action, watching the crew on the deck below hoist that winch and tote that bale—sometimes at four in the morning. Usually, the schedule includes stops at heritage sites, abandoned villages, or even a pebbly beach for an impromptu barbecue (if trolling for supper has proved successful). So in addition to a seafaring adventure, there are opportunities for shore explorations. From May to mid-September, all-inclusive fares are C$292 (US$190) a person, a day; from mid-September through October and from the end of March through April, all-inclusive fares are C$239 to $272 (US$155 to $177). The *MV Aurora Explorer* does not sail November through February. For information, contact **Marine Link Tours,** P.O. Box 451, Campbell River, BC V9W 5C1 (© **250/286-3347;** www.marinelinktours.com). If private charters are still your preference, be aware that most are geared for fishing (see "Fabulous Fishing," above). That said, **Rippingale's Fishing,** 2330 Steelhead Rd., Campbell River (© **800/988-8242** or 250/286-7290; www.rippingalesfishing. com), offers 3-night packages ranging from C$479 to $639 (US$300 to $402) per person, per day.

SIDETRIPS FROM CAMPBELL RIVER

When a pulp mill opened here in 1965, **Gold River** ✿ was built out of the wilderness, a British Columbia "instant community," whose existence was predicated on industry and economic need. Besides Tofino and Ucluelet (see chapter 5), Gold River is the only community on Vancouver Island's west coast reachable by a well-maintained paved road. Located 92km (57 miles) west of Campbell River along Highway 28, the trip will take you about 1½ hours by car. You'll drive through spectacular **Strathcona Provincial Park** and on to the remote **Muchalat Inlet.** Sport fishing, rugged scenery, and abundant wildlife have always been the region's trademarks, and since the pulp mill closed in 1998, hopes are high that these natural attractions will become the center of a tourist-based local economy. There are a number of modest restaurants, B&Bs, and motels, which makes Gold River a good base from which to explore places like **Nootka Sound** (see below). In addition to kayaking, hiking, and wildlife viewing, activities include spelunking in the **Upana Caves** ✿, 27km (17 miles) northwest of Gold River. A well-marked trail connects the five caves, which includes the two-chambered Main Cave with a waterfall at the end of one passage, the marble-smooth Resurgence Cave, with its toothy outcrops, and the spiraling Corner Cave. For more information about the Upana Caves and about Gold River in general, visit the **Gold River Visitor Information Centre** at 499 Muchalat Dr., Gold River BC V0P 1G0 (✆ **250/283-2202** or 250/283-2418; www.village.goldriver.bc.ca).

If you decide to venture farther west from Gold River, you'll have a tremendous opportunity to explore the coastal communities in and around **Tahsis, Nootka, and Kyoquot Sounds** ✿✿✿ —some of the most beautiful coastal scenery in the world. Doing so aboard the workboat *MV Uchuck III,* is not only a treat for the whole family, but is good value for money. It's a much more cost-effective option than chartering a private boat, and you'll see, hear, taste, and smell more along the way than you will in the more "sanitized" environment of a private vessel. A converted WW II minesweeper, the *MV Uchuck III* sails year-round on day-long and overnight trips. Depending on the day and time of year, your destination might be **Tahsis, Zeballos,** or **Kyoquot,** the ancestral home of the Mowachaht/Muchalaht people of the Nuu-chah-nulth (formerly Nootka) nation. June through August, the schedule extends to the almost uninhabited First Nations village of historic **Yuquot**

(Friendly Cove), where British explorer Captain James Cook first came ashore in 1778. As the workhorse of the sounds, and the lifeline of many of these isolated communities, the *MV Uchuck III* also puts in at remote logging camps and fishing ports, picking up passengers and offloading anything from stoves to Oh Henry! bars. On overnight trips, passengers stay in local B&Bs in whichever community they are visiting. This is included in the price of the trip.

The *MV Uchuck III* sails year-round, with departures every day of the week except Friday and Sunday. Day-trip rates range from C$45 (US$29) for adults, $C37 to $41 (US$24 to $27) for seniors, C$20 to $22.50 (US$13 to $15) for children 7 to 12. Children 6 and under sail for free. Overnight trip rates range from C$160 to $310 (US$104 to $201) for adults, C$70 (US$45.50) for children 7 to 12. Children 6 and under sail for free. There are no seniors' rates on overnight trips. For more information, contact **Nootka Sound Services,** P.O. Box 57, Gold River, BC V0P 1G0 (© **250/283-2325;** www.mvuchuck.com).

3 En Route to Port Hardy

Trees, trees, and more trees line either side of Highway 19 heading north from Campbell River. Every now and then, their guard breaks to reveal logging sites: mountainsides scalded by machinery or fields of blackened stumps, left to rot before replanting. While logging is still the mainstay for communities such as **Port McNeill,** smaller hamlets such as **Holberg** and **Telegraph Cove** seem to co-exist in their lumber-industry environment in a more peaceful dimension. As a result, they have developed distinct personalities, whether from the Finnish influence still holding court in **Sointula,** or the richness of First Nations culture in **Alert Bay.**

ESSENTIALS
GETTING THERE
BY CAR   Although the road north is a well-maintained two-lane highway, this is the only driveable route, and it's used by logging trucks as well as local traffic. Getting stuck behind one of these lumbering vehicles can slow travel time, since they aren't always easy to pass. Give yourself extra time, and relieve frustration by taking detours. In summer, the road gets particularly busy with ferry travelers heading to and from Port Hardy. The distance from Campbell River to Port Hardy is 238km (148 miles), which could take up to 3½ hours to drive. From Nanaimo to Port Hardy, it's 391km

(243 miles)—allow at least 5 hours. For the long haul from Victoria to Port Hardy, it's a whopping 502km (312 miles). For this killer road trip, set aside 7 hours.

BY PLANE   **Air Canada Jazz** (© **888-247-2262;** www.flyjazz.ca) operates daily flights between Vancouver, Victoria, Port Hardy, Comox, and Campbell River, as does **Pacific Coastal Airlines** (© **800/663-2872;** www.pacific-coastal.com). **Kenmore Air** (© **800/543-9595** or 425-486-1257; www.kenmoreair.com) flies from Seattle Harbor to Port Hardy, Port McNeill, and Quadra Island.

BY BUS   **Island Coach Lines,** operated by **Laidlaw Coach Lines** (© **800/318-0818** or 250/385-4411; www.victoriatours.com), runs daily service from Victoria to Port Hardy, stopping in Campbell River. The one-way fare from Victoria to Port Hardy is C$94 (US$61) for adults. From Nanaimo to Port Hardy, it's C$74 (US$48) for adults. Fares for seniors are 10% less; fares for children 5 to 11 are 50% less. The trip from Victoria to Port Hardy is just under 10 hours. From Nanaimo to Port Hardy, it's approximately 7 hours. Contact **Greyhound Canada** (© **800/661-8747;** www.greyhound.ca) for reservations.

BY FERRY   **BC Ferries** (© **888/223-3779;** www.bcferries.com) operates nine crossings daily between Port McNeill and the community of **Alert Bay,** on Cormorant Island, and between Port McNeill and **Sointula,** on Malcolm Island. One-way fares are C$5.50 (US$4) for adults, C$3 (US$2) for children 5 to 11. Crossing time is 45 minutes. BC Ferries also operates service between Port Hardy and Prince Rupert, a 15-hour journey via the famed **Inside Passage.**

VISITOR INFORMATION

There are visitor information centers in several of the communities dotting the route to Port Hardy, such as **Port McNeill Visitor Information** at 351 Shelley Cres. (P.O. Box 691), Port McNeill, BC V0N 2R0 (© **250/956-3131;** www.portmcneill.net) and **Alert Bay Visitor Information** at 116 Fir St. (P.O. Box 28), Alert Bay, BC V0N 1A0 (© **250/974-5213;** www.alertbay.net). Once in Port Hardy, head to the **Port Hardy Visitor Information Centre,** 7250 Market St. (P.O. Box 249), Port Hardy, BC V0N 2P0 (© **250/ 949-7622;** www.ph-chamber.bc.ca). These folks also provide an **accommodation reservations service** for Port Hardy and Prince Rupert (for those going to Prince Rupert with BC Ferries).

WHERE TO STAY & DINE

Glen Lyon Inn & Suites ☺☺   Once you make it past the rather daunting stuffed eagle showcased in the lobby, you'll find a clean, modern motel. Renovations carried out in 2000 include the addition of a third floor with 15 guest rooms. All rooms have an oceanview, and come in a mix of configurations to match your needs, whether it's a family suite with bunk beds for the kids, an executive-style room, or the honeymoon suite, with Jacuzzi and wet bar. The **Glen Lyon pub** opens for lunch and is a popular spot until last orders at around midnight. The tiny **Glen Lyon restaurant-cafe,** which bustles with activity, serves quality salads and burgers by day and dishes such as barbecued ribs and Thai chicken in the evening. The restaurant will have new ownership in the summer of 2002, so there could be a change of flavor and set-up. The hotel is beside the Fisherman's Wharf and the Adventure Centre, which offers several fishing, wildlife, and eco-adventure excursions.

6435 Hardy Bay Rd. (P.O. Box 103), Port Hardy, BC V0N 2P0. ℂ **877/949-7115** or 250/949-7115. Fax 250/949-7415. www.glenlyoninn.com. 44 units. May–mid-Oct C$85–$120 (US$55–$78) double; C$125–$170 (US$81–$110.50) suite. Mid-Oct–Apr C$62–$69 (US$40–$45) double; C$95–$125 (US$62–$81) suite. AE, MC, V. Small pets accepted C$10 (US$6.50). **Amenities:** Restaurant, pub; exercise room; laundry service. *In room:* TV, dataport, fridge, coffeemaker, hair dryer.

Oceanview B&B ☺   Although it has rather a grandiose exterior, this lovely home extends a warm welcome to weary travelers. Guest rooms are spacious—they have small sitting areas—and quaintly decorated, with brass or wrought-iron beds. Two of the rooms share a bathroom, while the third has a private ensuite bathroom. Thoughtful touches such as fresh-cut flowers, pillow chocolates, and a plate of homemade chocolate chip cookies greet you in your room. A European-style breakfast, with plenty of cold cuts and assorted cheeses, is served up in a bright and spacious kitchen. The sitting room is decorated with wicker furniture, and offers various reading materials, a piano, and a fireplace. The house has wonderful views of Hardy Bay and the snow-covered mountains on the mainland. An unexpected bonus is free parking for guests who wish to leave their vehicles while they take the ferry to Prince Rupert or to Discovery Passage.

7735 Cedar Place (P.O. Box 183), Port Hardy, BC V0N 2P0. ℂ and fax **250/ 949-8302.** www.island.net/~oceanvue. 3 units, 2 w/shared bathroom. C$85–$100 (US$55–$65). Rates include breakfast. Extra person C$15 (US$10). MC, V. Free parking. **Amenities:** Lounge. *In room:* TV.

Quarterdeck Inn & Marina ☆☆   A smart, if generic-looking hotel, the Quarterdeck opened in 1999 and still feels very new. Peppermint-tinted corridors (a favorite color of many Port Hardy buildings) lead to spacious, pastel-colored rooms, with comfortable beds and oceanviews from every window. Suites are larger, with sitting areas and fireplaces. The hotel is surrounded by a working boatyard and marina, so there's always something to see. The **Quarterdeck Pub,** a nautical-style pub-restaurant, situated on the marina a few steps from the inn, serves great fresh halibut and chips, oyster burgers, and calamari, in addition to pub fare. There are regular evening specials. If you're in a hurry, all items are available to go.

6555 Hardy Bay Rd. (P.O. Box 910), Port Hardy, BC V0N 2P0. ℂ **877/902-0459** or 250/902-0455. Fax 250/902-0454. www.quarterdeckresort.net. 40 units. May–Sept C$110 (US$71.50) standard; C$120 (US$78) suite. Oct–Apr C$80 (US$52) standard; C$95 (US$64) suite. Rates include continental breakfast. **Amenities:** Restaurant, pub; Jacuzzi. *In room:* TV, kitchenette, coffeemaker.

EXPLORING THE AREA

Considering all the trees you'll see, a visit to some of the mine- and timber-based communities en route to Port Hardy puts the landscape into perspective. The destinations that follow are listed geographically, heading north from Campbell River along Highway 19.

Located 191km (118 miles) north of Campbell River, at the end of a gravel road off Highway 19, historic **Zeballos** once produced more than $13 million worth of gold. Tailings from the mines were used to build up the roads and led to a local legend that the streets were literally "paved with gold." But when Zeballos lost its Midas touch, logging, fishing and tourism became its mainstays. Today, this pretty village is an eco-adventurer's dream, especially for recreational cavers and experienced spelunkers, who head to **Little Hustan Caves** with their sinkholes, canyons, and fast-moving river that disappears and reappears in the rock formations.

A highlight of your trip north must be **Telegraph Cove** ☆☆☆, a picture-perfect village, located 239km (180 miles) north of Campbell River. Overlooking Johnstone Strait, it epitomizes the West Coast, and is one of the few remaining **elevated-boardwalk villages** on Vancouver Island. This historic community got its start in 1912 as a one-room telegraph station that marked the end of a cable, strung tree to tree, all the way from Victoria. When messages were received, the operator hopped into a boat and rowed to the community of **Alert Bay,** on Cormorant Island, to deliver the news. Part of the cove's charm is that many of the original buildings still stand, including the telegraph station, an army mess hall, picturesque residences, and cozy cabins perched on stilts over the water's edge, joined by boardwalks. **Telegraph Cove Resorts** (℃ **800/200-HOOK** or 250/928-3131; www.telegraphcoveresorts. com) rents out many of the refurbished buildings. They have renovated the old saltery into the **Old Saltery Pub** and the **Killer Whale Cafe** (℃ **250/928-3131**); both are terrific stops for lunch. You can also schedule a whale-watching or other type of excursion while you're here, with **Stubbs Island Charters** (℃ **800/665-3066;** www. stubbs-island.com), BC's first orca- and wildlife-watching company. If you're traveling by RV and want to stay over, **Telegraph Cove Marina & RV Park** (℃ **877/835-2683** or 250/928-3160) dominates the other side of the cove. It's a rather overwhelming development that is dragging the sleepy 1930s feel of the cove kicking and screaming into the new millennium.

From Telegraph Cove, it's approximately 40km (25 miles) to **Port McNeill,** gateway to whale-watching expeditions and the island communities of **Alert Bay** and **Sointula.** Companies like **Mackay Whale Watching,** P.O. Box 66, Port McNeill, BC V0N 2R0 (℃ **877/663-6277;** www.whaletime.com) and **Sea Orca Whale Watching,** Government Dock, P.O. Box 483, Alert Bay BC V0N 1A0 (℃ **800/668-6722** or 250/974-5225; www.seaorca.com) will take you out. Hourly rates are about C$70 (US$45) for adults, C$50 (US$32) for children 3 to 12.

From Port McNeill, BC Ferries runs nine daily crossings to the 1,800-strong community of **Alert Bay** 𝕲𝕲 on Cormorant Island or to **Sointula** on Malcolm Island. One-way fares are C$5.50 (US$3.50) for adults, C$3 (US$1.90) for children 5 to 11. The crossing time is 45 minutes. A Kwagiulth tribal village, Alert Bay exudes its rich, cultural heritage, and is most proud of the 53-m (173-ft.) cedar totem pole featuring 22 hand-carved figures of bears, orcas, and ravens. It stands outside the Big House at the top of the hill. Near the ferry dock at Alert Bay, at the **U'Mista Cultural Centre** (℃ **250/974-5403;** www.umista.org), you'll find an extraordinary collection of carved-wood ceremonial masks, cedar baskets, copper jewelry, and other potlatch artifacts that were confiscated by the Canadian government in 1922, and repatriated in 1980. The modern building is modeled after a Kwakwaka'wakw Big House, and often hosts performances by 'Na'Nakwala dancers. Look also, at the

Anglican Church on Front Street, which reflects the arrival of Scottish immigrants into the area at the turn of the 20th century. Erected in 1881, the church's stained-glass windows are an interesting blend of Native Kwagiulth and Scottish design motifs.

Founded by Finnish settlers in 1901, the community of **Sointula,** on Malcolm Island, was to be a Utopian society, "a place of harmony." Although the concept collapsed, you can still feel the peaceful atmosphere of that dream. Finnish was the island's principal language until as recently as 30 years ago. But today, less than 50% of the 1,000-strong population is Finn. Sointula is a charming fishing village; it's a good place to absorb a maritime atmosphere. There's a local gallery, store, and the **Sointula Museum** (© 250/973-6764), next to the tennis courts by the ferry terminal, which tells the Finnish story.

Port Hardy is 44km (27miles) north of Port McNeill. Many visitors come via ferry, en route either to or from **Prince Rupert.** In fact, in summer this tiny town gets so busy with ferry travelers that decent accommodation gets full fast, leaving a motley assortment of tired motels to choose from. Until recently, the town's prosperity has always been fueled by forestry, mining, and commercial fishing, but the refurbished seaside promenade, and the fresh coat of paint here and there, is evidence of Port Hardy's efforts to diversify its economic base through tourism. Is this why the timbered **Port Hardy Visitor Information Centre,** 7250 Market St. (P.O. Box 294), Port Hardy, BC V0N 2P0 (© 250/949-7622), is the nicest building downtown? If you have an hour to spare, drop into the **Port Hardy Museum,** 7110 Market St. (© 250/949-8143), which has some interesting relics from early Danish settlers, plus a collection of stone tools, found nearby, which date from about 8,000 B.C.

Once you make it to **Port Hardy,** you may feel like you've reached the edge of the world, but in actual fact, Port Hardy is the jumping-off point for a myriad of exhilarating, year-round outdoor activities, such as **hiking in Cape Scott Provincial Park** (see below), fishing, kayaking, golf, and diving. Water clarity and tidal action have made this one of the best dive locations in the world. **Port Hardy Outdoor Experience,** 714B Market St. (P.O. Box 220), Port Hardy BC V0N 2P0 (© 866/902-0444 or 250/902-0440; www.island.net\~charters.com), comprises 27 different outfitters in the area, some of which will provide fully equipped dive boats. A 4-hour two-dive trip is C$125 (US$81) a diver.

CAPE SCOTT PROVINCIAL PARK 🐾🐾🐾

Clinging to the northwest tip of Vancouver Island, Cape Scott Provincial Park is 53,967 acres of untamed raincoast wilderness, where the wild Pacific Ocean pounds wide, windswept beaches and crashes against rocky headlands. In the late 1890s, enterprising Danish colonists from the American Midwest carved the tortuous route to Cape Scott itself out of the tangled bush. They hoped to build a community there. But the land was too isolated, and the weather too inhospitable to let the settlement grow. Today, their wagon roads are now hiking trails, and heritage markers along the way point out the remains of their endeavors: tumbledown cabins, sun-bleached driftwood fence posts, a dilapidated cougar trap, and cedar planked "corduroy roads."

Getting there is a 2-hour, 67-km (42-mile) drive west from Port Hardy down a heavily used logging road toward the tiny town of **Holberg,** a good place to break the journey, especially if you stop in at the **Scarlet Ibis Pub** (© **250/288-3386**). On the outskirts of Holberg, you'll find **Ronning Gardens.** Established in 1910 by a Norwegian settler, they are an extraordinary anomaly of exotic trees and plants from all over the world. Then continue on until the Cape Scott parking lot, where you'll find the trailheads to both the **San Josef Bay** and **Cape Scott trails.** *Note:* If you're making the trip to the park more to see the sights than to do any hiking, you may prefer to leave your vehicle in Port Hardy, and take a **guided boat tour** to the park. Tours leave from Port Hardy. Make your reservations through **Port Hardy Outdoor Experience,** 714B Market St. (P.O. Box 220), Port Hardy BC V0N 2P0 (© **866/902-0444** or 250/902-0440; www.island.net\~charters.com). You can also book a spot aboard an 11-passenger van that will take you right to the trailheads. The flat rate is C$50 (US$32.50) each way.

HIKING Heavy rainfalls (nearly 504 centimeters (200 in.) per year) and violent windstorms predominate in this wild landscape, turning hiking trails into muddy quagmires. But if you thrive on doing things off the beaten track, these trails deliver. The easiest and most popular hike is the 2.5-km (1.5-mile) **San Josef Bay Trail,** a fairly easy walk through marshy ferns, skunk cabbage, and along the San Josef River to San Josef Bay, where there's an expanse of sandy beach, and the ruins of a Danish settlement. More experienced and well-equipped hikers can opt for the challenging 24-km (15-mile) **Cape Scott Trail.** This grueling trek starts in mud, but once you're on your way, the scenery is pure wilderness: ocean bay beauty, weathered grass, high-rise canopies of Sitka spruce, and vast stretches of natural beach. Stops along the way include **Eric Lake,** an ideal spot for fishing and warm water swimming, and **Hansen Lagoon,** once a Danish settlement, and now a stopping place for Canada geese and a variety of waterfowl traveling the Pacific Flyway. Allow 3 days of heavy hiking, and a good week if you want to explore all the offshoot trails.

The Gulf Islands

Snuggled between Vancouver Island and the mainland, the Gulf Islands are pastoral havens. Their protected waterways provide some of the finest cruising in the world, and their semi-Mediterranean climate is enviable, even by West Coast standards. Add to this, sweeping scenes of woods and water, pebble and shell beaches, and placid lakes stocked with bass and rainbow trout—ideal for fly-fishing, and you can understand why the Gulf Islands have been described as "fragments of paradise."

The raggedly beautiful archipelago, the northern extension of Washington's San Juan Islands, is made up of more than 200 islands. Although most are small, uninhabited, and accessible only by private boat, the five larger islands, off the southeastern tip of Vancouver Island—Salt Spring Island, the Pender islands, Galiano, Mayne, and Saturna islands—are home to about 15,000 permanent residents and are served by a regularly scheduled ferry service.

From the beginning, the islands have attracted a polyglot of individuals: writers and artists, poets and cooks, ecologists and escapists. So, far from being an unsophisticated backwater, you'll find first-class restaurants throughout the region, as well as heritage B&Bs, galleries, farmhouses, and artisans' studios. In recent years, relocated urbanites have started to gentrify the islands' counterculture, and it's an uneasy mix. Land values have skyrocketed and petty crime is on the rise. Only the self-governing Islands Trust holds development in check. One example of the fallout from this concerns the islands' water supply. As more and more city folk migrate to the islands (prompting a population increase of almost 30% in the past decade), resources must stretch to accommodate their city habits. With the onslaught of multibathroom homes, dishwashers, and Jacuzzis, freshwater has become a precious commodity. Today, homesteaders must dig twice as deep for water as they did 20 years ago. Boiling and filtering is becoming a way of life, and there are often shortages in summer.

That said, the Gulf Islands are still a heavenly place to hike, kayak, and canoe, or simply enjoy a glass of wine from the deck of a private, self-catering cottage. Families usually resort to the latter since many of the islands' inns and B&Bs are geared to adults. When a hotel welcomes children, this information is included in the review. Refer to the "Where to Stay" sections for individual islands.

The islands may lack many urban amenities like bank machines and laundromats, but they do have a wealth of quirky features that will make your visit memorable. One example is the "honesty stands," which dot the sides of roads around the islands. You drop your money in the box provided, and walk away with honey, flowers, veggies, jams, and whatever else local folk have for sale. Deer are another feature. With no natural predators on the islands, they are free to roam roads, gardens, and forests, so be sure to drive carefully, especially at night.

Of all the islands, Salt Spring is the most dynamic, and the easiest to get to from Vancouver Island, especially if you only have a day to spare. Once on a Gulf Island, it is easy to hop to another, arriving in the early morning and departing late afternoon. You're best to incorporate at least one night on each island—it's the only way to experience the very different personality of each, although you might be tempted to stay far longer; after all, they are fragments of paradise.

GETTING THERE

BY PLANE   Seaplanes criss-cross the skies above the Gulf Islands at regular intervals, between Vancouver Island, Vancouver on the mainland, and Seattle. **Seair Seaplanes** (© **800/447-3247** or 604/273-8900; www.seairseaplanes.com) and **Harbour Air** (© **800/665-0212** or 604/278-3478; www.harbour-air.com) offer daily flights. One-way fares range from C$70 to $75 (US$45.50 to $49). **Kenmore Air** (© **800/543-9595**) flies from Seattle May through September. One-way fares are C$223 (US$145); round-trip fares are C$385 (US$250). There are no areas on the islands that accommodate commercial flights, although some islands have small, grassy airstrips for private aircraft.

BY FERRY   Juggling your schedule with ferry departures is an art that requires patience, if not a Master's degree in reading timetables. **BC Ferries** (© **888/223-3779** or 250/386-3431; www.bcferries.com) provides good basic service to the Gulf Islands, with at least two sailings a day from **Tsawwassen,** a 22-km (14-mile) drive south

The Gulf Islands

LEGEND

- ✈ Beach
- – – – Ferry Route
- 🐟 Fishing
- ⓘ Information
- ▲ Mountain
- 🍷 Winery

Reid Island
Alcala Point
DIONISIO POINT PROVINCIAL PARK
Hall I.
Norway I.
Secretary Islands
Kuper Island
Houston Passage
Bodega Ridge
Wallace Island
Retreat Cove
GALIANO
ISLAND
Devina Dr.
Porlier Pass Rd.
Bodega Beach Dr.
Vineyard Way
32
Tent Island
North N. Beach Rd.
Sunset Dr.
1
2 3
4
Fernwood
Walker's Hook Rd.
Porlier Pass Road
Strait of Georgia
31
Parminter Point
Saint Mary Lake
Vesuvius Bay
Vesuvius
Channel Ridge
Vesuvius Bay Rd.
Stark Rd.
5
Upper Ganges Rd.
Robinson Rd.
Trincomali Channel
Charles I.
Wise I.
Montague Harbour
Parker Island
Julia I.
30
29
Mortimer Rd.
Sturdies Bay Rd.
Georgeson Bay Rd.
Morgan Rd.
28
BLUFFS PARK
Mt. Galiano
Georgeson Bay
Stuart Channel
Crofton
Vesuvius Bay / Crofton
7
6 10
9
8
Ganges
11
Mansell Rd.
Long Harbour Rd.
Long Harbour
Ganges Harbour
SISTER ISLANDS
Captain Passage
Tsawwassen
Prevost Island
MAPLE MOUNTAIN PARK
Maple Mt.
Maple Bay
Maple Bay
Sansum Narrows
Maxwell Lake
Maxwell Rd.
Cranberry Rd.
MT. MAXWELL PROVINCIAL PARK
SALT
Blackburn Lake
Cusheon Lake
Fulton-Ganges Rd.
Beddis Rd.
12
Cusheon Stewart Road
SPRING
Burgoyne Bay
Fulford-Ganges Rd.
Stowell Lake
Beaver Pt. Rd.
Weston Lake
Fulford Harbour
RUCKLE PROVINCIAL PARK
Beaver Point Road
Vancouver Island
Mt. Sulivan
Mt. Bruce
ISLAND
Musgrave Rd.
Fulford Harbour
Fulford-Ganges Rd.
Beaver Pt. Rd.
Swartz Bay
Swartz Bay / Tsawwassen
PRINCESS MARGARET PROVINCIAL MARINE PARK
Portland Island
Cowichan Bay
Separation Point
Cowichan Bay
Mt. Tuam
ECOLOGICAL RESERVE
16
Satellite Channel
Piers Island
1

SALT SPRING ISLAND

Accommodations

Anchor Point B&B **11**
Anne's Oceanfront Hideaway B&B **1**
Beddis House B&B **12**
Cloud 9 **2**
Hastings House **8**
The Old Farmhouse B&B **5**
Salt Spring Island Hostel **3**
Salt Springs Spa Resort **4**

Dining

Bousaouki Greek Cafe ◆**9**
House Piccolo ◆**6**
Moby's Marine Pub ◆**7**
Tree House Cafe ◆**10**

THE PENDER ISLANDS

Accommodations & Dining

Alice's Shangri-La Oceanfront B&B **15**
Bedwell Harbour Island Resort **17**
Inn on Pender Island **14**
Oceanside Inn **13**
Sahhali Serenity Oceanfront B&B Inn **16**

SATURNA ISLAND

Accommodations & Dining

Breezy Bay B&B ◆**18**
Saturna Lodge & Restaurant ◆**19**

MAYNE ISLAND

Accommodations

A Coach-House on Oyster Bay B&B Inn **23**
Blue Vista Resort **21**
Oceanwood Country Inn **20**

Dining

Mayne Inn ◆**22**
Spring Water Lodge ◆**24**

GALIANO ISLAND

Accommodations

Bellhouse Inn **26**
Bodega Resort **32**
Driftwood Village **25**
Galiano Inn **27**
Island Time B&B **31**
Woodstone Country Inn **28**

Dining

La Berengerie ◆**30**
Hummingbird Pub ◆**29**

Strait of Georgia

Bellhouse Provincial Park
Georgina Point Lighthouse
Oyster Bay
Campbell Bay
Wilkes Rd
Active Pass
Village Bay
Mariners Way
MAYNE ISLAND
MT. PARKE PARK
Bennett Bay
Curlew I.
Horton Bay
East West Rd
Navy Channel
Samuel Island
Port Washington
Swartz Bay / Tsawwassen
Veruna Bay
WINTER COVE PROVINCIAL MARINE PARK
Port Washington Rd
Amies Rd
Lyall Harbour
East Point Rd
East Point Rd
Saturna Island Vineyards
Tumbo Island
Tumbo Channel
Tumbo Channel Rd
Otter Bay
Otter Bay Rd
Saturna Pt.
Harris Rd
SATURNA ISLAND
ECOLOGICAL RESERVE
Cliffside Rd
Bedwell Harbour Road
NORTH PENDER ISLAND
Browning Harbour
Narvaez Bay Rd
East Point Regional Park
Medicine Beach
Magic Lake
MT. NORMAN REGIONAL PARK
BEAUMONT MARINE P.P.
Porlier Rd
Bedwell Harbour
Canal Rd
Breezy Bay
Warburton Pike
Spalding Rd
SOUTH PENDER ISLAND
Brookes Pt.
Swanson Channel
Boundary Pass
Moresby Island

0   2 mi
0   2 km

of Vancouver, on the mainland, and from **Swartz Bay,** 32km (20 miles) north of Victoria, on Vancouver Island. Ferries also run frequently between islands. Schedules are available from **BC Ferries.** One-way fares from Tsawwassen to the Gulf Islands average C$9 (US$6) per person; C$35 (US$23) for a standard-size vehicle. One-way fares from Swartz Bay to the islands average C$6 (US$4) per person; C$21 (US$14) for a standard-size vehicle. Return fares are less, and vary according to which island you are returning from. One bonus to note is that return fares from the Gulf Islands to **Swartz Bay** are free. Inter-island trips average C$3 (US$2) per person; C$7 (US$4.50) for a standard-size vehicle. *Note:* Ferry travel can be costly if you're taking a vehicle, and long boarding waits are not uncommon. Ticket prices vary seasonally; mid-week travel is slightly less expensive than weekends and holidays, when reservations are essential. During these peak periods, book at least 3 weeks in advance to avoid disappointment. Reservations can be made with BC Ferries by phone or online. **Washington State Ferries** (© **888/808-7977** or 206/464-6400; www.wsdot.wa.gov/ferries) provides daily service from **Anacortes to Sidney,** a short distance from Swartz Bay (see "The Saanich Peninsula" in chapter 4). From Swartz Bay, you can transfer to a BC Ferries ferry to the Gulf Islands. One-way fares are C$17 (US$11) for adults, C$8.50 (US$5.50) for seniors, C$12 (US$7.70) for children; C$46 ($US29.75) for a standard-size vehicle. Reserve by 5:30pm the day prior to travel. Sailing time is 3 hours. The ferry dock in Anacortes is at 2100 Ferry Terminal Rd.

A local **inter-island water taxi** (© **250/537-2510;** www.salt spring.com/watertaxi) operates June through August on Wednesdays and Saturdays. When school is in session, September through June, it operates as a weekday school boat, and adults often hitch a ride for day excursions. The one-way fare between any two points is C$10 (US$6.50) per person. People often transport kayaks, C$5 (US$3.25). Transporting bicycles is free.

VISITOR INFORMATION

Services operate through the local chamber of commerce or general store on individual islands (see "Essentials," below, for the island in question). You can also check out **www.gulfislands.com** for general information. There is a **central reservations service** for island hotels and B&Bs (© **866/539-3089**). Not all islands have public campgrounds, and moorage facilities for pleasure craft vary considerably.

1 Salt Spring Island

Named for the briny springs on the island, Salt Spring Island is the largest and most accessible of the Gulf Islands. Lying just north of Vancouver Island's Swartz Bay, this thriving community is made up of almost 10,000 commuters, retirees, farmers, and artistic free spirits. You'll come across a number of home-based entrepreneurs: everything from potters and weavers, to llama farms and cheese-makers! There are two golf courses, a small movie theater, an ice rink, lots of restaurants, and a scattering of hotly debated condominium developments, mostly in the **Ganges** area. Tour Salt Spring's pastoral landscape and you'll quickly see why sheep are Salt Spring's insignia —they're everywhere. You'll also discover any number of lakes (many are hot fishing spots) and hiking trails, such as those in **Mount Maxwell Provincial Park,** which includes a 1.5-km (1-mile) trek up to **Baynes Peak.** Rising 595 metres (1,952 ft.), it is the third highest mountain on the Gulf Islands. You can drive to the trailhead but go easy, the paved road becomes a narrow, gravel surface that's too rough for RVs to negotiate.

ESSENTIALS

GETTING THERE

BC Ferries sails to **Fulford Harbour,** in the southern part of Salt Spring, or **Long Harbour,** toward the north. Seaplanes land in **Ganges Harbour,** in the center of the island. See "Getting There," above, for information about fares and schedules.

VISITOR INFORMATION

Head to the **Salt Spring Island Chamber of Commerce,** 121 Lower Ganges Rd., Salt Spring Island, BC V8K 2T1 (© **866/216-2936** or 250/537-5252; www.saltspringisland.bc.ca), in the village of Ganges. Open daily, year-round. Another good online resource is **www.saltspringtoday.com**.

GETTING AROUND

Silver Shadow Taxi (© **250/537-3030**) services the island. If you want to rent a car, there's **Budget Car Rentals,** 30 Upper Ganges Rd., Ganges (© **800/668-3233** or 250/537-6099). Rentals are about C$60 (US$39) a day. You can rent bicycles from **The Bike Shop,** 131 McPhillips Rd., Ganges (© **250/537-1544**), beside the library. Rentals cost C$20 (US$13) a day. **Salt Spring Kayaks,** 2933 Fulford-Ganges Rd., Fulford Harbour (© **250/653-4222**), rents both bikes (C$25 (US$16) a day) and kayaks (C$45 (US$29) a day), and will deliver them to anywhere on Salt Spring Island.

WHERE TO STAY
EXPENSIVE

Hastings House ✹✹✹   A member of the exclusive French hotel network Relais & Châteaux, this upscale inn lies an olive pip's throw from the village of Ganges, in a magnificent garden and orchard overlooking the Ganges Harbour. First a Hudson's Bay Company trading post, and then a farm, the homestead was bought in the 1930s by Barbara Wedgwood, the British pottery heiress, who turned the site into a replica of a 16th-century Sussex estate (all the while driving around Salt Spring's country roads in a Rolls-Royce!). Since then, the Tudor-style manor house, farmhouse, barn, and trading post have been superbly renovated into charming cottages and suites, each charged with character and filled with original art, antiques, and all the modern luxuries of a first-class hotel, save for TVs and VCRs, which are provided only on request. Its restaurant is equally impressive (see "Where to Dine," below). Reserve 6 months in advance for summer visits.

160 Upper Ganges Rd., Ganges, Salt Spring Island, BC V8K 2S8. ✆ **800/661-9255** or 250/537-2362. Fax 250/537-5333. www.hastingshouse.com. 18 units. Mid-June–mid-Oct C$430–$660 (US$279.50–$429) suite. Mid-Mar–mid-June and mid-Oct–mid-Nov C$330–$560 (US$214.50–$364) suite. Mid-June–mid-Nov C$3,360–$3,960 (US$2,184–$2574) cottage weekly rate. Rates include wake-up hamper, breakfast, and afternoon tea. Extra person C$85 (US$55). AE, DC, MC, V. Closed Mid-Nov–mid-Mar. Children 16 and under not accepted. **Amenities:** Restaurant, lounge. *In room:* Minibar.

MODERATE

Anchor Point B&B ✹   Surrounded by a courtyard garden and terraces, Anchor Point is a traditional Cape Cod–style B&B that exudes an ambience of home. Guests can use a comfortable lounge and dining area with lovely water views, as well as a TV/VCR den where the movie library comprises more than 450 titles. Guest rooms are sparkling clean, with fireplaces, designer linens, and quality amenities; two have private ensuite bathrooms, while the third has a private cross-hall bathroom. Robes and slippers are provided to all guests—pretty handy for scuttling to the outside Jacuzzi. Turndown service is a pampering touch, as is the never-ending supply of freshly baked cookies.

150 Beddis Rd., Salt Spring Island, BC V8K 2J2. ✆ **800/648-2560** or 250/538-0110. Fax 250/538-0120. www.anchorpointbb.com. 3 units. Mid-May–mid-Sept C$125–$145 (US$ 82–$94). Mid-Sept–mid-May C$135 (US$88). Rates include breakfast. Extra person C$15 (US$10). MC, V. **Amenities:** Jacuzzi; laundry service. *In room:* TV, VCR on request, hair dryer, no phone.

Anne's Oceanfront Hideaway B&B ⋒⋒   This beautiful oceanfront inn offers cozy lounges (one with a TV/VCR), comfortable furnishings, and a central staircase that leads to guest accommodation upstairs. Guest rooms are well appointed and individually decorated, ranging from French country styling to Queen Anne elegance. Lying on the edge of a cliff, from wherever you are in Anne's, the sweeping views of the island and sea, which stretch to the horizon, might tempt you to belly flop over the treetops and into the water. Thoughtful touches include a half bottle of private label champagne chilling in the guest room fridge upon arrival (perfect for sipping in front of the fireplace or on the balcony), slippers and robe to head outside to the Jacuzzi, and evening turndown service. An elevator makes the four upstairs guest rooms wheelchair accessible, as well as the lower level, where you can enjoy an aromatherapy massage.

168 Simson Rd., Salt Spring Island, BC V8K 1E2. ✆ **888/474-2663** or 250/537-0851. Fax 250/537-0861. www.annesoceanfront.com. 4 units. May–Sept C$195–$245 (US$127–$159). Oct–Apr C$165–$210 (US$107–$136). Rates include breakfast and afternoon tea. AE, MC, V. Children not accepted. **Amenities:** Lounge; Jacuzzi; limited water-sports equipment; massage. *In room:* Fridge, hair dryer, no phone.

Beddis House B&B ⋒⋒   This beautiful heritage farmhouse sits on the oceanfront, making walks along the beach a part of the package. The original turn-of-the-century wood-frame farmhouse is now a sunlit dining and lounge area. Deluxe guest rooms each have wonderful views of the sea, and gardens. Decorator accents in guest rooms include pine armoires, shaker chests, and rocking chairs by the fire, as well as ensuite bathrooms with clawfoot bathtubs, and showers. The surrounding orchard contains apple and plum trees, many of which were planted from seed around 1900. The seeds had been embedded in potatos for protection and shipped all the way from Ireland. Although children are not accepted in the main house, there is a delightful, self-contained guesthouse, perfect for families.

131 Miles Ave., Salt Spring Island, BC V8K 2E1. ✆ **250/537-1028.** Fax 250/537-9888. www.saltspring.com/beddishouse. 3 units. May–mid-Oct C$145–$190 (US$94–$123). Mid-Oct–April C$125–$170 (US$81–$110). Rates include breakfast and afternoon tea. MC, V. Closed Dec–Jan. Children not accepted in main house. **Amenities:** Lounge. *In room:* Hair dryer, no phone.

Cloud 9 🏵🏵   Perched atop one of Salt Spring Island's highest hills, Cloud 9 lives up to its name. Boasting magnificent 180-degree views, this upscale B&B, which opened in 2000, takes mountaineering to new heights—only this summit you can reach by car, and without any rappeling equipment. With vaulted ceilings, scores of large windows and over 152 m² (500 sq. ft.) of decks, views rule the roost. Even the Jacuzzi clings to the cliff, reached by a stone pathway that leads from the house to the edge of the mountain. Guest rooms are tastefully decorated, with enough pampering touches to encourage cocooning. Of special note are the individually controlled heated floors, fireplaces, down duvets and pillows, satellite TV, and genuine Persian rugs. Enormous bathrooms have deep double-soaker or jetted bathtubs. You even get two pairs of slippers: one for inside, the other for outside (to get to the Jacuzzi), as well as a pair of binoculars. The Cloud 9 Suite is completely self-contained, with full kitchen and barbecue.

238 Sun Eagle Dr., Salt Spring Island, BC V8K 1E5. ℂ 877/722-8233 or 250/537-2776. Fax 250/537-2776. www.cloud9oceanview.com. 3 units. June 28–Sept 30 C$160–$195 (US$104–$127). May 1–June 27 and Oct 1–15 C$150–$185 (US$98–$120). Oct 15–Nov 15 and Mar 1–Apr 30 C$135–$160 (US$88–$104). Extra person C$50 (US$32.50). AE, MC, V. Closed mid-Nov–Mar 1. Pets accepted w/prior approval. Children 12 and under not accepted. **Amenities:** 2 lounges; Jacuzzi; bike rental; laundry service. *In room:* TV/VCR, dataport, fridge, hair dryer, no phone.

The Old Farmhouse B&B 🏵🏵   The driveway is flanked by meadows and ancient orchards, and is a fitting prelude to this heritage B&B. The original white clapboard farmhouse has been lovingly renovated, retaining much of its yesteryear charm, but with modern conveniences such as private bathrooms, a private entrance, and a sophisticated European ambience. Cascading geraniums fall from porches and private patios; the farm-style kitchen is warm and inviting, and guest rooms are comfortable and spacious. A separate cottage is especially romantic. The homesite was staked in 1860 by black American settlers from Kentucky, who had been recruited north in return for their vote that British Columbia join Canada rather than the US.

1077 North End Rd., Salt Spring Island, BC V8K 1L9. ℂ 250/537-4113. Fax 250/537-4969. farmhouse@saltspring.com. 4 units. May–Oct C$170 (US$110.50). Closed Nov–Apr. Rates include breakfast. Extra person C$30 (US19.50). MC, V. Children not accepted. **Amenities:** Lounge. *In room:* No phone.

Salt Springs Spa Resort 🏵   This spa resort is the only spot where the island's salty spring waters can be enjoyed. The day spa offers a variety of facials, body wraps, and massages, and even if spa-ing isn't your thing, Salt Springs is a great getaway, made up of several one-, two-, and three-bedroom A-frame chalets. A handful are in the forest, but most sport an oceanview, looking across Trincomali Channel to Wallace Island, a marine park. All chalets have full kitchen, wood-burning fireplace, wide porch with barbecue, and an oversize, two-person mineral tub in addition to a regular bathtub. Clamming gear and crab traps are available for those wanting to try their luck on the beach across the road.

1460 North Beach Rd., Salt Spring Island, BC V8K 1J4. © **800/665-0039** or 250/537-4111. Fax 537-2939. www.saltspringspa.com. 12 chalets. Mid-June–mid-Sept C$239 (US$155) 1-bedroom; C$269–$299 (US$175–$194) 2- and 3-bedroom. Mid-Sept–Oct and Mar–Apr C$149–$169 (US$97–$110) 1-bedroom; C$199–$229 (US$77–$149) 2- and 3-bedroom. Nov–Feb C$119–$139 (US$77–$90) 1-bedroom; C$169–$199 (US$110–$129) 2- and 3-bedroom. 2-night minimum stay in summer, 3-night minimum holiday weekends. Nightly rates offered in low season. Weekly rates available. Extra person C$35 (US$23). Children not accepted. **Amenities:** Spa; limited water-sports equipment; bike rental; game room; coin-op washer and dryer. *In room:* Kitchen.

INEXPENSIVE

Salt Spring Island Hostel ⊛ *(Kids* *(Value* Here's budget accommodation that's worth rhapsodizing about, at least for backpackers, and for boomers looking to relive their youth. Located down a twisty, cedar-flanked road, 15 minutes from the Fulford Harbour ferry dock, it's a real find—literally. Situated on 10 forested acres along Cusheon Creek, the hostel is a collection of tepees, dormitories, tent camping, and enchanting tree houses, designed to give Pooh Bear a run for his honey. The lodge, a higgledy-piggledy two-storey home, has a comfy shared guest lounge and large kitchen, as well as dorm rooms (men only, women only, and mixed) with private bathrooms, plus two private family rooms, one with ensuite shower and bathroom. The wood stove in the common room is a magnet for meeting fellow travelers, as is the nightly campfire, although you're just as likely to share a barbecue, a game of volleyball, or a walk around the many surrounding trails.

640 Cusheon Lake Rd., Salt Spring Island, BC V8K 2C2. © **250/537-4149.** www.beacom.com/ssihostel. Units vary: 1 6-bed women's dorm, 1 4-bed men's dorm, 1 4-bed mixed dorm, 2 family suites, 1 adult treehouse, 1 family treehouse, 3 tepees. Mar–Oct C$15.50 (US$10) tepee; C$19.50 (US$13) single occupancy dorm; C$60 (US$39) family suite; C$70 (US$46) adult treehouse and family treehouse. Extra person C$19.50 (US$13). Children 6–12 C$7.75–$17.50 (US$5–$11). Children 5 and under stay free w/parents. MC. Closed Nov–Feb. **Amenities:** Lounge. *In room:* No phone.

WHERE TO DINE

Bousaouki Greek Cafe ✶✶ GREEK   With a lovely view of Ganges Harbour, and a delightful waterfront patio, Bousaouki is one of the few ethnic eateries you'll find on Salt Spring Island. It recently changed hands, and improvements are noticeable. The decor is cheery, the atmosphere is casual, and food, deliciously authentic. Selections include all the classics such as Ouzo cake—which oozes with Ouzo, is glazed in Ouzo, and is topped with half a pear and fresh cream. In summer, kebabs and souvlakis are barbecued on the deck.

115 Fulford Ganges Rd., Grace Point Sq. ℂ 250/537-4181. Reservations recommended July–Aug. Main courses C$10–$20 (US$6.50–$12). MC, V. Mon–Thurs 10am–3pm; Fri–Sat 10am–8pm.

Hastings House ✶✶✶ PACIFIC NORTHWEST   Impeccable cuisine, attentive service, and a gracious setting have helped make Hastings House one of the most sought-after destination restaurants—and inns—in the Pacific Northwest (see "Where to Stay," above). The superb, multicourse menus change daily; many of the ingredients come from the estate's gardens and orchards. Dinner is a sophisticated, evening-long affair, starting with cocktails and canapés served by the fireplace, then continuing through five courses; hence there's only one sitting each night. The choice of entrees always features Salt Spring lamb, the house specialty, as well as three other selections. The Snug Lounge, a cosy retreat away from the main dining room, offers less formal dining. If you're a true foodie, ask for the "kitchen table," and front row seats to the chef and his artistry.

160 Upper Ganges Rd. ℂ 250/537-2362. Reservations required. Jacket required for men. 5-course prix fixe dinner C$85 (US$55.25). AE, DC, MC, V. June–mid-Oct daily seating at 7:30pm; mid-Oct–mid-Nov and mid-Mar–May daily seating at 7pm. Closed mid-Nov–mid-Mar.

House Piccolo ✶✶✶ SCANDINAVIAN CONTINENTAL   This small blue-and-white farmhouse-turned-restaurant is wonderfully intimate. Two-person tables are scattered through two connecting country-style dining rooms accented with copper kettles set high on shelves. Everything on the European-styled menu is enticing, particularly the fresh bread, broiled sea scallop brochettes, and roasted British Columbia venison with juniper berries. Save room for homemade ice cream or the signature chocolate terrine. House Piccolo recently garnered coveted recognition by Chaine des Rôtisseurs, an international gastronomic society dedicated to the promotion of fine dining around the world.

108 Hereford Ave. ℂ 250/537-1844. Reservations recommended July–Sept. Main courses C$25–$32 (US$16–$21). DC, MC, V. May–Sept 5–10pm; Oct–Apr 5–8pm.

Moby's Marine Pub ✶✶ PUB FARE   This is a contemporary marine pub with big beams, multilevel wood floors, and great views of Ganges Harbour from cathedral-size windows. It's a local favorite, especially on live entertainment nights when an eclectic mix of R&B, folk, jazz, and rock, takes to the stage. If it's a local headliner, such as Valdy, performing, get there early to grab a table. The menu includes burgers and fajitas alongside savory entrees like Caribbean fish pot (to die for) and Louisiana lamb curry. Jazz on Sunday nights is a dinner tradition. Enjoying any one of the 10 beers on tap is a lively affair. Moby's deck hangs over the water, within inches of bullwhip kelp and minnows. It's a great place to catch some summer rays over a cold one.

124 Upper Ganges Rd. ℂ **250/537-5559.** Main courses C$8–$17 (US$5–$11). MC, V. Sun–Thurs 10am–midnight; Fri–Sat 10am–1am.

Tree House Cafe ✶ CAFE   Set in the heart of Ganges, this funky 12-seat cafe spills over onto a larger patio that stakes its claim around and beneath a sprawling old plum tree. In summer, the place is jammed, in part because of the folksy musical entertainment, but also because of the great food that includes everything from Thai peanut tofu and vegetarian chili, to burgers and BLTs. The organic Salt Spring coffee sidelines Starbucks.

In the heart of Ganges, under the plum tree. ℂ **250/537-5379.** Main courses C$5–$7 (US$3–$5). MC, V. Oct–May daily 8am–3pm; June–Sept daily 8am–11pm.

EXPLORING SALT SPRING ISLAND

The bustling seaside village of **Ganges** ✶✶✶ belies the notion that the Gulf Islands are sleepy hideaways. The sheer number of realtors is a gauge of Salt Spring's "love-at-first-sight" appeal. Historic buildings and bright new commercial structures harbor banks and shopping malls, liquor stores, cafes, bakeries, and a busy marina. As the cultural center of the island, you'll also find several quality galleries of locally crafted goods. In spring, this showcase expands into **Artcraft,** an exhibition of more than 250 Gulf Island artisans. Housed at Mahon Hall, Artcraft runs May through September daily from 10am to 5pm. Call ℂ **250/537-0899.** Salt Spring's Saturday morning **farmer's market,** held in Centennial Park in the heart of Ganges, is another summer must-see (www.saltspringmarket.com). This weekly gathering is a glorious melee of islanders and visitors, dogs and children, craftspeople, food vendors, jugglers, and musicians. Everything for sale must be handmade or homegrown, so it's as much a feast for the eyes as it is for the stomach. Go to **www.salt**

springmarket.com for more information. As good as it is, the farmer's market pales in comparison to the **Salt Spring Island Fall Fair,** an annual 2-day event held toward the end of September. Filled with all the sights, sounds, tastes, and smells of a good old-fashioned country fair, it showcases everything from award-winning livestock and home-baked pies, alongside rides and classic games like balloon darts. The sheepdog trials are superb. Inspired to explore Ganges further? Ask the bartender at **Moby's Marine Pub,** 124 Upper Ganges Rd. (© **250/537-5559**), about Moby's kayaking, boat, and fishing charters. (See "Where to Dine," above). Nearby in **Fulford Harbour, St. Paul's Church** is another worthwhile place to visit. Founded by a Roman Catholic missionary in 1878, it was built by immigrants from Hawaii who worked for the Hudson's Bay Company, descendants of whom still live on the island.

RUCKLE PROVINCIAL PARK 𐀀𐀀

This 1,070-acre park starts out along 8km (5 miles) of shoreline around **Beaver Point,** and sweeps up to an expanse of open and grassy meadow. Once owned by the Ruckle family, part of the park is still operated as a sheep farm, and several of the original buildings still stand. It's by far the easiest hiking ground on Salt Spring Island, with an abundance of wildlife, so remember your binoculars. The park has 70 walk-in campsites with fire pits (firewood is provided in the summer), plus some new group sites, a picnic area, a large kitchen shelter, drinking water, several pit toilets, and a security patrol for the entire camping area. From mid-March to October, a camping fee of C$10 (US$6.50) per night applies, and you must reserve your campsite in advance. Camping is free from November to mid-March, on a first-come, first-served basis. No firewood is supplied November through mid-March. Call **Discover Camping** at © **877-559-2115** or 250/539-2115 for reservations and information, or log on to **www.discovercamping.ca**.

VESUVIUS

Located at the western edge of Salt Spring Island, the village, which consists of old seaside cottages knitted together by winding lanes, got its name for its wonderful sunsets that are made all the more dramatic by the clouds of smoke that spew forth across the Stuart Channel, from a pulp mill in Crofton, on Vancouver Island. Unfortunately, this artistry also carries an off-putting pulpy odor. **BC Ferries** runs a regular service across the Stuart Channel, to Crofton.

One-way fares are C$6 (US$4) for adults, C$3 (US$2) children; C$17 (US$11) for a standard-size vehicle. The crossing takes 20 minutes. A time-honored pit stop is **The Vesuvius Inn,** 805 Vesuvius Bay Rd. (✆ **250/537-2312**). A replica of the original 1873 inn, which was built by a wandering Portuguese sailor, it serves home-cooked meals and 15 kinds of wine by the glass. Next to the Vesuvius ferry dock is a little Catholic chapel known as **The Ark,** 782 Vesuvius Bay Rd. (✆ **250/537-9451**), now an intriguing home/gallery.

2 The Pender Islands

Known for their secluded coves, beautiful beaches, and islets, the Penders are a tranquil escape, and a boater's nirvana. With a population of barely 2,000, they remain small enough that, as one resident says, "The sight of another human being still conjures up a smile!"

The Penders are actually two islands, linked by a short wooden bridge, which spans a canal between **Bedwell and Browning harbours.** Until 1903, when the canal was dug, island pioneers were forced to haul their boats laboriously over a wide neck of land known as "Indian Portant." Centuries before, the Coast Salish, a local First Nations group, used to set up seasonal camps in the area, and several shell middens, some dating from 4500 B.C., have revealed thousands of artifacts, including carved spoons and lip ornaments.

With several parks, picnic areas, and overnight camping facilities, the Penders are a delight to tour by car or bicycle. Picturesque cottages, orchards, and a dozen or so artisan's home galleries add to the idyllic setting. The nine-hole golf course is a pleasant diversion, as is the golf Frisbee–throwing park, where the "tees" are metal poles tucked in between trees. The real trick is to keep your Frisbee from ricocheting off the trees on its flight to the target.

ESSENTIALS
GETTING THERE
BC Ferries sails to **Otter Bay,** on the northwest side of North Pender Island. Pleasure boats can dock at **Bedwell Harbour,** on the southern cove where North and South Pender meet. See "Getting There," at the beginning of the chapter, for information on ferry fares and schedules.

VISITOR INFORMATION
The **Pender Island Visitor Information Centre,** 2332 Otter Bay Rd. (P.O. Box 75), Pender Island, BC V0N 2M1 (✆ **250/629-6541**),

is located just up from the ferry terminal at Otter Bay. Open daily from mid-May to Labor Day (first Monday in September). Closed from September to mid-May. Ask for information at local businesses during the off-season.

GETTING AROUND

Pender Island Carriage & Taxi (© **250/629-6050**) provides service to various points around the islands. Bike rentals are available at **Otter Bay Marina** (© **250/629-3579**) at C$8 (US$5) per day.

WHERE TO STAY & DINE

Alice's Shangri-La Oceanfront B&B 𝒦𝒦 (North Pender) Perched on Pender's Oaks Bluff with 10 acres of wilderness at its feet, this sprawling house has a billion-dollar view plus 1,676 m² (5,500 sq. ft.) of wraparound balconies to drink it all in. Staying here is like nesting in your own deluxe aerie, complete with private deck and Jacuzzi. Guest rooms have fireplaces, and are comfortably furnished. The Star Trek Suite is for unabashed "Trekkies": with planetary swirls and galactic formations covering the walls. Escaping to the hammock outside has a more grounding effect. On the off chance that you tire of the view, or of your own company, guests share a comfortable games room with piano and pool table.

5909 Pirate's Rd., Pender Island, BC V0N 2M2. © **877/629-6555** or 250/629-3433. Fax 250/629-2007. www.alicesoceanfrontbnb.com. 3 units. May–Oct C$170–$195 (US$110–$127). Nov–Apr C$130–$150 (US$85–$98). Rates include full breakfast. MC, V. Pets accepted. Children not accepted. **Amenities:** Jacuzzi; complimentary bikes; game room. *In room:* TV, fridge, coffeemaker, no phone.

Bedwell Harbour Island Resort 𝒦𝒦 *Kids* (South Pender)   This seaside resort is as popular with families as it is with American boaters. Parents can sip drinks on poolside chaise longues, while youngsters enjoy the extensive children's programs. Or, you can give kayaking or ski-dooing a try. Accommodations range from deluxe two-bedroom villas complete with kitchens, dining rooms, balconies, and living rooms with fireplaces, to secluded two-bedroom cabins, studios, and budget-priced guest rooms. The marina provides 180 moorings and has a boating supplies store. The bright, airy **Poet's Cove restaurant** has a wide-ranging menu, so that on top of kid-friendly burgers, you can enjoy pan-seared scallops or Caribbean spiced pork tenderloin. The **Poet's Cove pub and bistro,** which opens in mid-April for the summer season, is usually jam-packed, likely because satellite TV is in short supply on a boat. The resort has bold plans to create a year-round destination, including the building of a deluxe spa. If permits are granted and things get under-way, construction might be evident during your stay. *Note:* The resort will be renamed during this transformation, to **Poet's Cove Resort at Bedwell Harbour.**

9801 Spalding Rd., South Pender Island, BC V0N 2M3. © **800/663-2899** or 250/629-3212. Fax 250/629-6777. www.bedwell-harbour.com. 24 units. May–Labor Day C$119 (US$77) standard; C$159–$179 (US$103–$116) studio and 2-bedroom cabin; C$269–$339 (US$175–$220) 2–3 bedroom villa. Rates up to 50% lower Mar–Apr. Extra person C$12 (US$8). Children 16 and under stay free in parents' room. MC, V. Closed Labor Day–Feb. **Amenities:** Restaurant, pub; large heated outdoor pool; 2 outdoor tennis courts; extensive water-sports rentals; children's programs. *In-room:* Fridge, coffeemaker, hair dryer.

Inn on Pender Island ✦ (North Pender)   Situated next to Prior Centennial Provincial Park, this unpretentious inn offers a choice of comfortable lodge rooms or studio log cabins, many with ocean-views and some with private Jacuzzis. Lodge rooms are clean and spacious; cabins have fireplaces and deck swings. Refreshingly, the inn welcomes children. **Memories at the Inn** is a fully licensed restaurant, and while the decor's a bit plain, it's a popular choice for affordable dining. The homemade pizza is exceptionally good.

4709 Canal Rd. (P.O. Box 72), Pender Island, BC V0N 2M0. © **800/550-0172** or 250/629-3353. Fax 250/629-3167. www.innonpender.com. 12 units. May–Sept C$79–$89 (US$51–$58) lodge room; C$130 (US$85) cabin. Oct–Apr C$69–$89 (US$45–$58) lodge room; C$120–$130 (US$78–$85) cabin. Rates include continen-tal breakfast. MC, V. Small pets accepted. **Amenities:** Restaurant; Jacuzzi. *In room:* TV/VCR, coffeemaker.

Oceanside Inn ✦✦ (North Pender)   You can't beat the location: minutes from the ferry terminal and nestled on secluded oceanfront. Refurbished in 2000, every guest room is well appointed, and includes extras like oversize towels and aromatherapy toiletries. The surrounding apple and pear orchards make it extra private, which is all the more appreciated when skinny-dipping in your very own Jacuzzi. Two-night packages include full breakfast daily and a four-course dinner for two. Check out the new health club; the only one on the island. The inn's **Oceanside Restaurant** is licensed and is reserved exclusively for guests. The food is unfussily prepared and tasty. The Gulf Island salmon is a house specialty, and is often freshly caught only hours before.

4230 Armadale Rd. (P.O. Box 50), Pender Island, BC V0N 2M0. © **250/629-6691.** www.penderisland.com. 4 units. June–Sept C$449–$539 (US$292) 2 nights. Oct–Mar (C$349–$429 (US$227–$279) 2 nights. Apr–May C$399–$489 (US$259–$318) 2 nights. 2-night minimum stay. Rates include breakfast and one dinner for two. V. Children not accepted. **Amenities:** Restaurant, lounge; health club. *In room:* Fridge, hair dryer, no phone.

Sahhali Serenity Oceanfront B&B Inn ⭐⭐⭐ *Finds* (North Pender) Sitting atop a majestic bluff with incomparable vistas, this intimate, stunningly designed B&B puts you eye-to-eye with eagles. Be careful as you wend your way up the 0.5-km (⅓-mile) gravel road. Guest rooms are so pampering, there's virtually no need (and even less desire) to leave the premises. Features include vaulted ceilings, woodburning fireplaces, wet bars, private Jacuzzis, and double marble showers. Glass walls are a beautiful touch that manage to be classic yet futuristic all at the same time. Although children are not accepted in the main house, a self-contained guest cottage, complete with private Jacuzzi, barbecue, and full kitchen opened in 2001, and is ideal for families.

5915 Pirates Rd. (P.O. Box 83), Pender Island, BC V0N 2M0. ✆ 877/625-2583 or 250/629-3664. www.sahhali-serenity.com. 4 units. Mar–Sept C$195–$275 (US$127–$179). Oct–Feb C$125–$235 (US$81–$153). Rates include full breakfast. Extra person C$20 (US$13). MC, V. Pets accepted w/prior approval. **Amenities:** Complimentary canoe. *In room:* TV/VCR, fridge, coffeemaker.

EXPLORING THE PENDERS
NORTH PENDER

The larger of the two islands, **North Pender** is more populated and more developed than its southerly neighbor. Surprisingly, there's no real town center in the traditional sense on North Pender, so the modern **Driftwood Centre** (on Bedwell Harbour Rd. near Razor Point Rd.) in the center of the island, does double duty as a mini-mall and the nucleus of island life. The **Saturday Market** (May through October) is a fine place for mixing with the locals, sampling island-grown produce, and browsing through artisan stalls. Otherwise, most activity happens around **Otter Bay,** where the ferries arrive, and **Port Browning.** At **Port Washington,** northwest of Otter Bay, you'll find orchards and charming old cottages, reminiscent of a turn-of-the-century coastal village. Nearby, **Otter Bay Marina** (✆ **250/629-3579**) is a good place to rent boats, kayaks, and bikes. Check out **Kayak Pender Island,** at the Otter Bay Marina (✆ **250/629-6939;** www.kayakpenderisland.com), for guided kayaking tours and lessons. Two-hour guided tours are C$35 (US$23) for adults, C$30 (US$19.50) for children 11 and under; 3-hour tours are C$45 (US$29.50) per person; lessons are C$50 (US$32.50) each. **Port Browning Marina,** 4605 Oak Rd. (✆ **250/629-3493**), on the northern cove where North and South Pender meet, is an inviting "watering hole," with First Nations decor, including a totem pole. It's cheerfully downscale from the **Bedwell Harbour Island Resort,** on the other side of the narrow neck of land that separates the two islands, and a definite local favorite for good food and relaxed fun. (See "Where to Stay & Dine," above, for a review of the Bedwell Harbour Island Resort.) North Pender parks include **Medicine Beach,** one of the last wetlands in the Gulf Islands, and home to many native plants once used for food and medicine; and **Roseland,** a new, 568-acre park that includes a headland, a freshwater lake, beaches, and lots of forest. Take the trail past the Davidson home to the headland, to see the rotting remains of a 220-year-old Indian canoe.

SOUTH PENDER

This remote part of the island has always attracted independent, sometimes eccentric, fun-loving spirits who don't mind the isolation. Although the only services to be found are at the **Bedwell Marina,** 9801 Spalding Rd. (© **250/629-3212**), part of the Bedwell Harbour Island Resort (see "Where to Stay & Dine," above), there are lots of beaches, parks, and trails to enjoy. Hikers should head for **Mount Norman Regional Park.** Mount Norman is the highest point on the Penders. The gravel access road up to Mount Norman is uninteresting, but the 1-km (0.5-mile) hike to the summit is well worth the effort; the panoramas are stunning. From Mount Norman Regional Park, you can access **Beaumont Marine Provincial Park** 🐾🐾🐾, without a doubt the prettiest marine park in the Gulf Islands; its picturesque coastal wilderness seemingly tamed by gentle waters, moss-covered rocks, and grassy verges. It's about a 40-minute hike into the park from Mount Norman. Another favorite recreation area, **Brookes Point,** is one of the last undeveloped headlands in the Gulf Islands. The coastal bluff is ecologically important as it hosts rare types of native grass, and more than one hundred bird species, some of which are endangered. Large pods of **killer whales** sometimes swim right under the point in the nearby kelp beds, as do mink, seal, otter, and Dall's porpoise. Tidal pools contain abalone, sea anemones, and coral.

3 Galiano Island

Galiano Island is a magnet for outdoor enthusiasts. It's a long, skinny island that stretches more than 26km (16 miles) from top to bottom, and is no more than 2km (1.5 miles) across. Two harbors and several parks provide abundant opportunity to hike, camp, fish, boat, and birdwatch; activities that have, in fact, been hard won. Until recently, logging was Galiano's biggest industry, and was changing the landscape dramatically. Determined that clear-cuts should cease, the community rallied, and has managed to purchase key tracts of land with the intention that it return to, and remain, as wilderness. Remnants of lumber operations are still evident in parts, including a shoreline strewn with salt-laden, sun-bleached logs. In spite of their activism, the folks on Galiano are actually very laid back. It's as if they've not quite outgrown their obsession with growing marijuana back in the seventies. For boomers, it's strangely comforting.

Most of the 1,000 or so permanent residents live on the southern part of the island, close to **Sturdies Bay,** which, for all intents and purposes, is the island's downtown. So this is where you'll find accommodations, restaurants, and stores, as well as in the surrounding areas of **Georgeson Bay, Montague Harbour,** and **Spotlight Cove.** North Galiano is much wilder, and although you'll find pockets of housing, the country is dense with cedar and fir trees, maple and alder stands.

ESSENTIALS
GETTING THERE
BC Ferries sails to **Sturdies Bay,** on the southern tip of the island. Boaters dock at **Montague Harbour,** on the west coast, about a 20-minute drive from Sturdies Bay.

VISITOR INFORMATION
Contact the **Galiano Chamber of Commerce,** 2590 Sturdies Bay Rd., (P.O. Box 73), Galiano Island, BC V0N 1P0 (© **250/539-2233;** www.galianoisland.com). Open daily in July and August; on weekends from September to June.

GETTING AROUND
The **Go Galiano Island Shuttle** (© **250/539-0202**) provides year-round taxi service. You can also rent mopeds from **Galiano Mopeds,** at Montague Harbour (© **250/539-3443**), and bicycles from **Galiano Bicycle,** 36 Burrill Rd., Sturdies Bay (© **250/539-9906**). Mopeds are available from May to September and cost C$18 (US$12) per hour. Bike rentals are C$28 (US$18) for a 24-hour period.

WHERE TO STAY
Bellhouse Inn ⋆⋆ Built in the 1880s, this scenic waterfront farmhouse is surrounded by meadows, grazing sheep, and orchards. Views of Active Pass are up close and personal, whether you're

playing croquet on the lawn, lazing on the sandy beach, or sprawling in a hammock. Guest rooms are small, though tastefully decorated, with lovely bathrooms and private balconies. Thankfully, the main lounge is large and extremely comfortable. The owners will arrange an in-room massage, just in case lazing around hasn't worked out all the muscle knots. This inn even provides guests with hot water bottles—not because the rooms are cold, but because the owners are English—so have a natural predisposition to these homey comforts. In summer you'll probably spend most of your time on the expansive decks, unless you're tempted to go sailing; the owners also charter a 13-m (43-ft.) yacht.

29 Farmhouse Rd. (P.O. Box 16), Site 4 Galiano Island, BC V0N 1P0. ℭ **800/ 970-7464** or 250/539-5667. Fax 250/539-5316. www.bellhouseinn.com. 3 units. June–Sept C$95–$195 (US$62–$127) standard; C$125 (US$81) cabin. Oct–May C$85–$125 (US$55–$81) standard; C$90 (US$59) cabin. 2-night minimum stay required in cabin. Rate includes full breakfast. Children not accepted. **Amenities:** Lounge, library, in-room massage. *In room:* Hair dryer, no phone.

Bodega Resort 𝕽 *(Kids)* *(Value)*   Located near Spanish Hills, at the island's northern end, this hilltop resort and sheep farm is a rambling collection of hand-hewn cottages, offering majestic views and basic comforts. The immaculate two-level log chalets are simply decorated and feature full kitchens, making them ideal for families. They do feature stained-glass doors and tasteful wood furnishings, however—pretty touches. While kiwi and grape vines clamber over the main farmhouse, landscaped gardens are sprinkled with Celtic standing stones, ponds, and miles of hiking trails. The resort has riding stables, so you can climb on and ride clear across the island, if you want. Riding is not included in the room rates. Costs are C$25 (US$16) for adults and C$15 (US$10) for children.

120 Manastee Rd. (P.O. Box 115), Galiano Island, BC V0N 1P0. ℭ **250/539-2677.** Fax 250/539-2677. www.cedarplace.com/bodega. 7 units. Year-round C$90 (US$58.50). Extra person C$10–$20 (US$6.50–$13). MC, V. **Amenities:** Lounge. *In room:* Kitchen, no phone.

Driftwood Village Resort 𝕽 *(Kids)* *(Value)*   Set in a delightful, meandering garden filled with fruit trees, every one of these 11 cottages is charming, cozy, and decorated with original artwork. While various bed-linen combinations give each cabin a different feel, all cottages have oceanfront views, private bathrooms, well-equipped kitchens, and private decks with barbecues. All but one of the cottages have wood-burning fireplaces. There's a Jacuzzi in the center of the garden—a great spot to stargaze. A footpath leads down to a sandy beach on Matthews Point, one of Galiano's many birdwatching spots.

205 Bluff Rd. East, Galiano Island, BC V0N 1P0. ℂ **888/240-1466** or 250/539-5544. www.driftwoodcottages.com. 11 units. Mid-June–mid-Sept C$98–$149 (US$64–$97). Mid-Sept–mid-Oct C$79–$129 (US$51–$84). Mid-Oct–mid-June C$65–$120 (US$42–$78). Extra person C$10 (US$6.50). Children 12 and under stay free in parents' cottage. MC, V. Pets accepted. **Amenities:** Jacuzzi; free ferry pick-up/drop-off. *In room:* TV, kitchen, no phone.

Galiano Inn 𝒜𝒜𝒜   Located only 2 blocks from the ferry dock, this Mediterranean-style country inn, which opened in 2001, exudes West Coast ambience. Furnishings are elegant, and all guest rooms overlook Active Pass, with private balconies or terraces, fireplaces, and ensuite bathrooms featuring Jacuzzis or soaker tubs—with 24-karat gold fixtures! The **Atrevida! restaurant** is fast becoming an island favorite (see "Where to Dine," below). The full-service **Oceanfront Spa** opens in summer 2002, offering a number of luxurious spa treatments, massage, hydrotherapy, and a steam room.

134 Madrona Dr., Galiano Island, BC V0N 1P0. ℂ **877/530-3939** or 250/539-3388. Fax 250/539-3338. www.galianoinn.com. 10 units. Year-round C$185–$225 (US$120–$146). Rates include breakfast. Extra person C$25 (US$16). MC, V. Children not accepted. **Amenities:** Restaurant, lounge; spa (opening summer 2002); laundry service. *In room:* Hair dryer, no phone.

Island Time B&B 𝒜𝒜𝒜   Standing in the living room is like being on the prow of a ship heading out to sea, because of the amazing views. If you look through the telescope, focused due North onto Grouse Mountain, above Vancouver, you can actually see skiers slaloming down the slopes. Add deep-seated sofas and crackling fireplaces to the picture, and you might never want to leave this place. Guest rooms are exceptional. All have fireplaces; one has two marble bathrooms as well as a double Jacuzzi. Shared guest areas include a movie-viewing lounge and library. Recreational facilities outside, such as tennis, table tennis, and a universal gym, make this bed-and-breakfast more like a mini resort.

952 Sticks Allison Rd., Galiano Island, BC V0N 1P0. ℂ **877/588-3506** or 250/539-3506. Fax 250/539-3507. www.gulfislands.com/islandtime. 3 units. Mid-May–June C$135–$195 (US$88–$62). July–early Sept C$175–$215 (US$114–$140). Early Sept–Dec C$125–$185 (US$81–$120). Jan–mid-May C$115–$175 (US$75–$114). 2-night minimum June–Aug. Rates include full breakfast. MC, V. Pets accepted w/prior approval. Children not accepted. **Amenities:** Lounge; 1 night-lit outdoor tennis court; Jacuzzi; free ferry pick-up/drop-off. *In room:* No phone.

Woodstone Country Inn ✿✿✿   This elegantly classy inn is set amid towering fir trees overlooking an expanse of meadow and cultivated gardens. In summer, both meadow and garden overflow with flowers, and birds are everywhere. Inside, the inn is graciously decorated with quality antiques, folk art, and exotic sculptures, all garnered during the owner's travels around the world. Guest rooms are exceptionally spacious and bright, with bathrooms that positively sparkle. Pampering touches include luxury Lord & Mayfair toiletries. All main floor guest rooms have private patios. The inn's restaurant is one of the finest in the Gulf Islands (see "Where to Dine," below).

743 Georgeson Bay Rd., RR1, Galiano Island, BC V0N 1P0. ✆ 888/339-2022 or 250/539-2022. Fax 250/539-5198. www.gulfislands.com/woodstone. 12 units. Mid-May–mid-Oct C$115–$185 (US$75–$120) 2 nights. Mid-Oct–Nov and Feb–mid-May C$105–$185 (US$68–$120) 2 nights. 2-night minimum stay. Rates include breakfast, afternoon tea, 4-course dinner for two. AE, MC, V. Closed Dec–Jan. Children not accepted. **Amenities:** Restaurant, lounge. *In room:* Hair dryer, no phone.

WHERE TO DINE

Atrevida! ✿✿✿ PACIFIC NORTHWEST   Galiano Island's only oceanfront restaurant, this dining room is a treat. Watch the ferries ply through Active Pass as you chow down on garlic prawns with creamy risotto or Italian-style lamb shanks braised in red wine. If you've a ferry wait, park your car in the lineup and head over to the outdoor patio to chill out over a cold drink. The West Coast crab pot is hard to resist, and it beats ferry food any day.

In the Galiano Inn, 134 Madrona Dr. ✆ **250/539-3388**. Reservations required. Breakfast C$9 (US$6); lunch C$8–$14 (US$5–$9); dinner C$20–$23 (US$13–$15). MC, V. May–Oct daily 7am–10pm. Nov–Apr Mon–Fri 5–9pm; Sat–Sun 7am–9pm.

La Berengerie FRENCH   Shrouded by evergreen clematis, this tiny log cabin is a jewel in the forest. Floral linen tablecloths, soft classical music, and watercolor paintings by local artists set a romantic tone. The food rarely disappoints. Described as French-Algerian, a canny use of herbs brings a Middle Eastern flavor to classics like duck à l'orange and red snapper with gingered tomato sauce. A four-course menu features a choice of appetizers, entrees, and desserts. The homemade breads and comfort desserts are a must. In summer, there's also a sundeck and a garden patio.

Montague Harbour Rd. ✆ **250/539-5392**. Reservations recommended on weekends. 4-course prix fixe dinner C$27.50 (US$18). MC, V. Daily 5–9pm.

Hummingbird Pub ⟨⟩ PUB FARE Serving hearty pub grub at reasonable prices, the Hummingbird is the local watering hole. The classic West Coast cedar and beam architecture creates a warm atmosphere, and although there's no water view, the garden more than makes up for it. From mid-May to October, this resourceful pub runs its own shuttle bus to the ferry at Sturdies Bay, and from the Montague Park Marina. This tip could be of particular interest to boaters seeking some liquid libations on dry land.

47 Sturdies Bay Rd. ℂ 250/539-5472. Main courses C$7–$17 (US$4.50–$11). MC, V. Sun–Thurs 11am–midnight; Fri–Sat 11am–1am.

Woodstone Country Inn ⟨⟩⟨⟩ FRENCH/INTERNATIONAL This enchanting restaurant is one of the best on the Gulf Islands. Service is impeccable and the cuisine is a blend of classic French and vivid international flavors: roast halibut with a macadamia nut crust is prepared with a lemon-coconut sauce, while seared duck breast is served atop wild-rice pancakes with a Saskatoon berry sauce. Each day's menu offers a choice from three entrees (which determines what you'll pay) and also includes homemade bread, soup, and salad. Desserts are decadent, and the wine list is an interesting mix of Okanagan, Californian, and French vintages. There are no additional a la carte items.

743 Georgeson Bay Rd. ℂ 250/539-2022. Reservations required. 4-course dinner C$22–$29.50 (US$14–$19). AE, DC, MC, V. Sun–Thurs 5–9pm; Fri–Sat 5–10pm.

EXPLORING GALIANO ISLAND

In and around **Sturdies Bay,** you'll find picturesque B&Bs, a few galleries, and a handful of shops. Nearby, **Bellhouse Provincial Park** ⟨⟩⟨⟩ is one of prettiest spots on the island, with a rocky, moss-covered peninsula, sculpted sandstone, and magnificent groves of coppery-red arbutus trees. Situated at the entrance to **Active Pass,** it's an ideal place to picnic and watch the myriad kinds of wildlife. Tides run up to 5 knots here, and the shoreline drops sharply into deep water, making it an excellent point to spincast for salmon. **Galiano Bluffs Park** ⟨⟩, another favorite area, is also at the entrance to Active Pass but sitting 120m (394 ft.) above it. The views from the bluffs deserve rave reviews. Watch BC Ferries' largest ships rumble past, take your binoculars and see eagles catching the updrafts, as well as seals, sea lions, and other marine life. Seasonal wildflowers are an equal delight. Go easy on the approach road; it has some serious potholes. **Montague Harbour Marina** (ℂ 250/ 539-5733) is a fun place to visit, if only to yacht watch or grab a light meal in the marina restaurant. While there, check out **Galiano Island Kayaking** (© **250/ 539-2442;** www.seakayak.bc.ca/tour). The 3-hour tours are C$38 (US$25) a person; full-day paddles are C$68 (US$44) a person.

MONTAGUE HARBOUR PROVINCIAL MARINE PARK 🐾🐾

One of the Gulf Islands' most popular provincial parks, here's where to watch giant American yachts arriving, and chattering kingfishers diving for salmon. Swim and beachcomb to your heart's content along gorgeous shell and gravel beaches, enjoy a picnic on the bluff, and search through shell middens dating back 3,000 years. The protected waters are perfect for beginner rowers, and hiking trails include an easy 3-km (2-mile) forest and beach walk around Gray peninsula. There are two caves along the southern shore, reached by foot at low tide, or by boat.

If you want to stay awhile, the park has two campgrounds: one with 15 walk-in sites for boaters and cyclists, another with 25 drive-in sites for motorists. *Note:* There are no RV hookups. There's a boat ramp, 23 mooring buoys, and a store. Free interpretive talks are offered during July and August. Check the **Nature House** for schedules. Buoys are C$6 (US$4) per vessel; campsites are C$15 (US$10) each. The campgrounds are open year-round. Call **Discover Camping** at © **800/689-9025** or 250/391-2300 for information and reservations, or go online to **www.discovercamping.ca.**

4 Mayne Island

Mayne has always been a transfer point between islands. This began in the 1860s, when prospectors rested up in Miners Bay before crossing the Georgia Strait on their way to the gold mines in the Fraser Valley and the Cariboo. But as gold fever faded, so did Mayne's importance, and today, stopovers are somewhat tamer. The 800 or so permanent residents like it this way, as it's enabled the island to retain much of its charm and heritage.

Because most of Mayne Island is privately owned, there are few public trails, so walkers and cyclists take to the network of hilly roads, traveling past 19th-century buildings, farms, beaches, and home studios. Avid cyclists could circuit Mayne in a day. There are numerous sheltered bays, including **Village Bay, Miners Bay,** and **Horton Bay,** all with docking facilities and accommodations that run the gamut from bare bones to luxurious. There are no public campgrounds on Mayne Island.

ESSENTIALS
GETTING THERE
BC ferries sails to **Village Bay,** on the northwest side of the island. Pleasure boaters dock at **Horton Bay,** at the southwest corner of the island.

VISITOR INFORMATION
Head to the **Mayne Island Community Chamber of Commerce (Windermere Realty)**, 425 Fernhill Rd. (P.O. Box 2), Mayne Island, BC V0N 2J0 (© **800/665-8577** or 250/539-2031; www.mayneislandchamber.ca).

GETTING AROUND
M.I.D.A.S. taxi company (© **250/539-3122**) offers pick-up and drop-off service to the ferry, as well as island tours.

WHERE TO STAY
A Coach-House on Oyster Bay B&B Inn 🌟🌟   Located on Oyster Bay, on the northwest corner of the island, this snazzy barn and tack-room renovation is filled with artwork and antiques. Spacious suites have many luxury touches, including private bathrooms, fireplaces, patios or balconies, and private entrances. The Landau, a converted hayloft, is the most romantic, with a four-poster bed, secluded deck, and private Jacuzzi. It adjoins a shared guest living room, where a 135-year-old square piano holds court. A path from the inn leads to a Jacuzzi perched just steps from the tide line, and to a pagoda a little farther on. Both spots are perfect for watching oyster catchers skim across the water. A neat touch: flashlights in each guest room, so night forays to the Jacuzzi don't have to depend on moonlight.

511 Bayview Dr., Mayne Island, BC V0N 2J0. © **888/629-6322250** or 250/539-3368. Fax 250/539-2236. www.acoachhouse.com. 3 units. Year-round C$130–$150 (US$84.50–$97.50). Rates include full breakfast. MC, V. Children not accepted. **Amenities:** Lounge; Jacuzzi; complimentary bikes. *In room:* Hair dryer, no phone.

Blue Vista Resort 🌟 *Value*   Blue Vista's value-for-money one- and two-bedroom cabins are ideal for family vacations. Comfortable, but not fancy, each of the blue-painted wood-framed units comes with a fully equipped kitchen, private bathroom, fireplace, deck, and barbecue. The resort's open, park-like setting encourages children to play with newfound friends. Complimentary bikes are available for guest use. If you're staying over a weekend, be sure to catch the resort's Saturday Sundaes, when they provide all the fixings for a delicious sundae. Somehow, each session becomes a contest between guests.

563 Arbutus Dr., Mayne Island, BC V0N 2J0. ℂ 877/535-2424 or 250/539-2463. Fax 250/539-2463. www.bluevistaresort.com. 8 units. Mid-May–Oct C$50–$95 (US$33–$62). Nov–mid-Jan and mid-Feb–mid-May C$45–$86 (US$29–$56). Weekly rates available. MC, V. Closed mid-Jan–mid-Feb. Pets accepted w/prior approval. **Amenities:** Complimentary bikes; free ferry pick-up/drop-off; coin-op washers and dryers. *In room:* Kitchen, no phone.

Oceanwood Country Inn 𝔊𝔊𝔊   This waterfront English country inn is as upscale as you can get on Mayne. Since it's a gated property, the deer haven't ravaged the gardens of tulips, irises, and other tasty morsels, as they have most Mayne gardens. Every guest suite is decorated in a floral or bird theme, with names like Kingfisher, Daffodil, and Geranium. Most are exceptionally romantic with deep-soaker bathtubs and private balconies. Many have fireplaces. The Wisteria Suite even has a sunken living room and private outdoor soaking tub—perfect for a moonlit soak *à deux*. The living room in the main lodge features a crackling fireplace, abundantly full bookshelves, board games, and good listening music. Enjoying dinner at Oceanwood's gourmet restaurant is a highlight of most people's stay (see "Where to Dine," below).

630 Dinner Bay Rd., Mayne Island, BC V0N 2J0. ℂ 250/539-5074. Fax 250/539-3002. www.oceanwood.com. 12 units. Mid-June–mid-Sept C$159–$329 (US$103–$214). Mar–mid-June and mid-Sept–Nov C$119–$279 (US$77–$181). 2-night stay required if staying over Sat. Rates include breakfast and afternoon tea. MC, V. Closed Dec–Feb. Children not accepted. **Amenities:** Restaurant, lounge, library; Jacuzzi; sauna; complimentary bikes. *In room:* Hair dryer, no phone.

WHERE TO DINE

Mayne Inn PACIFIC NORTHWEST   Perched on a grassy bank leading down to a would-be marina, the Mayne Inn could be so much more than it is. The marina concept was quashed by islanders who didn't want big American yachts disturbing their peace, so the inn makes do with a fairly decent restaurant, eight guest rooms, and a small, licensed TV lounge that gets particularly crowded when a hockey game is on. In summer, the deck's a quieter spot than the Spring Water Lodge (see below), and more family-friendly. Children can play on the grass while parents enjoy the views of Bennett Bay.

494 Arbutus Dr. ℂ 250/539-3122. Breakfast C$7 (US$4.50); lunch C$9 (US$6); dinner C$15 (US$10). MC, V. Daily 9am–8pm.

Oceanwood Country Inn 𝔊𝔊𝔊 PACIFIC NORTHWEST Opening onto a terrace overlooking the water, Oceanwood's restaurant dishes up extravagant daily creations. Four-course menus change nightly, but are posted a week in advance on notice boards throughout the island so diners can plan a visit according to their taste buds. Cuisine highlights fresh local ingredients, as imaginative to read as they are to experience. Try the Oceanwood day lilies stuffed with smoked salmon mousse, fennel snap bread and nasturtium flower oil, and flying fish roe and cornmeal soufflé with nettle cream. Oceanwood's wine list, too, is an award-winner.

In the Oceanwood Country Inn, 630 Dinner Bay Rd. *C* 250/539-5074. Reservations required. 4-course prix fixe dinner C$44 (US$29). MC, V. Daily 6pm.

Spring Water Lodge PUB FARE/PACIFIC NORTHWEST Built in the 1890s, this pub and restaurant is the heart of the Mayne Island community. In summer, people crowd the flower-brightened outdoor decks to watch the boats thread through Active Pass. In winter, the pub overflows with boisterous gossip. Live bands are often featured on Saturday nights. Food is good. Fish and chips are great. Onion rings are the best. Despite service that's rather offhand, it's a great place to kick back and grab a meal. Unfortunately, this good review doesn't extend to the guest rooms. Despite what you might hear, they are nothing to write home about, and the beach cabins are even less appealing.

400 Fernhill Rd. *C* 250/539-5521. Pub main courses C$7.50 (US$5); restaurant main courses C$19 (US$12). MC, V. Mid-May–mid-Sept daily 9am–9pm. Mid-Sept–mid-May Mon–Thurs 11am–8:30pm; Fri–Sun 9am–8:30pm. Pub open until 1am.

EXPLORING MAYNE ISLAND

Miners Bay *★★* is the hub of Mayne, housing a surprisingly well-stocked supermarket, a small library, and a bakery-cafe. The liquor store, which is actually only a counter with a separate till, is part of a store that has sold goods and groceries since World War I. On summer Saturdays, a small farmer's market is held outside the **Agricultural Hall,** which on other days doubles as a theater, bingo hall, and exhibition center. On the lawns opposite the Spring Water Lodge (see "Where to Dine," above), you'll find kayaks for rent from **Mayne Kayaks,** 411 Fernhill Rd. (*C* 250/539-5599; www.maynekayak.com). Rates range from C$26 (US$17) per person for a 2-hour rental, to C$45 (US$29) a person for a 24-hour rental fiberglass kayak, with an option to extend the rental. The **Mayne Island Museum,** dating from 1896, when it was a jail, now displays all manner of local artifacts from the early 1900s. Located on Fernhill Road, just up from the Springwater, it usually opens on July and August weekends, as well as holiday weekends, from 10am to 3pm. Admission is by donation; C$2 (US$1.20) is suggested.

The road from Miners Bay to **Georgina Point** ☀☀☀ and the **Active Pass Lighthouse** is the most picturesque on Mayne Island. En route, you'll pass **St. Mary Magdalene Anglican Church,** built in 1898, on a hill amidst a beautiful grove of red arbutus trees. Overlooking Active Pass, its steeple has been a landmark for sailors for more than a century. Many of the headstones in the mossy grave-yard are silent testament to Mayne Island's history. The lighthouse, now automated, is open daily, free, from 9am to 3pm, and is a great spot from which to see seals, seabirds, and the occasional whale. Because most of Mayne Island is privately owned, there are few pub-lic parks to hike. **Mount Parke Park** ☀ however, is one exception. Although many islanders have "back routes" to the top of Mount Parke itself, officially, there's only one public hiking trail up, and it's a fairly strenuous 30- to 40-minute uphill hike. At 255m (836 ft.), it's the highest point on Mayne, and if you can forgive the obligatory antennae towers, you'll be rewarded with wonderful views and maybe an air show of soaring eagles and turkey vultures. Cyclists must leave their bikes at the trailhead rack. Six beaches on the island are open to the public, but since a distinct lack of signs makes access to them easy to miss, keep your eyes peeled for road markers that lead down to the shoreline to avoid tromping on private land. Two of the best beaches for picnics are at **Georgina Point** and **Dinner Bay,** so-called because it once teemed with fish and shellfish. "When the tide goes out," the old prospector's slogan goes, "the table is laid for breakfast." **Bennett Bay** is pebbly, and home to herons, king-fishers, and unusual pink seashells. **Oyster Bay, Piggot Bay,** and **Campbell Bay** are good for swimming. The latter has eye-catching rock formations, which served as models for the artificial rocks around the killer whale pool in the Vancouver Aquarium.

5 Saturna Island

Time seems to have bypassed Saturna Island, making remote tran-quility the island's star attraction. Home to approximately 350 per-manent residents, Saturna is still fairly primitive. Covering an area of only 31 km² (19 sq. mi.), this strip of an island is great for hiking, boating, and communing with nature. It also boasts British Columbia's largest estate winery, **Saturna Island Vineyards,** which is worth the ferry trip alone.

Of all the Gulf Islands, Saturna is the most ecologically vigilant, and visitors quickly note the drawbridge mentality. Saturna people aren't unfriendly—they just prefer to keep their own company.

Laced with trails through mixed forest and marshland, the island is ideal for hikers, who usually head for **Winter Cove Marine Park,** a sanctuary to eagles, shore birds, kingfishers, seals, and otters. Kayakers will prefer **Thomson Park,** or **Cabbage Island Marine Park,** near **Tumbo Island,** while **Russell Reef** is the hot spot for family swimming. What commerce there is happens around the community centre at **Lyall Harbour,** where the ferry docks. Here you'll find a grocery store, pub, gas station, kayak rentals, and a gallery, as well as a couple of B&Bs. There are no public campgrounds.

ESSENTIALS
GETTING THERE
BC Ferries sails to **Lyall Harbour.** Most trips involve a transfer at Mayne island. Boaters dock at **Winter Cove Marine Park,** north of Lyall Harbour.

VISITOR INFORMATION
Head to the **Saturna Island General Store,** 101 Narvaez Bay Rd., Saturna Island, BC V0N 2Y0 (☏ **250/539-2936;** www.saturna tourism.bc.ca).

GETTING AROUND
If you arrive by foot, the **Saturna Island Shuttle** (☏ **250/539-5359**) operates a pick-up and touring service.

WHERE TO STAY & DINE
Breezy Bay B&B ☏ *(Kids)*   This charming 1890s heritage house lies in the heart of a 50-acre farm approximately 2km (1 mile) from the ferry dock. You enter beneath a canopy of century-old Lombardy poplars that gives way to gardens filled with walnut trees, maple, scented linden, and hawthorne. Inside, you'll find detailing, such as Victorian wainscoting and period wood paneling. The guest library is full of assorted titles to spark curiosity, while the spacious piano lounge is comfortable, without being pretentious. The three guest rooms are small, simply furnished, but inviting; they share two bathrooms. On the first floor, an outside veranda runs the length of the house, and overlooks the orchard, waterfowl pond, and pastures of sheep and llama. The beach at the end of the garden is ideal for swimming and launching kayaks. The kids will love it.

131 Payne Rd., Saturna Island, BC V0N 2Y0. ☏ **250/539-5957** or 250/539-3339. www.gulfislands.com/saturna/breezybay. 3 units. Apr–Sept C$65–$85 (US$42–$55). Rates include full breakfast. No credit cards. Closed Oct–Mar. **Amenities:** Lounge, library. *In room:* No phone.

Finds **Saturna Island Vineyards** ★★

The location is idyllic, and offers visitors more than just a taste of wine. Nestled between the Pacific Ocean, a soaring granite cliff face, and picturesque Campbell farm, these south-facing vineyards—the largest estate winery in British Columbia—are a pleasure to explore. The first wines from the 1998 harvest were released to critical acclaim and no wonder: Saturna has managed to lasso one of BC's finest winemakers, Eric Von Krosigk. Look for good Chardonnays and Merlots for less than C$20 (US$13) in the wine shop, as well as other merchandise. The vineyards are at 8 Quarry Rd. (P.O. Box 54), Saturna Island, BC V0N 2Y0 (© **877/918-3388** or 250/539-5139). They are open May through October from 11am to 4:30pm. Take East Point Rd. from Lyall Harbour, and then Harris Rd for 2.5km (1.5 miles).

Saturna Lodge & Restaurant ★★★ *(Kids)* Set amidst the rustic, rural charms of the island, a stone's throw from the critically acclaimed **Saturna Island Vineyards,** this elegant country inn comes as an unexpected delight. A revamp in 2000, as well as a change in ownership, has turned this place into a destination lodge offering deluxe, well-appointed guest rooms, all with views of Plumber Sound. Of note are private decks, ensuite bathrooms, and comfortable queen- or king-size beds. TV-hungry urbanites can cozy up in the downstairs lounge in front of the fireplace, or pick a VCR title from the lodge's small library. The other surprise is the quality of its small restaurant, where an ever-changing prix fixe menu features superb Pacific Northwest cuisine (Saturna Island lamb, organic produce, and local seafood). The wine list features many award-winning labels; on midsummer evenings, there's nothing better than a chilled Chardonnay on the outdoor deck overlooking the cove. If you're off on a day-long excursion, be sure to pre-order a picnic lunch.

130 Payne Rd. (P.O. Box 54), Saturna Island, BC V0N 2Y0. © **888/539-8800** or 250/539-2254. Fax 250-539-3091. www.saturnavineyards.com. 7 units. Mid-June–Sept C$135–$195 (US$88–$127). Mid-May–mid-June and Oct–mid-May C$120–$175 (US$78–$114). Rates include full breakfast. Children 12 and under stay free in parents' room. MC, V. Closed mid-Oct–mid-May. Pets accepted w/prior approval. **Amenities:** Restaurant, lounge, library; Jacuzzi; complimentary bikes; free shuttle to and from vineyard. *In room:* No phone.

EXPLORING SATURNA ISLAND

East Point Regional Park ✹✹, on the island's southeastern tip, is a naturalist's delight. It starts with the oceanviews from the sculptured sandstone headlands and just gets better. Strong tides curl around the point to create back eddies where salmon and small fish congregate; rocks, honeycombed by wind and waves, form tidal pools filled with starfish, limpets, spider crabs, and more; and waving kelp beds attract cormorants, oyster catchers, eagles, seals, and even whales. Take the trail down to the **East Point Lighthouse,** built in 1888, and you'll be standing at the easternmost edge of the Gulf Islands, looking over to **Patos Island Lighthouse,** on the US side of the border. Together, the lights guide large vessels through the channel's surging waters. Some of the area is on private land; be careful not to trespass off the trails. If you've time, make the 4.5-km (3-mile) drive or hike up to the summit of **Warburton Pike** ✹, and if you can disregard the unbecoming sprawl of TV towers, the sweeping vistas from the top are nothing short of fantastic. The way up is via a winding gravel road that's narrow and sometimes slippery in wet weather, but the beautiful Douglas fir forest more than makes up for the occasional rough patch of road. Look out for feral goats, wild descendants of domestic goats imported here in the early 1900s, along the paths at the edge of the bluff.

The San Juan Islands

Lying just off the coast of Vancouver Island, south of the Gulf Islands, the San Juan Islands are a mostly blue-sky oasis in a region better known for its clouds. Like their island neighbors, they provide mariners with spectacular waters, hundreds of small, protected coves, and a landscape where stands of coastal trees give way to grassy meadows and gardens resembling Eden. The ferry trip between the San Juan Islands and Sidney, on Vancouver Island, is a delightful 1½-hour mini-cruise, and provides the opportunity to create a really diverse islands adventure. From Sidney, you can choose to explore Vancouver Island, or take a ferry to the Gulf Islands, creating an itinerary that can stretch from a few days to a few weeks.

Although many of the 700 or so islands in the archipelago disappear at high tide, there are still about 400 or so to explore. Some are no more than a raised tuft of land; others are wildlife sanctuaries or privately owned paradises. For years the San Juans' pastoral tranquility was a favorite getaway for Washingtonians, but this is now taking its toll. Today, land deals for would-be homeowners are long gone. There are nearly 30 different real estate dealers on the San Juans—that's one for every 40 residents; and assessed property values are almost three times the state average. Although development is controlled somewhat by the San Juan Preservation Trust, monumental homes are appearing in what was once humble rock and farmland.

In the 1800s, because of their proximity to British Columbia (San Juan Island lies only 26km (16 miles) from Sidney), many British settlers moved to the islands alongside their American counterparts. Remnants of those pioneering years are seen throughout the islands, and many landmarks are listed in the National Register of Historic Places. On San Juan Island, in particular, you'll find the Anglo-American rivalry especially well documented in the American and English camps.

The three largest islands, San Juan, Orcas, and Lopez, are home to about 12,000 people. For much of the year, the residents' easygoing lifestyle is quite solitary, but when summer arrives, the population triples, with eco-adventurers and holidaymakers suddenly peopling the streets. *Note:* If you're traveling with children, be aware that family fun is derived mainly from beachcombing, kayaking, and hiking, with the larger resorts providing children's programs and supervised swimming. (Consult the individual hotel reviews to see whether an establishment offers these programs.) Also note that despite the annual influx of visitors, accommodations on the San Juans are limited, and pre-arranged accommodation is highly recommended. Touring all three islands can be done in 3 or 4 days, but chances are that you'll acclimatize to "island time," slow down, and wish you had set aside a day or two longer. But leave your jet skis at home. When locals complained that the incessant buzzing of city folk zipping around their waterfront was disrupting the serenity of the islands, San Juan County promptly outlawed the noisy watercraft! As a result, the only wild time you'll find on the San Juan Islands is pretty much what nature provides.

GETTING THERE

BY PLANE **Kenmore Air Seaplanes** (© 800/543-9595; www.kenmoreair.com) provides daily flights from **Seattle** to the three major San Juan Islands. One-way fares are C$148 (US$96) for adults, C$131 (US$85) for children 2 to 11, free for children 1 and under. Kenmore Air also offers daily departures from Seattle to Victoria. One-way fares are C$178 (US$116) for adults, C$140 (US$91) for children 2 to 11, free for children 1 and under. These fares include a US$6 immigration fee. **NW Seaplanes** (float and land planes) (© 800/690-0086; www.nwseaplanes.com) flies out of **Renton,** just outside of Seattle, with daily service to the San Juan Islands, including Friday Harbor and Roche Harbor on San Juan Island, and Rosario and West Sound on Orcas Island. The one-way fare is C$115 (US$75) per person. **West Isle Air** (© 800/874-4434 or 360-293-4691; www.westisleair.com) has daily land plane flights from **Seattle** (C$131 (US$85) per person), **Anacortes** (C$48 (US$31) per person), and **Bellingham** (C$58 (US$38) per person), to Orcas, San Juan, and Lopez islands. Private plane arrivals can be accommodated at small public airstrips on San Juan, Orcas, and Lopez islands.

BY FERRY **Washington State Ferries,** Column Dock/Pier 52, Seattle, WA 98104 (© 888/808-7977 or 206/464-6400; www.wsdot.wa.gov/ferries), offers multiple daily sailings between **Anacortes** and the San Juan Islands, and limited service from **Sidney,** on Vancouver

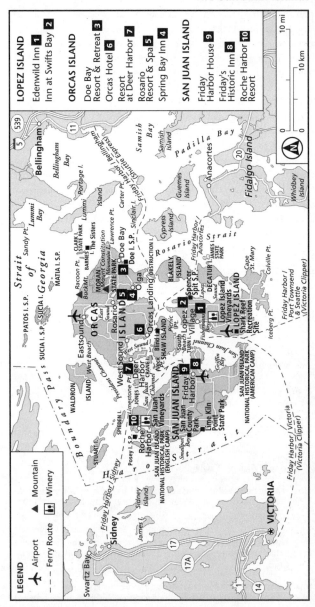

The San Juan Islands

LOPEZ ISLAND
Edenwild Inn **1**
Inn at Swifts Bay **2**

ORCAS ISLAND
Doe Bay Resort & Retreat **3**
Orcas Hotel **6**
Resort at Deer Harbor **7**
Rosario Resort & Spa **5**
Spring Bay Inn **4**

SAN JUAN ISLAND
Friday Harbor House **9**
Friday's Historic Inn **8**
Roche Harbor Resort **10**

LEGEND
✈ Airport
▲ Mountain
🏠 Winery
- - - Ferry Route

Island. From Anacortes, loading is on a first-come, first-served basis. It's a good idea to get in line about 30 minutes in advance of the scheduled sailing. If you bring a vehicle, allow for at least an hour's wait—up to 3 hours at peak travel times on summer and holiday weekends. Also, be sure to fill your tank in Anacortes. Gas stations on the islands charge at least 30% more for gas than on the mainland. Some food service and a picnic area are available near the terminal. Check out **www.ferrycam.net** to see live images of the ferry lanes.

One-way passenger fares during the high season, from May 3 to October 1, are C$12.50 (US$8.20) for adults, C$9 (US$5.80) for children, C$6 (US$4.10) for seniors, C$47 (US$30.50) for a standard-size vehicle, C$40 (US$26.40) for seniors and a standard-size vehicle. Inter-island travel is C$8.50 (US$13) for a driver and standard-size vehicle.

Once a day, the ferry continues to Sidney, 26km (16 miles) north of Victoria, and returns. Summer vehicle reservations are recommended to and from Canada, and must be made by 5:30pm the day prior to travel, at least 24 hours in advance. One-way passenger fares from May 3 to October 1 are C$19 (US$12.40) for adults, C$9.50 (US$6.20) for seniors, C$13.50 (US$8.70) for children, C$63 (US$41) for a standard-size vehicle and driver. From mid-October to April, return fares are C$17 (US$11) for adults, C$8.50 (US$5.50) for seniors, C$12 (US$7.70) for children, C$46 (US$29.75) for a standard-size vehicle and driver. Crossing time is 3 hours. From the San Juan Islands to Sidney, one-way fares are C$7 (US$4.50) for adults, C$3.50 (US$2.25) for seniors, C$5 (US$3.25) for children, C$33 (US$21.25) for a standard-size vehicle, C$29 (US$19) for seniors and a standard-size vehicle. Fares are lower October 2 through May 2.

Tips Makes Cents

Ferry foot passengers are only charged in the westbound direction; eastbound travel within the San Juan Islands or from the San Juan Islands to Anacortes is free (the only exception to this is for travelers leaving from Sidney, BC). If you're planning to visit all the San Juan islands, save money by heading straight to Friday Harbor on San Juan Island, the most westerly of the islands, and work your way back through the others at no additional charge.

Victoria Clipper (𝒞 800/888-2535 or 206/448-5000; www.victoriaclipper.com) is a popular way to reach the San Juan Islands from either **Seattle or Victoria.** This passenger-only boat departs from Seattle's **Pier 69** daily from May 1 to September 8. One-way fares from Seattle to Friday Harbor, on San Juan Island, are C$60 (US$39) for adults, C$30 (US$19.50) for children 1 to 11; fares from Seattle to Rosario Resort, on Orcas Island, are C$69 (US$45) for adults, C$34.50 (US$22.50) for children 1 to 11; fares from Victoria to Friday Harbor are C$44.50 (US$29) for adults, C$22.50 (US$14.50) for children 1 to 11. **Puget Sound Express** (𝒞 360/385-5288) offers passenger-only service between **Port Townsend,** northwest of Seattle, and Friday Harbor, May through September. The captain takes the 3-hour scenic route. Round-trip fare is about C$83.50 (US$52.20) per person. The **San Juan Island Shuttle Express** (𝒞 360/671-1137) runs a seasonal passenger ferry from Bellingham to the three major San Juan Islands, from April 5 to October 31. Round-trip fares are C$51 (US$33) for adults, C$45 (US$29) for seniors, C$41.50 (US$27) for students and children. They also offer whale-watching and adventure tours. Call for more information.

VISITOR INFORMATION

The **San Juan Islands Visitor Information Service,** P.O. Box 65, Lopez Island, WA 98261 (𝒞 888/468-3701 or 360/468-3663; www.guidetosanjuans.com), offers a range of maps and information. **San Juan Central Reservations** (𝒞 888/999-8773 (from the US only) or 360/378-8773; www.sanjuancentral.com) has accommodation leads throughout the islands. For live images of the San Juan Islands, check out **www.islandcam.com**. San Juan, Lopez, and Orcas islands also operate visitor services through their local Chambers of Commerce (see "Essentials," in separate sections devoted to each island).

1 San Juan Island

Compared to sleepier Orcas and Lopez islands, San Juan Island is "downtown central." Home to about 7,000 people, most of whom prefer this island's quicker pace, and covering over 88 km² (55 sq. mi.), San Juan is a popular holiday destination, offering visitors the most in terms of urban amenities, relaxing hideaways, and wilderness hikes. It is the most practical destination in the San Juan Islands if you're traveling without a car, since restaurants, shops, and museums are within walking distance of the ferry landing. Car and moped rentals are available all the same. The island even has a small winery, the **San Juan Vineyards,** housed in a century-old schoolhouse near **Roche Harbor.**

San Juan Island has a fair bit of historic appeal, too. Its colorful past stems from a boundary dispute between the US and Great Britain when, from 1860 to 1872, both countries occupied the island. In one of the stranger pieces of history, the killing of a British homesteader's pig by an American settler nearly sent the two countries to the battlefield. Ill will quickly escalated, but fortunately cooler heads prevailed, so that what is now referred to as the Pig War of 1869 only resulted in one casualty: the pig. The San Juan Islands were eventually declared American territory. The history of this little-known war is chronicled through the interpretive centers in **San Juan Island National Historical Park,** divided into **English Camp** and **American Camp** (see "Exploring the Area," below).

ESSENTIALS
GETTING THERE
Washington State Ferries arrive at **Friday Harbor** on the island's eastern coast. See "Getting There," at the beginning of the chapter, for information about fares and schedules.

VISITOR INFORMATION
The **San Juan Island Chamber of Commerce,** 1 Front St. (P.O. Box 98), Friday Harbor, WA 98250 (℃ **360/378-5240;** www. sanjuanisland.org), will be happy to tell you what you need to know about the island.

GETTING AROUND
There are two island taxi services, **Bob's Taxi & Tours** (℃ **360/ 378-6777**) and **San Juan Taxi** (℃ 360/378-3550). In summer months, **San Juan Transit** (℃ 360/378-8887) provides bus transportation. Rental cars are available year-round from **M&W Rental Cars,** 725 Spring St., Friday Harbor (℃ **800/323-6037** or 360/ 378-2886; www.interisland.net/mandw). Rates for a mid-size car are C$71 (US$45.95) May 1 through October 31, per day; C$55.50 (US$35.95) November 1 through April 30, per day. Bicycling and, especially, touring the island via scooter or moped is great fun. Rent bikes at **Island Bicycles,** 380 Argyle Ave., Friday Harbor (℃ **360/378-4941;** www.islandbicyles.com). Rates for mountain and hybrid bikes are C$46 (US$30) per day. Hourly and multiple-day rates are available. Rent mopeds at **Susie's Mopeds** (℃ **800/ 532-0087** or 360/378-5244; www.susiesmopeds.com), located above

the ferry parking in Friday Harbor. Susie's is the only place to find "scootcars," an inventive composite of a car and scooter. Moped rentals are C$25 (US$16) per hour; scootcars are C$61.50 (US$40) per hour. Per-day rates are available.

WHERE TO STAY & DINE

Friday Harbor House 𝒜𝒜𝒜   This elegant hotel on the bluff above the harbor offers the finest modern accommodations on San Juan Island, if not the best views of the harbor to boot. In fact, the inn is a welcome relief from all the Victorian-styled B&Bs found elsewhere on the San Juan Islands. The interior is distinctly West Coast, with lots of windows, wood, slate tiles, and plush carpets. Guest rooms are beautifully appointed. A standout feature is a double-person (but noisy) Jacuzzi strategically situated so that you can see through into the bedroom, enjoying the views beyond. It's also within sight of the fireplace, so you can enjoy its warmth, too. The continental breakfast includes extraordinary scones and muffins. If you're on the early morning ferry, park your car in the lineup and return to enjoy these goodies; and be sure to ask for a treat box "for the road." Open daily from 5pm, you'll find the **Harbor House Restaurant** first class in creativity, service, and wine selections. Although hotel guests have preferred seating, reservations are still recommended; it's a popular spot for locals to celebrate special occasions. Main dinner courses range from C$21.50 to $40 (US$14 to $26).

130 West St., Friday Harbor, WA 98250. ℭ **360/378-8455.** Fax 360/378-8453. www.fridayharborhouse.com. 20 units. May 24–Sept C$308–$408 (US$200–$265) standard; C$462 (US$300) 1-bedroom suite. Oct–May 23 C$215–$300 (US$140–$195) standard; C$392 (US$255) 1-bedroom suite. 2-night minimum stay required in summer and on weekends. Rates include continental breakfast. Extra person C$54 (US$35). Children 17 and under stay free in parents' room. AE, MC, V. **Amenities:** Restaurant. *In room:* TV/VCR, fridge, hair dryer, iron.

Friday's Historic Inn 𝒜   In the last few years, this historic inn has undergone a complete facelift. The hotel has had several lives since opening in 1891, and many still remember it as the Elite Hotel, an economy-rate youth hostel. But what a change; its current incarnation is as a sassy little boutique hotel, even though it manages to maintain the gracious atmosphere of yesteryear. There's a bit of an oenophilic theme at work here: guest rooms are named after wines, so be prepared to be handed the key to the Chardonnay or Riesling room. Guest rooms are tastefully decorated in rich colors with a blend of modern and period furnishings. Three of the rooms share two bathrooms; the other 12 have private bathrooms. Several rooms have Jacuzzis. All bathrooms have heated floors. Suites include the Garden Suite, which has a private outdoor Jacuzzi, while the new Lighthouse Suite can sleep seven. The Eagle Cove Suite is a favorite. As its name suggests, it's near the top of the house, offering a kitchen, a private deck, and a bird's-eye view of the harbor. Just note that the inn is right downtown, 2 blocks from the ferry landing and from a couple of boisterous bars; noise can sometimes be a factor.

35 1st St. (P.O. Box 2023), Friday Harbor, WA 98250. ② **800/352-2632** or 360/378-5848. Fax 360/378-2881. www.friday-harbor.com. 15 units. June–mid-Sept C$138–$184 (US$90–$120) economy; C$215–$246 (US$140–$160) standard; C$300–$408 ($195–$265) suite. Mid-Sept–May C$85–$131 (US$55–$85) economy; C$177–$208 (US$115–$135) standard; C$238–$346 ($155–$225) suite. Rates include continental breakfast. Extra person C$13 (US$20). Children 3 and under stay free in parents' room. MC, V. **Amenities:** Lounge. *In room:* TV, minibar, coffeemaker, no phone.

Roche Harbor Resort ⭐⭐ *(Kids)*   A village unto itself, Roche Harbor offers many different kinds of lodging, as well as a marina large enough for 377 vessels, for seafaring guests. First, there is the century-old **Hotel de Haro,** where lacy-trimmed beds, antiques, and roaring fireplaces transport you back to an earlier time. Originally a log bunkhouse, the hotel evolved into the distinctive three-story structure you see today, sophisticated enough to entertain company brass and dignitaries, including President Theodore Roosevelt (look for his signature in the guestbook). Suites have killer views, welcoming big beds, and large, clawfoot soaking bathtubs. Some single guest rooms share a bathroom. The one on the second floor contains the bathtub that John Wayne used to soak in. Now doesn't that drum up a few fantasies? In addition to the hotel, there are nine former **workers' cottages** that have been converted into two-bedroom units, close to the swimming pool, as well as one- to three-room **condominiums,** renovated in 2000. Cottages and condos both have contemporary furnishings, kitchen facilities, and of course, great views. In summer, there's dancing and live entertainment in the lounge. Dining options are numerous, and include **McMillin's Restaurant,** housed in the former home of John S. McMillin, Roche Harbor Lime & Cement Company President, and the less formal **Madrona Grill** on the waterfront, an espresso bar, cafe, and ice-cream emporium.

4950 Reuben Tarte Memorial Dr., Roche Harbor, WA 98250. ② **800/451-8910** or 360/378-2155. Fax 360/378-6809. www.rocheharbor.com. 60 units. Mid-June–Aug C$152 (US$99) shared bathroom; C$254 (US$165) private bathroom; C$306–$460 (US$199–$299) condominium and luxury suite; C$275–$353 (US$179–$229) cottage. Sept–mid-June C$131–$12 (US$85–$99) shared bathroom; C$192–$245 (US$125–$159) private bathroom; C$214–$408 (US$139–$265) condominium and luxury suite;

C$183–$315 (US$119–$205) cottage. Children 18 and under stay free in parents' room. AE, MC, V. **Amenities:** 3 restaurants, lounge; large outdoor heated pool; 2 tennis courts; playground; activities desk. *In room:* TV/VCR, coffeemaker, hair dryer.

EXPLORING THE AREA

The busy fishing village of **Friday Harbor** was first populated by a feisty bunch of scalawags in the mid-1800s, and only gained respectability when it became the county seat in 1873. Today it's the business center of the San Juan Islands: its harbor teems with commercial fishing boats and pleasure craft. From the docks of the Friday Harbor marina, **Trophy Charters** (© 360/378-2110; www.globaltelesis.com/trophy) runs salmon fishing trips, starting from C$131 (US$85) per person. **Western Prince Cruises** (© 360/ 378-5315; www.orcawhalewatch.com) offers nature and **whale-watching** expeditions from C$75 (US$49) for adults, C$49 (US$32) for children 13 and under. **San Juan Kayak Expeditions** (© 360/ 378-4436; www.sanjuankayak.com) will set you up for 3- and 4-day kayaking trips around the islands from C$500 to $646 (US$325 to $420) per person. The area's maritime history is best seen at the **San Juan Historical Museum,** 405 Price St., Friday Harbor (© 360/378-3949; www.sjmuseum.org). Housed in an 1890s wood-frame farmhouse, the museum includes fascinating antiques, old photos, and American Indian artifacts, plus intriguing old farm equipment seemingly stranded outside. Open from May to September, Thursday through Saturday from 10am to 4pm, and on Sundays from 1pm to 4pm. November through February by appointment. Admission is C$2 (US$1.20) for adults, C$1 (US65¢) for children 6 to 18. **The Whale Museum,** 62 1st Street North, Friday Harbor (© 360-378-4710; www.whale-museum.org), is also worth a visit. Maritime displays, huge whale skeletons, and informative videos explain orca behavior: the difference between breaching, spy hopping, and tail lobbing, as well as the many vocalization patterns. If whale watching is on your agenda, check out the photo collection with the names and identification markings of some of the 90 or so resident orcas in the area. The museum also has an orca adoption program to help fund ongoing research, and it operates a **24-hour hotline** (© 800-562-8832) to report whale sightings and marine mammal strandings. The museum is open May through September daily from 10am to 5pm. Hours vary from October to April; call to confirm. Admission is C$8 (US$5) for adults, C$6 (US$4) for seniors, C$2 (US$1.20) for children 5 to 18.

AMERICAN CAMP 𝔊

When British and American settlers were tilling the soil of San Juan Island, soldiers on both sides attempted to stake a national claim to these fertile lands. Sovereignty was eventually settled and, although not entirely accurate, today Americans refer to that time as the British occupation. However you view it, the American Camp, 10km (6 miles) south of Friday Harbor, serves as a historic reminder of those early days. The windswept grassy peninsula is a wonderful place to spend a sunny summer afternoon. On any other day, though, the winds make it barren and rather inhospitable, though some might say deliciously lonely. Two buildings remain, an officers' and a laundress's quarters, along with a cemetery and a defensive fortification built by Henry M. Roberts, of *Roberts Rules Of Order* fame. A white picket fence circles the grounds, which include a Hudson's Bay Company farm on Grandma's Cove at the southern border of the park, along the water. Trails lead to various beaches: the most popular is **South Beach,** the longest public beach on San Juan Island. The most secluded beach is **Fourth of July Beach,** where, appropriately, eagles nest nearby. **Picnic Cattle Point** is arguably the prettiest beach on the island, but it's a precarious scramble down a rocky ledge to get there. Hardy hikers usually opt for the upward trail to reach **Mount Finlayson**—90m (295 ft.) from where you can see the Coastal Mountains—as well as the Olympic and Cascade Ranges on the horizon and seascape below. Birders come to the camp to catch a glimpse of the only nesting Eurasian skylarks in the US. An on-site **Visitor's Center** (𝒞 **360/378-2902**) is open year-round daily from 8:30am to 4:30pm.

ENGLISH CAMP 𝔊𝔊

In sharp contrast to American Camp, English Camp is located in an area of protected waters, with maple trees spreading out overhead. About 16 km (10 miles) from Friday Harbor, the site includes a restored hospital, a commissary, an impressive formal garden, and small white **barracks,** which are open to the public mid-May through Labor Day. The blockhouse, built right on the beach, served to protect the marines from marauding Natives, not Americans, and was later used as a guard house for miscreant troopers. You'll find interpretive displays on a hillside terrace overlooking the camp, close to where the officers' quarters were built. A small cemetery holds the graves of six British Marines who died accidentally during the occupation from 1860 to 1872 (there were no war-related casualties, other than the pig), and a trail leads through second-growth forests up to **Mount Young,** a fairly easy 198-m (650-ft.) ascent. A **Visitor's Center** (© **360/378-4409**) operates mid-May through Labor Day daily from 8:30am to 4:30pm. For information at any time of year, for English and American Camps, contact the **Park Headquarters,** 125 Spring St., Friday Harbor (© **360/378-2240**). Admission is free to both.

ROCHE HARBOR ☆☆

Lying on the northwest peninsula of San Juan Island, about 14km (9 miles) from Friday Harbor, Roche Harbor is worth a visit, even if you're staying elsewhere on the island. A first-class destination resort complex (and a favorite getaway of the late John Wayne), Roche Harbor is a mix of historic buildings, modern conveniences, and marine-related activities. Listed on the National Register of Historic Places, Roche Harbor was once the home of a lime and cement tycoon, John S. McMillin. In its heyday during the 1890s, the town had the largest limeworks west of the Mississippi, operating kilns that each burned 10 cords of wood every 6 hours—just to keep functioning. The remains of several kilns are still visible. Much of the lime sweetened the huge salt marsh that was filled in and became the tulip fields of the Skagit Valley. The renovated Hotel de Haro still maintains much of its historic character, and a number of the heritage cottages used by workers in the lime kiln business have been converted to overnight lodgings. (See "Where to Stay & Dine," above). The resort has a terrific view of the Spieden Channel and smaller San Juan islands; meandering paths are paved with the same bricks that lined the original lime kilns. There are pretty Victorian gardens, and the still-operating original general store. Make sure you visit **Afterglow Vista,** a bizarre McMillin family mausoleum. The structure itself is fascinating and packed with Masonic symbols: an open, Grecian-style columned complex surrounds six inscribed chairs, each containing the ashes of a family member, set before a round table of limestone. Rumors abound as to why the seventh chair and column have been removed. Some say it was part of Masonic ritual, others believe a family member was disinherited. Or was it because the seventh member considered life to be everlasting?

LIME KILN POINT STATE PARK ☆ (Kids)

Head due west from Friday Harbor, through the center of the island, and you'll wind up at Lime Kiln State Park. Named for an early lime kiln operation on-site (remnants of its old structures are still evident), this is the only park in the world dedicated to whale watching.

Researchers use the **Lime Kiln Lighthouse,** built in 1914 and listed on the National Register of Historic Places, to watch for whales and to determine whether passing boats are affecting their behavior. Other whale-watching enthusiasts crowd the bluff, or set up camp around picnic benches scattered along the beach. Your chances of sighting success are especially good in late August and early September, when major salmon runs head for the Fraser River spawning grounds. En route, they pass through **Haro Strait** in front of the park, along the west side of San Juan Island, attracting whales, which feed on them. You might spot orca, minke, and pilot whales, or their smaller cousins, harbor and Dall's porpoises. Bring your binoculars and cameras with telephoto lenses. The park is open year-round, daily from 8am to dusk. It operates a pre-recorded information line, at © **360/378-2044.**

2 Orcas Island

Named for the viceroy of Mexico in 1792, and not, in fact, for the orca whales common to its waters, Orcas Island is the largest (92 km² (57 sq. mi.)), hilliest, and most beautiful of the San Juan Islands. Half the fun of exploring this island is traveling its roads, which, in addition to going up and down, twist and turn between hedgerows, fields, and orchards. Around any bend might lie a jewel of a bay or an unexpected hamlet filled with quaint cottages and wildflower gardens. You can climb to the top of the 610-m (2000-ft.) **Mount Constitution,** in **Moran State Park,** where the panorama stretches from The Lions, over Vancouver, to Mount Rainier, south of Seattle, or meander down lanes that give way to picturesque havens such as **Deer Harbor** and **Orcas Landing.** Early settlers logged, fished, and farmed, but today most of the island's 4,500 population are artisans, entrepreneurs, retirees, and eco-adventurers. In **Eastsound,** the heart of "commercial" activity on Orcas, you'll find horseback and kayaking excursions, in addition to galleries, restaurants, and some shops. The **Rosario Resort,** an elegant mansion that regularly graces the pages of travel magazines, is probably the island's most prominent landmark. It employs almost 200 people, and is the largest private employer on the islands (see "Where to Stay & Dine," below).

ESSENTIALS
GETTING THERE
Washington State Ferries dock at **Orcas Landing,** at the central southern peninsula of the island. See "Getting There," at the beginning of the chapter, for information about fares and schedules.

VISITOR INFORMATION

Stop in at **Orcas Island Chamber of Commerce**, Moran State Park, Olga Rd. (P.O. Box 252), Eastsound, WA 98245 (© **360/376-2273;** www.orcasisland.org), which operates from June to Labor Day (second Monday in September) daily from 8:30am to 4:30pm. During these months, a **lodging hotline** is also available at © **360/376-8888.**

GETTING AROUND

Once there, **Orcas Taxi** (© **360/376-TAXI**) provides pick-up and drop-off service throughout the island, year-round. From May to September, **Island Petroleum Services** (© **360/376-3883**) offers a limited number of mid-size rental cars for about C$79 (US$49.95) a day. Bike rentals are available from **Dolphin Bay Bicycles** (© **360/ 376-4157**), located at the ferry landing, as well as from **Wildlife Cycles,** 350 North Beach Rd., Eastsound (© **360/376-4708;** www. wildlifecycles.com). Mountain bike and hybrid bike rentals are C$46 (US$30) per day.

WHERE TO STAY & DINE
VERY EXPENSIVE

Rosario Resort & Spa ☆☆☆   This wonderful turn-of-the-century mansion, originally the private residence of shipping magnate Robert Moran, is worth the look even if you don't have the money to stay. Listed on the National Register of Historic Places, the building has been beautifully restored, and boasts 1,829 m² (6,000 sq. ft.) of teak parquet floors and a music room that features a Tiffany chandelier and a working 1,972-pipe Aeolian organ. Don't miss the free hour-long concerts held nightly—a nostalgic reminder of when Moran used to play the complicated organ for his guests. The mansion is one of 10 buildings that make up the Rosario Resort & Spa, which is spread out over 8 acres, and that is surrounded by several more acres of countryside. Guest rooms vary from standard accommodation either scattered along the waterfront in motel-style buildings or near the mansion, to one- and two-bedroom suites, with kitchens and private balconies, perched on the hillside. All are spacious (especially those on the hill), with bright, modern decor, and terrific views of Cascade Bay. The **Avanyu Spa** offers everything from early morning yoga and cardio workouts, to aromatherapy wraps, massage, and other personalized body treatments. There are four restaurants, suitable to all tastes and budgets. The **Compass Room** is the *pièce de résistance* for fine dining. The menu features popular steak and salmon dishes as well as organic island-grown produce. According to the chef, one of the nearby farmers actually uses a horse and plow to till his fields. In summer, a poolside bar and grill is also open.

1 Rosario Way, Eastsound, WA 98245. © **800/562-8820** or 360/376-2222. Fax 360/376-2289. www.rosarioresort.com. 127 units. July–mid-Sept C$506–$568 (US$329–$369) standard; C$675–$1,000 (US$439–$650) suite. Mid-Sept–June C$352–$414 (US$229–$269) standard; C$506–$846 (US$329–$550) suite. Extra person C$13 (US$20). Children 17 years and under stay free in parents' room. AE, DC, DISC, MC, V. Pets accepted w/prior approval. **Amenities:** 3 restaurants, lounge; small heated indoor pool; large heated outdoor pool; health club; spa; sauna; concierge; activities desk; car-rental desk. *In room:* TV, VCR on request, dataport, kitchen, coffeemaker, hair dryer.

EXPENSIVE

Resort at Deer Harbor ✦✦✦ Deer Harbor lies at the end of a winding country lane. The resort is perched on a quiet beachfront alongside a small, picturesque marina. It offers a range of new and historic guest cottages. The most accurate way to describe the newer ones is that they are a hybrid between a luxurious hotel room and a miniature townhouse. Most are designed to accommodate two people; the Grand Suite can sleep five. Inside any one of the newer cottages, a fireplace, viewed from two sides, divides the lounge from the bedroom, where you sink onto a plush king-size mattress. Remember to bring your favorite CDs, since cottages come equipped with CD players. The kitchenette is well stocked, with a fridge, microwave, and Starbucks coffee. Sensibly, the private Jacuzzi is within easy access of the expansive spa-style bathroom, so you can scurry out of one into the other without dripping water all over the place. Coupled with the harbor views, it's little wonder that the Resort at Deer Harbor has been touted as one of the most romantic spots on Orcas Island. The **Starfish Grill** (© **360/376-2482**) has star billing. Serving dinner daily May through October, this bistro-style restaurant lies steps away from the Deer Harbor docks and the blue herons that skim across the water. Start your evening on the wide-view deck, sipping a cold drink and nibbling a tasty appetizer, then dive into an entree such as salmon with ginger lime teriyaki sauce or crab cakes with basil aioli. Main dinner courses average C$26 (US$17).

11 Jack and Jill Place (P.O. Box 200), Deer Harbor, WA 98243. © **888/376-4480** or 360/376-4420. Fax 360/376-5523. www.deerharbor.com. 26 units. July–Sept C$290 (US$189) cottage; C$337–$414 (US$219–$269) deluxe suite. Oct–June C$198.50 (US$129) cottage; C$229–$306 (US$149–$199) deluxe suite. C$460 and way up (US$299) Grand suite. 2-night minimum stay summer season, weekends, and holidays. Rates include continental breakfast. **Amenities:** Restaurant; small heated outdoor pool. *In room:* TV/VCR, kitchenette, coffeemaker.

Spring Bay Inn 🌟🌟 *(Finds*   It's a long drive on a dirt road to get here, but your efforts are amply rewarded. Situated on 57 wooded acres, the Spring Bay Inn is as stylish indoors as it is scenic outside. The angular Great Room, with its fieldstone fireplace and vaulted ceiling, showcases a stunning view of Spring Bay. The four guest rooms upstairs feature waterfront views, wood-burning fireplaces, feather beds, high ceilings, fresh flowers, and private bathrooms. The fifth guest room, the Ranger's Suite, downstairs, has—count them—27 windows, and its own outdoor Jacuzzi. In the morning, coffee, muffins, and fresh fruit are delivered to your door—a little sustenance for the 2-hour guided kayak tour to follow, included with the room rate. Brunch is served on your return. The innkeepers are an engaging pair of retired State Park Rangers, who go out of their way to share their knowledge and make beginner kayakers feel like pros.

464 Spring Bay Trail (P.O. Box 97), Olga, WA 98279. ✆ 360/376-5531. Fax 360/ 376-2193. www.springbayinn.com. 5 units. Year-round C$338–$400 (US$220–$260). Rate includes continental breakfast, brunch, and kayaking trip. AE, DISC, MC, V. **Amenities:** Lounge; Jacuzzi. *In room:* Fridge, hair dryer, no phone.

MODERATE

Doe Bay Resort & Retreat Center   Spread over 50 acres, this funky resort is a throwback to the 1970s, offering a New Age atmosphere alongside a wide range of different accommodation: rustic cabins (one-, two-, and three-bedroom configurations, some with full kitchen), yurts (a canvas and wood structure) with skylights, treehouses, greenhouse cabins, tents, limited RV sites, and a hostel. There are shared central bathrooms and a community kitchen. A wonderful, clothing-optional, three-tiered sauna and a creekside mineral springs Jacuzzi perch on a covered deck. Bring an oversize towel or two, and a flashlight. Sea kayak tours and bike rentals are available. The **Cafe Doe Bay** is decorated with lava lamps, and it dishes up good vegetarian and seafood selections, although you might have to wait a bit since service can be casual. The cafe is housed in a former general store and post office (built in 1908 and listed in the National Register of Historic Places). It's open daily in summer, weekends in winter.

P.O. Box 437 (Star Route 86), Olga, WA 98279. ✆ 360/376-2291. Fax 360/ 376-5809. www.doebay.com. 64 units. June–Sept C$38 (US$25) tent and hostel; C$100–$285 (US$65–$185) cabin and yurt. Rates 20% lower Oct–May. MC, V. Pets accepted June–Sept C$30 (US$20). **Amenities:** Restaurant; Jacuzzi; sauna; limited water-sports rentals; bike rentals. *In room:* No phone.

Orcas Hotel ☞   Built in 1904 as a boarding house, this pretty home overlooking the water and ferry terminal features period pieces inside and white wicker on the deck outside. For the longest time, the place was all rather tired, but a recent change in ownership has brought about a marked improvement. The hotel is really quite romantic, and although guest rooms aren't deluxe, they're tastefully decorated, clean, and intimately comfortable. Some share bathrooms; others have private toilets but shared showers. The newer guest rooms have private balconies and Jacuzzis. For those who really want to get away from it all, there's also a small, self-contained cottage that sleeps six. In summer, a continental breakfast of home-baked yummies is served in the adjoining **Orcas Cafe.** In the off-season, you're on your own as far as food goes. The cafe has a grandstand veranda to wait out the ferry with a beer or a sandwich, and even one or two fancier dishes.

P.O. Box 155 (Orcas ferry landing), Orcas, WA 98280. ℂ **888/672-2792** or 360/ 376-4300. Fax 360/376-4399. www.orcashotel.com. 12 units, cottage. May–Oct and year-round holiday weekends C$122–$260 (US$79–$169) standard; C$305 (US$198) Jacuzzis. Nov–Apr C$77–$168 (US$50–$109) standard; C$198 (US$129) Jacuzzi. Year-round C$308 (US$200) cottage or C$1846 (US$1200) weekly. Rates include breakfast May–Oct. Extra person C$6.50–$23 (US$10–$15). AE, MC, V. **Amenities:** Restaurant, pub, lounge. *In room:* TV, VCR on request, hair dryer, no phone.

EXPLORING THE AREA

From the ferry dock, head due north 23km (14 miles) to **Eastsound Village,** at the center of the island. This is the commercial center of Orcas Island, and it's both lovely to look at and a delight to stroll through. Catering to backpackers and the well-to-do alike, Eastsound sports galleries, potters, and a charming village green that hosts a number of special events. Check out the **Saturday morning market,** or watch a craftsperson whittle all manner of furniture and kitchen utensils with a foot-powered lathe at a pioneer display. One restaurant worth noting that's been a local favorite for more than two decades is **Christina's,** 310 Main St., (ℂ **360/376-4904**), built on the waterfront above a 1930s gas station.

Eastsound is also where you'll want to base any **outdoor activities.** You may want to go horseback riding at **Walking Horse Country Farm,** 180 Westbeach Rd. (ℂ **877/376-9423** or 360/376-5306). Each session costs C$77 (US$50), and includes a demonstration, some instruction, and a trail ride.

You can rent kayaks from **Shearwater Adventures,** 259 A St. (ℂ **360/376-4699;** www.shearwaterkayaks.com). Three-hour trips cost C\$69 (US\$45) for adults, C\$39 (US\$25) for children 11 and under; full-day trips cost C\$131 (US\$85) per person. For a historical twist to kayaking, take a look at what **Osprey Tours,** P.O. Box 580, Eastsound, WA (*©* **360/376-3677**), has to offer. These folks use handcrafted Aleutian-styled kayaks and every kayaker is given an Aleutian whale-hunter's hat. Shaped like conical visors that resemble bird beaks, these hats served to disguise hunters, while their shape amplified the sounds of whales moving through the water. Osprey Tours specializes in private tours, and will accommodate families. Call for reservations and to arrange a venue based on your itinerary. Half-day trips cost C\$77 (US\$50) per adult; full-day trips cost C\$185 (US\$120); overnight trips cost C\$285 (US\$185). Children's rates are negotiable.

For history that's more terra firma, **The Orcas Island Historical Museum,** 5 North Beach Rd. (*©* **360/376-4849**), is an interesting spot to visit, for the building alone. It is comprised of six one-room log cabins constructed by homesteaders in the 1880s. Between 1951 and 1963, cabins were disassembled and transported to Eastsound Village, where they were painstakingly reconstructed and connected to create the museum you see today. Admission is C\$3 (US\$2) for adults, C\$1 (US65¢) for seniors, students, and children 5 and up, C50¢ (US30¢) for children 4 and under. The museum is open June through September daily from 10am to 4pm.

MORAN STATE PARK

A favorite destination for visitor and islander alike, Moran State Park's 4,605 acres offer a cornucopia of outdoor recreational activities, including camping, picnicking, canoeing and kayaking, hiking, horseback riding, and more. Over 48km (30 miles) of hiking trails cover everything from easy nature loops through old-growth forest, to rugged out-of-the-way hikes, while five crystal clear lakes tempt water enthusiasts to fish, canoe, or swim. In summer, the largest of these, **Mountain** and **Cascade lakes,** offer rowboat and paddleboat rentals. The park's landmark, **Mount Constitution,** is the highest point in the islands. Rising 610m (2000 ft.) above sea level, the summit is reached by a steep, paved road, where you'll discover a 16-m (52-ft.) stone tower patterned after a 12th-century fortress. You can drive to the top; if you take your bike, you'll find the hard ride up rewards with an exhilarating ride back down. Because the gradient is so steep, the road is generally closed from mid-November to mid-April, as it can get slick and dangerous. Information on trails, campsites, and activities in the park is available from **Washington State Parks,** 7150 Cleanwater Lane, Olympia, WA 98504 (© **360/ 902-8844**). You can also go online to **www.orcasisle.com/moran**.

Finds Shaw Island

Shaw Island is the most remote of the accessible San Juan Islands, and makes for a terrific bike trip. If you visit, however, take care to be as self-sufficient as possible, bringing along enough food, water, and other supplies to last. For some visitors, arriving at Shaw Island could be a religious experience, since the Franciscan Sisters of the Eucharist have operated its ferry landing every day for almost 20 years. Rain or shine, you're likely to see a nun standing at the dock in her habit, waiting to pull the big metal lever that lowers the ramp. Home to approximately 230 permanent residents, most of Shaw Island's 12.5 km^2 (7.7 sq. mi.) are undeveloped. With the exception of a **wildlife refuge** and a tiny county park offering limited picnicking and camping facilities, the island is completely privately owned. Its store, **Little Portion,** on Blind Bay Rd. (© **360/468-2288**) is, by law, the only commercial business allowed, which is why it acts as ferry terminal, grocery store, gas station, and post office. Although it sells a number of tourist trinkets, there is also a surprising selection of gourmet items, such as mustards, herbs, and vinegars, produced by the nuns of Our Lady of the Rock, a cloistered Benedictine order that runs a large dairy farm to the west. While tours are rarely available, you are welcome to take in the beautiful marine-themed chapel, where mass is held each Sunday. Nearby, **The Little Red Schoolhouse** (listed on the National Register of Historic Places) is one of the few one-room schools still in use. Across the road, a tiny log cabin houses the **Shaw Island Museum.**

---

3 Lopez Island

Laced with country lanes, picturesque farms, and orchards, Lopez Island is just about as bucolic and pastoral as it gets. Cows and sheep are a common sight, as are bright fields of daffodils, tulips, lilies, and delphiniums. Home to approximately 2,100 people, and covering

47.5 km² (29.5 sq. mi.), Lopez has a rich, agricultural heritage. Once known as the "Guernsey Island" for its exports of cream, eggs, and poultry, the land supports more than 50 working farms. In summer, cyclists flock to the gently rolling hills, and birdwatchers take to the expanses of protected tidal flats to watch a myriad of shorebirds: horned grebes, double crested cormorants, yellow legs, peeps, ospreys, and peregrine falcons.

Shark Reef Recreation Area is a favorite spot to watch harbor seals, sea lions, and bald eagles diving for dinner. Or you can head for **Agate Beach,** one of the few beaches open to the public, and one of the most romantic places to watch the sun go down. Come winter, Lopez Island seems to go into virtual hibernation, save for a fairly recent phenomenon: when one of the original Microsoft team built his compound here a few years back, techies followed, and mega-houses have been popping up all along the waterfront ever since. Real estate prices are soaring. Lopez village has developed a new gentrified air, and now has street names and sidewalks. Lopez is, however, still the friendliest of the San Juan Islands. Waving to passing cars and cyclists is a time-honored local tradition. Be careful not to make it a royal salute, though, or you will be instantly labeled the tourist you are!

ESSENTIALS
GETTING THERE
The ferry arrives at the most northerly tip of the island. See "Getting There," at the beginning of the chapter, for information about fares and schedules.

VISITOR INFORMATION
The **Lopez Island Chamber of Commerce,** P.O. Box 102, Lopez, WA 98261 (© **360/468-4664;** www.lopezisland.com), distributes literature and maps in shops and galleries throughout the island.

GETTING AROUND
For folks on foot, **Lopez Cab** (© **360/468-2227**) provides courier, as well as pick-up and drop-off passenger services. One of the best bike routes around the island is a 48-km (30-mile) circuit that's suitable for the whole family to bike in a day. If you don't have your own wheel power, here are some rental options: **Lopez Bicycle Works & Kayaks,** 2847 Fisherman's Bay Rd., (© **360/468-2847**) offers mountain bikes, tandems, and children's bikes, as well as repairs and sales. The **Bike Shop on Lopez,** Lopez Village, (© **360/468-3497**)

has a good selection of family and mountain bikes, and will deliver a bike to any location on the island, including the ferry landing.

WHERE TO STAY

Edenwild Inn 🐝🐝   This pretty little inn is a Victorian center-piece of Lopez Village, complete with picturesque flower garden and large wraparound porch. Although the inn is not located on the water, many guest rooms have views of the San Juan Channel. Pleasant antique furnishings decorate the rooms, and there are qual-ity amenity packages and deliciously sinful Bavarian chocolates. Three guest rooms also have large wood-burning fireplaces. All have private bathrooms, some of which feature deep-soaker clawfoot bathtubs. Room 6 is the most comfortable, notable for its cozy sit-ting area and vistas of Fisherman's Bay. In answer to the island's lack of cable TV, there are books everywhere—you can actually take them home thanks to Lopez's phenomenal recycling program. Breakfast is generous, with entrees such as fresh fruit crepes, Florentine quiche, or sourdough orange French toast.

132 Lopez Rd. (P.O. Box 271), Lopez Island, WA 98261. ℂ **800/606-0662** or 360/468-3238. Fax 360/468-4080. www.edenwildinn.com. 8 units. May–Sept C$169–$261 (US$110–$170). Rates 20% lower Oct–Apr. Rates include full breakfast. Extra person C$38 (US$25). AE, MC, V. Children under 10 not accepted. **Amenities:** Lounge. *In room:* Coffeemaker, no phone.

Inn at Swifts Bay 🐝🐝🐝   Set among tall cedars above Swifts Bay, this elegant Tudor inn, formerly a summer home, offers luxury in a casual atmosphere. It is, arguably, the best bed-and-breakfast on the island, mixing California-style furnishings with antique reproduc-tions. You'll notice details such as fresh flowers, crocheted anti-macassars, and needlepoint pillows. Shared areas are warm and inviting; the lounge contains a fireplace, a piano, decanters of sherry and port, oodles of books, and a movie library of over 350 films. The two-person sauna and tiny exercise studio are unexpected finds, with just enough equipment to work up a sweat: a universal gym, tread-mill, stationary bike, and some weights. Three of the comfortable guest rooms have fireplaces, fridges, and private bathrooms; the remaining two guest rooms share a bathroom. The breakfasts are Epicurean feasts: crab cakes are the reputed favorite, although the hazelnut waffles with fresh Lopez Island berries, potato galette with smoked salmon, and bread pudding can't be far behind.

856 Port Stanley Rd., Lopez Island, WA 98261. ℂ **800/375-5285** or 360/468-3636. Fax 360/468-3637. www.swiftsbay.com. 5 units. Year-round C$146–$169 (US$95–$110) shared bathroom; C$238–$285 (US$155–$185) private bathroom. Rates

include full breakfast. AE, DISC, MC, V. **Amenities:** Lounge; exercise room; Jacuzzi; sauna. *In room:* No phone.

WHERE TO DINE

The Bay Cafe 𝕴𝕴 *(Finds* *Value* PACIFIC NORTHWEST   Located at the entrance to Fisherman's Bay, this bright, spacious restaurant is a delight. Funky art adorns the walls, while row upon row of windows give way to terrific sunsets and waterside views. Thankfully, the views are only outdone by the food. The ever-changing selection of seafood tapas is imaginative (the prawns stuffed with basil and goat cheese are to die for), and the entrees cover all the bases, with dishes to please carnivores, herbivores, and everything in between. The Thai curry is exceptionally good, as is the beef filet in a roasted garlic Roquefort sauce. Homemade soup and salad are included with your meal, which makes the menu particularly good value. There's a patio in summer. In winter, call ahead.

9 Old Post Rd, Lopez Village. *©* 360/468-3700. Reservations required July–Aug. Main courses C$26–$38 (US$17–$25). AE, DISC, MC, V. May–Oct daily 5–10pm; Nov–Feb Fri–Sun 5–10pm; Mar–Apr Mon–Fri 5–10pm.

EXPLORING THE AREA

Lopez Village is the business center of the island, and has a scattering of cafes, shops, a charming farmers' market (held Wednesday and Saturday), and, of course, real estate offices. The **Library,** 2225 Fisherman Bay Rd. (*©* **360/468-2265**), housed in a bright red-and-white 19th-century schoolhouse, is the *only* place to get the Sunday *New York Times,* the *Los Angeles Times,* and *The Wall Street Journal.* Copies are donated, which might mean you're reading 2-day-old news. Well, call it being on island time. Nonresidents pay a refundable C$6.50 (US$10) fee to check books out while on the island. When you're browsing through Lopez Village, be sure to drop in to the **Soda Fountain & Pharmacy** (*©* **360/468-4511**), where you'll find an old-fashioned ice cream parlor with a slew of fountain treats: killer banana splits, hand-dipped malts, and suck-'til-your-brains-hurt thick-and-creamy milkshakes. The lunch counter is gossip central for Lopez locals, just in case you're interested in the lowdown on island life. The **Lopez Historical Museum,** 28 Washburn Place (*©* **360/468-2049**), houses artifacts such as a foot-powered cow-milking machine, and a 1903 Orient buckboard—the first car driven on the island. The museum puts out an island tour map of historic landmarks, which, believe it or not, has 34 destinations! Its operating hours are sporadic, particularly in winter, although you can usually count on Friday through Sunday from 10am to 3pm. To avoid disappointment, call first. Admission is C$2 (US$1.50) for adults, C$1.30 (US$1) for children 18 and under.

Touring island farms is another fun excursion, especially if you're into market produce, herbs, or handwoven blankets. Call the **Lopez Community Land Trust** (© 360/468-3723) for information. If you're a wine lover, or even just learning to love it, pay a visit to **Lopez Island Vineyards,** 724 Fisherman Bay Rd. (© **360/ 468-3644**). This small, family-owned winery is the oldest in San Juan County, producing organically grown grapes and some pretty drinkable wines. Until recently, if you bought any wines with labels stating an origin of Friday Harbor or Orcas Island, they were tourist gimmicks. The wine was actually made in the Yakima Valley. These folks, however, have matured their early-ripening vines from the mid-1980s, so they now produce grapes that create more flavor. In addition to a Cabernet and Merlot, there's a medium-dry white apple-pear wine, as well as a full-bodied blackberry dessert wine, all of which are made on the premises. The vineyard is open for free tastings from April 15 to December 15, Friday and Saturday, from noon to 5pm. It's also open on Wednesday in July and August.

Index

See also Accommodations and Restaurant Indexes below.

GENERAL INDEX

Accommodations (resorts), best, 4–6. *See also* Accommodations index; Campgrounds
Adventure activities, best, 3
Airlines, 22–23
All Fun Recreation Park (Cowichan Valley), 82
American Camp (San Juan Island), 180
American Express, 29, 38
ATMs (automated teller machines), 13
Automobile associations, 13, 28

Bamfield, 102–103, 111
Banks, 13, 38
Bars and clubs (Victoria), 60
BC Forest Museum Park/BC Forestry Discovery Centre (Cowichan Valley), 83
Beaches, 67–68, 74–76, 113, 180
Beaumont Marine Provincial Park (South Pender), 157
Bed-and-breakfasts. *See* Accommodations index
Bellhouse Provincial Park (Galiano Island), 162
Bicycle rentals, 154, 158, 176, 183, 189–190
British Columbia Aviation Museum (Saanich), 66
Broken Group Islands (Central Vancouver Island), 112
Brookes Point (South Pender), 157
Bus travel, 23, 33, 34, 68, 78, 86–87, 93, 104, 116, 126, 133
Butchart Gardens (Saanich), 8, 66

Calendar of events, 16–20
Campbell River, 3, 124–125
accommmodations, 126–128
fishing, 129
getting there, 125–126
Queen Charlotte Strait, cruising, 130
restaurants, 128–129
side trips, 131–132
transportation, 126
visitor information, 126
Campgrounds, 98, 112, 152
Canada, customs regulations, 9–10, 11
Canadian Consulate, 10
Cape Scott Provincial Park (Northern Vancouver Island), 138–139
Car insurance, 14
Car rentals, 28, 183
Car travel, 25–26, 28–29, 34, 61–62, 68, 86, 93, 99, 103, 115, 125–126, 132–133
Caving, 2, 97, 135
Central Vancouver Island, 85–113. *See also* Bamfield; Pacific Rim National Park; Parksville/Qualicum Beach; Port Alberni; Tofino; Ucluelet
Chemainus, 77–78
accommodations, 80
Children, traveling with, 10. *See also* Family-friendly activities
Clayoquot Sound, 3, 8
accommodations/dining, 104–108
Clayoquot Sound Biosphere Reserve, 110
Climate, 14, 16
Courtenay/Comox Valley
accommodations, 118–119
exploring, 121–124
getting there, 115–117
restaurants, 120–121
transportation, 118
visitor information, 117–118

Cowichan Bay, restaurants in, 81–82
Cowichan Native Village, 83
Cowichan Valley, 77–78
Cowichan Valley, en route to Nanaimo
  attractions, 82–83
  getting there, 78
  visitor information, 78
  restaurants, 71–82
  wineries, 83–84
Craigdarroch Castle (Victoria), 51
Credit cards, 13
Crystal Garden (Victoria), 52
Currency exchange, 12–13, 38
Customs regulations, 11–12

Dentists (Victoria), 38
Disabilities, travelers with, 20–21
Distances, from Victoria, 28
Doctors (Victoria), 38
Drinking age, minimum, 30
Driving times, from Victoria, 28
Drugstores, 29, 38
Duncan, 77
  accommodations, 80
  restaurants, 82

East Point Regional Park (Saturna Island), 170
Electricity, 30
Emergencies, 30, 38
English Camp (San Juan Island), 180
Entry requirements, 9–10
Events calendar, 16–20
Exchange rates, 12–13. See also Money

Family-friendly activities, 2, 20–21
Female travelers, 21
Ferries, 23–24, 25–27, 34, 36, 61–62, 87, 17, 133, 141, 144, 172, 174, 182
Festivals calendar, 17–20
Fishing, 3, 56–57, 125, 129
Forecasts, 31
Fort Rodd Hill & Fisgard Lighthouse National Historic Site (Sooke Region), 72

Gabriola Island, 90–92
Galiano Bluffs Park (Galiano Island), 162
Galiano Island (Gulf Islands), 157–158
  accommodations, 158–161
  exploring, 162–163
  getting there, 158
  restaurants, 161–162
  transportation, 158
  visitor information, 157
Ganges (Salt Spring Island), 151
Gastronomic tours, 63
Gay & lesbian travelers, 21
  bars (Victoria), 60
Golf, 3, 57, 98–99
Goods & Services Tax (GST), 12
Gulf Islands, 140–170. See also Galiano Island; Mayne Island; Pender Islands; Salt Spring Island; Saturna Island
  getting there, 27, 141, 144
  visitor information, 144

Health insurance, 13
Hiking, 3, 73–74, 111–112, 123, 138–139, 157
Holidays, 16
Horne Lake Caves Provincial Park, 2, 97–93
Hospitals, 30, 38
Hotels. See Accommodations index
Hot springs, 110

Inns. See Accommodations index
Inside Passage, 9
Insurance, 13–14
Internet access, 30, 39

Kayaking, 3, 156, 163, 166, 186–187
Kwagiulth Museum and Cultural Centre (Campbell River), 125

Ladysmith, accommodation, 81
Lesbian travelers. See Gay & lesbian travelers
Lighthouses, 72, 167, 170, 182
Lime Kiln Point State Park (San Juan Island), 3, 181–182

Liquor laws, 30
Little Hustan Coves (Campbell River), 135
Long Beach Unit (Pacific Rim National Park), 113
Lopez Island (San Juan Islands), 188–189
    accommodations, 190–191
    exploring, 191–192
    getting there, 189
    restaurants, 191
    transportation, 189–190
    visitor information, 189

Malahat, the (Cowichan Valley), 77
    accommodations, 79
    restaurants, 81
Maritime Museum of British Columbia (Victoria), 52
Mayne Island (Gulf Islands), 163
    accommodations, 164–165
    exploring, 166–167
    getting there, 163
    restaurants, 165–166
    transportation, 164
    visitor information, 164
Meares Island, 110
Medicine Beach (North Pender), 157
Miniature World (Victoria), 20, 52–53
Money, 12–13, 38
Montague Provincial Marine Park (Gulf Islands), 163
Moped rentals, 3, 158, 176
Moran State Park (San Juan Islands), 187–188
Mount Norman Regional Park (South Pender), 157
Mount Parke Park (Mayne Island), 167

Nanaimo, 77, 85–86. See also Cowichan Valley, en route to Nanaimo
    accommodations, 87–89
    getting there, 86–97
    outdoor activities, 90
    restaurants, 89–90
    visitor information, 87

side trip, Gabriola Island, 90–92
    transportation, 87
Newspapers, 39
North Pender, 156–157
    accommodations/dining, 154–155
North Vancouver Island, 114–139. See also Campbell River; Courtenay/Comox Valley; Port Hardy, en route to

Orcas Island (San Juan Islands)
    accommodations/dining, 183–186
    exploring, 186–188
    getting there, 182
    transportation, 183
    visitor information, 183

Pacific Rim National Park (Sooke Region), 3, 8, 74, 103, 111–113
Pacific Underseas Gardens (Victoria), 53
Parksville/Qualicum Beach, 92–93
    accommodations, 93–96
    getting there, 93
    restaurants, 96–97
    visitor information, 93
Parliament Buildings (Victoria), 53
Pender Islands
    accommodations/dining, 154–156
    exploring, 156–157
    getting there, 153
    transportation, 154
    visitor information, 153–154
Performing arts (Victoria), 58–59. See also Events calendar
Pets, traveling with, 10
Police (Victoria), 39
Port Alberni
    accommodations, 100
    exploring, 100–102
    getting there, 99
    restaurants, 100
    visitor information, 100
Port Hardy, en route to
    accommodations/dining, 134–135
    exploring, 135–139
    getting there, 132–33
    visitor information, 133
Port Renfrew, 76–77, 111
Postal information, 30, 39

Precipitation, average, 16
Provincial sales tax (PST), 12

Quadra Island, 125
Qualicum Beach. See
   Parksville/Qualicum Beach
Queen Charlotte Strait (Northern
   Vancouver Island), 130

Rainfall, average, 16
Rathtrevor Provincial Park (Central
   Vancouver Island), 2, 98
Resorts. See Accommodations index
Restaurants
   best, 6–7. See also Restaurants
      index
   tipping etiquette, 31
Roche Harbor (San Juan Island), 181
Roseland (North Pender), 157
Royal British Columbia Museum
   (Victoria), 2, 8, 53–54
Ruckle Provincial Park (Salt Spring
   Island), 152

Saanich Peninsula (Southern
   Vancouver Island)
   accommodations, 62–64
   attractions, 66–67
   getting there, 61–62
   parks & beaches, 67–68
   restaurants, 64–65
   visitor information, 62
Safety, 39
Sales tax, 12
Salt Spring Island
   accommodations, 146–149
   exploring, 151–152
   getting there, 145
   restaurants, 150–151
   transportation, 145–146
   visitor information, 145
San Juan Island, 175–176
   accommodations/dining, 177–179
   exploring, 179–182
   getting there, 176
   transportation, 176–177
   visitor information, 176
San Juan Islands, 9, 171–192. See
   also Lopez Island; Orcas Island;
   San Juan Island

Saturna Island (Gulf Islands),
   167–168
   accommodations/dining, 168–169
   exploring, 170
   getting there, 168
   transportation, 168
   visitor information, 168
Saturna Island Vineyards, 167, 169
Scenic drives, best, 4
Scooters, rentals, 3, 177
Seniors, 21
Shaw Island (San Juan Islands), 188
Shopping (Victoria), 55–56
Sidney Historical Museum (Saanich
   Peninsula), 66–67
Sidney Marine Centre (Saanich
   Peninsula), 67
Skiing, 123
Smoking, 30
Soft-adventure activities, best, 3
Sointula (Malcolm Island), 136, 137
Sooke Region (Southern Vancouver
   Island)
   accommodations, 69–71
   attractions, 72–73
   getting there, 68
   hiking trails, 73–74
   parks & beaches, 74–76
   Port Renfrew, 76–77
   visitor information, 68–69
Sooke Region Museum, 73
South Pender, 157
   accommodations/dining, 154–155
Southern Vancouver Island, 61–84.
   See also Cowichan Valley; Saanich
   Peninsula, Sooke Region
Special needs travelers, 20
Speedway, 82
Strathcona Provincial Park
   (Northern Vancouver Island),
   123–124
Students, 21–22

Tax, 12, 39
Taxis, 34, 154, 176, 183, 189
Telegraph Cove (Campbell River,
   135–136
Telephones, 31
Temperatures, average, 16
Time zones, 31

Tipping etiquette, 31
Tofino. *See also* Pacific Rim National
  Park; Ucluelet
    accommodations/dining, 104–108
    exploring, 109
    getting there, 103–104
    outdoor activities, 109–110
    side trips, 110
    visitor information, 104
Trains, 23, 29, 33, 78, 87, 93,
  116–117
Transportation, 22–29
Traveler's checks, 13

Ucluelet
    accommodations/dining, 108–109
    exploring, 110–111
    outdoor activities, 109–110
U'Mista Cultural Centre (Northern
  Vancouver Island), 136
United States
    customs regulations, 10, 11
    holidays, 16

Vancouver Island, 1–2. *See also*
  Central Vancouver Island;
  Northern Vancouver Island;
  Southern Vancouver Island;
  Victoria
    accommodations, best, 4–6
    adventure activities, best, 3
    events calendar, 16–20
    family-friendly activities, best, 2
    getting there, 22–27
    regional description, 8–9
    restaurants, best, 6–7
    scenic drives, 4
    temperature/precipitation,
      average, 16
    transportation, 28–29
    visitor information, 9
Vesuvius (Salt Spring Island),
  152–153
Victoria, 8
    accommodations, 39–46
    attractions, 51–54
    distances, driving times from, 28
    getting there, 32–34
    layout, 35
    nightlife, 60

    outdoor activities, 56–58
    performing arts, 58–59
    shopping, 55–56
    tours, 36–37
    transportation, 24, 26, 28
    visitor information, 34
Victoria Bug Zoo, 2, 20, 54
Victoria Butterfly Gardens (Saanich
  Peninsula), 67
Vineyards, 83–84, 167
Visitor information, 9

Washington State, holidays, 16
Wax museum (Victoria), 54
Weather updates, 31, 39
West Coast Trail Unit (Pacific Rim
  National Park), 3, 8, 74, 111–112
Whale watching, 3, 57–58, 110,
  136, 157, 179
Wickaninnish Centre (Long
  Beach), 113
Wild Pacific Trail, 2, 110–111
Wineries. *See* Vineyards

Zeballos, 135

ACCOMMODATIONS

Abigail's Hotel (Victoria), 5, 44
Aerie, The (the Malahat), 4, 79
Alice's Shangri-La Oceanfront B&B
  (North Pender), 154
Anchor Point B&B (Salt Spring
  Island), 146–147
Anne's Oceanfront Hideaway B&B
  (Salt Spring Island), 147
Bahari B&B (Qualicum Beach),
  93–94
Beach Acres Resort (Parksville),
  94–95
Beddis House B&B (Salt Spring
  Island), 147
Bedford Regency, The (Victoria),
  45–46
Bedwell Harbour Island Resort
  (South Pender), 154–155, 157
Bellhouse Inn (Galiano Island),
  158–159
Best Western Barclay Hotel (Port
  Alberni), 100

Bird Song Cottage/Castlebury Cottage (Chemainus), 80

Blue Vista Resort (Mayne Island), 164–165

Bodega Resort (Galiano Island), 159

Breezy Bay B&B (Saturna Island), 168

Cable Cove Inn (Tofino), 104–105

Canadian Princess Resort (Ucluelet), 108

Cherry Bank Hotel (Victoria), 50

Clarion Hotel Grand Pacific (Victoria), 40

Cloud 9 (Salt Spring Island), 148

Coast Westerley Hotel (Courtenay), 118

Clayoquot Wilderness Resort (Tofino), 5, 105

Coach-House on Oyster Bay B&B, A (Mayne Island), 164

Coast Bastion Inn (Nanaimo), 87

Coast Discovery Inn & Marina (Campbell River), 127

Coast Hospitality Inn (Port Alberni), 100

Crown Isle Resort (Courtenay), 3, 118–119

Delta Victoria Ocean Pointe Resort and Spa (Victoria), 40–41

Doe Bay Resort & Retreat Center (Orcas Island), 185

Driftwood Village Resort (Galiano Island), 159–160

Edenwild Inn (Lopez Island), 190

Fairburn Farm Country Manor (Duncan), 80

Fairmont Empress Hotel, The (Victoria), 4, 41–42

Friday Harbor House (San Juan Island), 6, 177

Friday's Historic Inn (San Juan Island), 177–178

Galiano Inn (Galiano Island), 160

Gatsby Mansion (Victoria), 42

Glen Lyon Inn & Suites (Port Hardy), 134

Haig-Brown House (Campbell River), 127–128

Hartmann House B&B (Sooke Region), 69

Hastings House (Salt Spring Island), 5, 146

Holland House (Victoria), 42

Hotel Bachmair Suite Hotel (Campbell River), 126–127

Hotel Nanaimo (Nanaimo), 77–89

Humboldt House B&B (Victoria), 44

Hummingbird Pub (Galiano Island), 162

Inn at Swifts Bay (Lopez Island), 6, 190–191

Inn at Tough City (Tofino), 7, 105–106

Inn on Pender Island (North Pender), 155

Island Time B&B (Galiano Island), 6, 160

Kingfisher Oceanside Resort & Spa (Courtenay), 119

Laurel Point Inn (Victoria), 42–43

Long Beach Lodge Resort (Tofino), 106

Maclure House (Parksville), 95

Magnolia Hotel & Spa, The (Victoria), 45

Malahat Farm (Sooke Region), 69

Markham House B&B (Sooke Region), 70

Mount Washington Alpine Resort (Northern Vancouver Island), 123

Oak Bay Beach Hotel and Marine Resort (Saanich Peninsula), 4–5, 62–63

Oceanside Inn (North Pender), 155

Oceanview B&B (Port Hardy), 134

Oceanwood Country Inn (Mayne Island), 165

Old Farmhouse, The (Salt Spring Island), 148

Orcas Hotel (Orcas Island), 186

Pacific Sands Resort (Tofino), 106–107

Painter's Lodge Holiday & Fishing Resort (Campbell River), 128

Poet's Cove Resort at Bedwell Harbour. See Bedwell Harbour Island Resort

Point No Point Resort (Sooke Region), 4, 70–71

Port Renfrew Recreational Retreat (Sooke Region), 76–77

Prancing Horse (on the Malahat), 79

Quarterdeck Inn & Marina (Port Hardy), 135

Resort at Deer Harbor (Orcas Island), 184

Roche Harbor Resort (San Juan Island), 168–179

Rosario Resort & Spa (Orcas Island), 5, 183–184

Royal Scot, The (Victoria), 43–44

Sahhali Serenity Oceanfront B&B Inn (North Pender), 6, 156

Salt Spring Island Hostel, 149

Salt Springs Spa Resort (Salt Spring Island), 148–149

Saturna Lodge & Restaurant (Saturna Island), 169

Shoal Harbour Inn, The (Saanich Peninsula), 63–64

Snug Harbour Inn (Ucluelet), 108

Sooke Harbour House (Sooke Region), 5, 70–71

Spring Bay Inn (Orcas Island), 185

Strathcona Park Lodge (Vancouver Island), 3

Swans Hotel (Victoria), 46

Tauca Lea Coast Resort (Ucluelet), 108–109

Telegraph Love Resorts (Northern Vancouver Island), 136

Tigh-Na-Mara Resort Hotel (Parksville), 95–96

West Coast Trail Motel, The (Sooke Region), 77

Wickaninnish Inn (Tofino), 5, 107–108

Woodstone Country Inn (Galiano Island), 161

Yellow Point Lodge (Ladysmith), 81

Restaurants

Aerie, The (the Malahat), 81

Atrevida! restaurant (Galiano Island), 160, 161

Baan Thai (Campbell River), 128

Barb's Place (Victoria), 6, 48

Bay Cafe, The (Lopez Island), 191

Beach House Cafe (Qualicum Beach), 96

Black Fin Pub (Comox), 120

Blethering Place (Victoria), 47

Blue Crab Bar & Grill (Victoria), 6, 47

Boat Basin Lounge and Restaurant (Ucluelet), 109

Bousaouki Greek Cafe (Salt Spring Island), 150

Bowman's Rib House (Victoria), 50

Cafe Brio (Victoria), 48–49

Cafe Doe Bay (Orcas Island), 185

Christina's (Orcas Island), 186

Cola Diner (Qualicum Beach), 96

Compass Room (Orcas Island), 183–184

Crow & Gate (Cowichan Bay), 81–82

Deep Cove Chalet (Saanich Peninsula), 64–65

Glen Lyon Pub (Port Hardy), 134

Glen Lyon restaurant-cafe (Port Hardy), 134

Harbour Grill (Campbell River), 129

Harbor House Restaurant (San Juan Island), 177

Hastings House (Salt Spring Island), 150

Herald Street Caffe (Victoria), 50

Hime Sushi (Victoria), 50–51

House Piccolo (Salt Spring Island), 7, 150

Il Terrazzo Ristorante (Victoria), 49

Inn at Tough City (Tofino), 7, 105–106

James Bay Tea Room & Restaurant, The (Victoria), 48

La Berengerie (Galiano Island), 161

Latch, The (Saanich Peninsula), 65

Legends (Campbell River), 128

Maclure House Restaurant (Parksville), 97

McMillan's Restaurant (San Juan Island), 178

Madrona Grill (San Juan Island), 178

Mahle House (Nanaimo), 89–90

Mark, The (Victoria), 47

Mayne Inn (Mayne Island), 165

Memories at the Inn (North Pender), 155

Moby's Marine Pub (Salt Spring Island), 151, 152

Mom's Cafe (Sooke Region), 71

Monte Cristo on the River (Courtenay), 120

Oceanside Restaurant (North Pender), 155

Oceanwood Country Inn (Mayne Island), 165–166

Old House Restaurant (Courtenay), 120

Orcas Cafe (Orcas Island), 186

Pagliacci's (Victoria), 6, 51

Poet's Cove pub and bistro (South Pender), 154

Poet's Cove restaurant (South Pender), 154

Pointe Restaurant (Tofino), 107

Quarterdeck Pub (Port Hardy), 135

Restaurant Matisse (Victoria), 49

Rock Cod Cafe (Cowichan Bay), 82

Saturna Lodge & Restaurant (Saturna Island), 169

Six Mile Pub (Sooke Region), 71–72

Sooke Harbour House (Sooke Region), 72

Spinnakers (Victoria), 47

Spring Water Lodge (Mayne Island), 166

Starfish Grill (Orcas Island), 184

Sticky Wicket Pub (Victoria), 47

Swans Brewpub (Victoria), 47

Toscanos Trattoria (Comox), 121

Tree House Cafe (Salt Spring Island), 151

Vesuvius Inn, The (Salt Spring Island), 153

Victorian, The (Victoria), 48

Vinoteca (Duncan), 82

Wesley Street Cafe (Nanaimo), 90

White Heather Tea Room (Victoria), 47

Woodstone Country Inn (Galiano Island), 162